The Comeback Blueprint

The Comeback Blueprint

A Battle Plan for Taking Back Your Life

Matt Farnsworth

©2025 Matt Farnsworth. All Rights Reserved. No portion of this book may be reproduced, stored in a retrieval system, or transmitted in any form or by any means—electronic, mechanical, photocopy, recording, scanning, or other—except for brief quotations in critical reviews or articles without the prior permission of the author.

Published by Revlation Media LLC

Paperback ISBN: 979-8-9926862-0-3
Hardcover ISBN: 979-8-9926862-1-0
Digital ISBN: 979-8-9926862-2-7

The Comeback Blueprint

A Battle Plan for Taking Back Your Life

Matt Farnsworth

PROLOGUE

Rock Bottom Isn't Your Grave

They say the sound of your neck breaking is like a tree branch snapping in winter.

POP. CRACK. SILENT SCREAM.

Let me tell you about salvation. Let me tell you about eating cocaine straight from a cup holder at eighty miles an hour while God decides your **fate.**

ONE SHOT OF TEQUILA.

That's all it takes. Eleven years of sobriety **DIES IN YOUR THROAT LIKE A SICK JOKE.**

Bottoms up. What's the harm?
When you're about to die, time stretches like **pulled taffy.**
The California sun becomes a spotlight for your execution.
Your guardian angel clocks out early.

The median comes at you—**JUDGMENT DAY IN CONCRETE AND STEEL.**

Metal tears against metal—the sound of your past catching up with you at terminal velocity. Your body becomes a pinball in Satan's arcade game.

FRONT SEAT TO BACK SEAT. DASHBOARD TO ROOF.

The windshield crowns me in blood as **my forehead SHATTERS it.**

Fun fact: Your ribs don't break.

They EXPLODE.

Like dry twigs in a bonfire. Like all the promises you ever made.

The car flips **SIX TIMES.**

Count them.

**One for every lie you told yourself.
One for every person you betrayed.
One for every time you said, "I've got this under control."**

Then—silence.

Just the soft ping, ping, ping of the engine cooling.

SATAN'S METRONOME COUNTING DOWN YOUR FINAL MOMENTS.

You know what gas and blood smell like mixed together?
REGRET.

The taste in your mouth **isn't just copper.**

It's eleven years of **sobriety coming back up to say goodbye. It's every compromise, every excuse, every time you swore** this was the last time.

I'm crawling out of twisted metal, and this isn't even **the lowest I will go.**

The **neck I don't know is broken SCREAMS** with every movement.

Glass confetti **celebrates my failure.**

Here's a secret: Sometimes, God has to **BREAK EVERY BONE IN YOUR BODY** to get your attention.

Here's another secret: The darkness you've been running from? It's **WEARING YOUR FACE.**

You want to know about control?

Try lying on sun-baked asphalt while your blood makes **abstract art on the concrete.**
Try watching your old life **leak out between your fingers.**

This isn't a crash.
This is a DEATH SENTENCE.
And the **DEVIL IS CASHING IN.**

The battle **wasn't physical.**

IT WAS SPIRITUAL.

And it had only begun.

A GHOST PAINTED IN HIS OWN BLOOD.

They didn't expect me to live.

NEITHER DID I.

But here's the thing about **failing at life—**
it doesn't have to be **THE END.**

The same fire that **burns you down** can also **light your way back.**

Now let me tell you about a **KING BABY** I used to know.

*"Pain isn't your enemy—it's your teacher. If you're willing to listen, it'll teach you how to grow, rebuild, **and become unbreakable**."*

Table of Contents

Chapter 1: The Seeds of Struggle 1
Chapter 2: Pretending to Be Normal 43
Chapter 3: The Demon in the Basement 71
Chapter 4: Addicted to Misery 89
Chapter 5: One Shot of Tequila 117
Chapter 6: The Kids 157
Chapter 7: The Pink Cloud 181
Chapter 8: The Judgment 207
Chapter 9: Online Dating 221
Chapter 10: The Real Gold 241
Chapter 11: The Indwelling 267
Chapter 12: All In 281
Chapter 13: The Calling 297
Epilogue 315

CHAPTER 1

The Seeds of Struggle

This is not a self-help book.

If you're looking for inspirational quotes to hang neatly framed on your wall, or gentle whispers about manifesting your dreams—put this down now. Walk away. What you're about to read isn't sanitized spirituality wrapped neatly with a bow. It isn't gentle. It isn't soft. It's nothing you want—but maybe everything you need.

This is blood on concrete.
This is prison cells, Hollywood excess, and rehab nightmares.
This is going toe-to-toe with demons in pitch-black rooms—and barely making it out alive.

You're holding the story of a man who crawled through earthly hell on broken glass, chasing soul-crushing desires while his spirit drowned in filth—unreachable for decades. Redemption didn't come to me gently; there were no trumpets, no white lights. It came screaming through the wreckage I'd created.

I'm a Midwesterner by blood. We don't speak of our demons. We bury them deep beneath stoic nods and calloused hands. That makes this confession brutal. The journey I'm sharing doesn't come wrapped in a glossy cover promising salvation through positive thinking and feel-good mantras.

No.
No.
No.

This is a roadmap etched from the debris of a life I nearly destroyed, a life reclaimed after thirty-eight stubborn years running from a God who refused to stop watching over me. This is a battle-tested blueprint, forged in fire, that if you follow **might just set you free**.

The pain He allowed shaped me.

From an unlovable man to a man who found love.

I wouldn't take back a moment of this story.

I have no regrets.
Because how can we who died to sin still live in it?

So let me take you back to the beginning—back to 1975, to childhood soil where the first seeds of darkness took root, back to where the whispers from the deep first began their seductive call.

I come from rural Iowa roots, a lineage of farmers and quarry workers who pulled life from stubborn soil. My dad's people knew cold so deep it could crack stone—a cold that seeped through dirt floors and followed them to outhouses in subzero dawns. By age twelve, my father was dropping sticks of dynamite down boreholes at my grandfather's limestone quarry, each detonation revealing fresh rock that kept food on their table. My parents, high school sweethearts, fled their small-town fate. Dad long-distanced his way to college on a cross-country scholarship—the first in his family to leave home. Mom, with her flute and sharp mind, followed. They married, working on the American dream, and soon after, I arrived. My dad was a **successful** salesman at IBM. Success meant moving. IBM—I've Been Moved—became our family motto. Thirteen schools before graduation. Illinois. Missouri. New Jersey. Arizona. Kansas City. Those schools weren't just buildings, but fortresses I had to breach, each with its own dialect of adolescent power. I became fluent in the universal language of fists and bloody noses—the unspoken tattoo of the perpetually new kid.

Inside our home, life gleamed with the artificial perfection of a department store display window. I was spoiled, insulated from the hardships that had shaped my parents' youth. But beneath our laminate countertops and wall-to-wall shag carpeting ran darker currents. A curse threaded through my mother's bloodline, disguised as religious devotion but infecting us with profound dysfunction. Alcoholism and depravity braided through generations of my family like perverse roots. My great-uncle robbed banks with the same methodical precision my grandfather used to quote Scripture—both of them meticulous in their chosen violations. His final chapter played out in woodland isolation—his only company—a bottle of whiskey that eventually claimed him.

We did not have those afflictions early on, but the curse had us in its sights. It's woven into the soul. The curse activated in our family when my brother arrived. Not his fault—his birth simply triggered what was already festering beneath the surface. When I was approaching five years old, my dad left—the world went from the crisp certainty of family dinner routines to something thin and insufficient. That same insufficient feeling followed us to Missouri, where it mingled with the musty breath of my grandparents' farmhouse. Dad began living a new life and relocated to New Jersey, while Mom, my newborn brother, and I retreated to her parents' farm—a backward step into a darkness that did not welcome her return.

That farmhouse wasn't just a building but a living organism with malice in its bones. The walls seemed to inhale when I entered a room, exhale when I left—as if the very structure fed on our collective dread. My grandfather—a pillar of Mormon respectability—had passed down this curse to my mother, a truth she buried so deep that it poisoned her from within. My grandmother carried chronic depression like a storm cloud, her resentment toward my mother manifesting in a curled upper lip and eyes that never quite met anyone else's. When she spoke, her sentences ended in deflation. They charged us rent, treated us like unwelcome tenants, and disguised contempt in thin religious courtesy.

My grandfather's voice carried the grit of pulverized rock—abrasive, yet somehow hollow. When he preached about Joseph Smith, I didn't fear the words but the calloused hand on my shoulder, heavy with unspoken intent. He'd squeeze until he knew he had caused discomfort. My only solace was Buddy, their blind terrier who navigated by memory and trust, and the fireflies I captured in Mason jars, their intermittent glow a reminder that even in darkness, light persists—if only in brief, desperate pulses.

I'd stare down that mile-long desolate gravel road, fingertips tracing patterns on fogged glass, willing my father's car to materialize. The whispers found me there, rising from some bottomless place inside:

Maybe it's your fault Dad left.

My younger brother fell gravely ill during this dark chapter; his tiny body seemed to absorb the toxicity around us and it manifested as a physical crisis. Hospital rooms with their antiseptic cleanliness became preferable to that house of secrets. Desperation made my mother reach for the phone, pride dissolving in the face of her son's suffering. She gave him an ultimatum: come back or it's over for good. Dad returned with a caveat—no questions permitted. Silence became their treaty, the terms non-negotiable.

We packed quickly, each cardboard box another step away from that suffocating farmhouse. But silence has weight and follows you like a shadow. I didn't know then that silence was addiction's favorite breeding ground, that unspoken pain never disappears—it finds new ways to speak.

My father's return lifted shadows but didn't banish them. The light that returned to my mother's eyes carried a wariness that never quite faded. We moved to New Jersey, another chapter, another challenge—this time to a place that held my father's secrets. The whispers never left—they followed, growing louder, weaving themselves into the fabric of who I was becoming.

This was the beginning—the first crack in a foundation.

We arrived in New Jersey carrying the wreckage of the unspoken sin—fragments held together by a thin veneer of forgiveness that hadn't yet taken root. The drive there was a masterclass in unspoken hurt. My parents bickered with the practiced precision of two people who knew exactly where to plant the knife. Wrong turns became personal betrayals. Minor inconveniences exploded into evidence of fundamental character flaws. My father's jaw would clench so tight I could hear his molars grinding. My mother's words came sharp and fast, like sleet against a windshield. Every wrong turn could be the end of the world. It was like being strapped into a seat, forced to listen to someone scrape a fork against fine china for hours—the sound piercing my skull with no way to stop it. They did love us. They just didn't know how to love each other at the time.

A five-year-old shouldn't understand the geography of adult warfare, but I mapped it perfectly—how they circled the real battlefield, engaging in proxy wars over directions and bathroom stops, neither willing to name the actual enemy. I was grateful to arrive and settle in.

Our new house was perched on a quaint cul-de-sac. My mother walked through it like a ghost haunting unfamiliar halls.

"We'll make it work," she said repeatedly, to no one in particular.

There was something that gave me joy. That hill—a perfect, steep slope ending at the bottom of our cul-de-sac. I fixated on riding my Big Wheel straight down that concrete mountain from day one. Three weeks later, I did it. What my kindergarten brain couldn't calculate was how to stop. I hit the bottom like a meteor, my elbows skinned raw—but the brief moment of weightlessness, of pure thrill—the wheels spinning so fast I had to lift my legs—was worth every drop of blood.

At the bottom of that hill lived Loraine, gap-toothed and freckled, who became the North Star of my five-year-old universe. I'd drag my Big Wheel up that punishing incline a dozen times a day to meet her playing in her front yard. Some days, I'd see her, and other days brought me face-to-face with the real New Jersey welcoming committee: her brother Keith.

Keith inhabited that terrible bridge between childhood and adolescence—twelve, maybe thirteen—his face distorted behind thick glasses that magnified eyes already swollen with cruelty. His laugh came high and wild, like a hyena that had discovered the joy of inflicting pain.

One fall afternoon, with leaves crunching under my Big Wheel's plastic tires and the air carrying that autumn bite, I made my usual pilgrimage down the hill. Before I could complete my circuit past Loraine's house, Keith and his friend materialized like dark conjurings, grabbed my front wheel, and yanked me to a stop.

"Where you going, stupid?" Keith's grin split his face like a **wolf panting**.

They dragged me behind the house, through a yard of dying grass, and into the woods behind the house. My stomach liquefied as the trees closed around us. Keith pulled something from his jacket—a BB gun—its barrel, a perfect black circle, aimed between my eyes.

"Take off your clothes," he said, voice flat as a stone.

Confusion collided with fury inside me, but before my brain could process what was happening, Keith lowered the gun and fired. A sharp sting exploded in my thigh; **pain shot outward like spilled ink.**

"Do it!" his friend screamed, spit flying from his mouth.

"Your shoes, too," Keith ordered, raising the gun again.

My fingers trembled against buttons and zippers. The cold air raised goosebumps across my exposed skin, shame burning hotter than the autumn chill as I stood naked before them, hands desperately trying to cover myself.

They grabbed me by the hair—pain shooting across my scalp—and dragged me toward what looked like a massive tunnel formed from dead branches. A natural formation where trees had grown into a circular pattern, maybe ten feet long, every inch **bristling with thorns.** They sprinted to the other side, leaving me alone, exposed—humiliated.

"Now walk!" Keith shouted, leveling the gun through the thorny passage.

I swallowed bitterly. *"If I do it, you have to let me go."*

"I promise," Keith called, the lie hanging in the air between us.

The first step wasn't terrible—a few scratches. The second brought thorns digging into my sides, my arms, my bare legs. Each movement invited fresh stabs of pain. Their laughter echoed through the woods, the sound bouncing off trees and multiplying until it seemed to come from everywhere at once.

"Come on, you wimp!"

I bit my lip until I tasted copper. I wouldn't cry. I wouldn't give them that **satisfaction.**

By the time I reached the end, my body was a roadmap of tiny cuts and scratches, beads of blood rising like crimson dew. They doubled over, wheezing with delight. My pain—my humiliation—was the funniest thing they'd ever witnessed.

They grabbed me by the hair again, dragging me back through the woods, across the yard, and finally to the street. With a final shove, they threw me onto the pavement. My clothes followed, landing in a twisted heap beside my Big Wheel. I dressed as quickly as my shaking hands would allow, rage building inside me like magma beneath a dormant volcano.

I wasn't scared anymore. I burned with **incandescent hatred.**

I dragged my Big Wheel back up that hill, legs burning with each step, blood trickling down my arms and legs, shame weighing more than any physical burden I'd ever carried.

When my mother asked about the scratches later, I told her I'd been racing down the hill and fell. The lie came easily—my first step into a lifetime of hiding pain behind fabricated stories. How could I tell her what happened? How do you explain to your mother that your dignity has been shattered, that two boys had their fun with you?

That day, I became someone different—hypervigilant, calculating risks and escape routes before venturing outside. My parents noticed the change: how I stopped playing outdoors and how I got defensive when older kids approached. They attributed it to the normal struggles of adjusting to a new place. They couldn't see the armor I was forging inside my skin, the vow I made to myself that no one would ever make me feel that powerless again.

When Dad announced IBM was transferring him to Scottsdale, Arizona, relief washed over me like a desert monsoon. I needed to escape that cul-de-sac, those woods, Keith and his BB gun, the thorns that had marked more than my skin. The night before we left, I stood at my bedroom window, staring down at the quiet street, and promised myself that someday strength and vengeance **would be mine**.

Scottsdale arrived like **salvation**—sunshine flooding every corner of our lives, the dry desert air burning away New Jersey's chill. Our house sat on half an acre with a swing set, pool, and a view that stretched toward forever. We had a dune buggy for weekend adventures, and sometimes Dad would let me shoot his .22 caliber pistol at bottles lined up against ridges of red rocks. For the first time since that day in the woods, I began to relax, to unfurl from the tight ball I'd wound myself into.

I struggled when I first started school in Scottsdale. I'd sit at my desk, hyperaware of everyone around me, jumping at sudden movements, my mind constantly scanning for threats instead of absorbing lessons. My grades suffered. My behavior swung erratically—withdrawn one moment, explosive the next—reactions I didn't fully understand. Teachers didn't know what to make of me.

Mrs. Kush, my second-grade teacher with her kindness and bicep-flexing humor, saw something in me that needed nurturing rather than correction. She gave me extra recess when my energy overflowed, created lessons that engaged my restless mind. Under her care, school transformed from punishment to possibility.

Those Arizona years were an oasis—a chance to breathe between storms. My parents' relationship found stable ground; my mother's eyes lost their haunted look. We were becoming what families are supposed to be: a refuge rather than a battlefield. Our house with its backyard pool and sweeping desert views felt like permanence. That pool was a lifeline for me. I worked out every ounce of negative energy in that pool daily.

Then came the news of another transfer. Back to the Midwest—to Kansas.

"It's a promotion," Dad explained, voice tight with a familiar mix of excitement and apology.

I felt the ground shift beneath me again. Precisely when stability had taken root and I'd started to believe in permanence, the cycle repeated itself. Everything is temporary. Nothing lasts. I kicked the table leg, earning a sharp glance from my mother.

"I don't want to go," I said, the words flat and useless.

I sat by our pool that night, watching the desert sunset paint the sky colors I knew I'd never see in Kansas. I was grieving Arizona before we'd even left, already bracing for whatever new school, new challenges, new humiliations awaited me.

In Kansas, I discovered my shield: sports. The contempt that had been building since New Jersey—that had temporarily retreated in the Arizona sun—found a constructive channel. On basketball courts, football fields, and soccer fields, I transformed that festering darkness into something that earned approval. Being good at sports gave me what I craved most: control. **Power**—a place where I let out **my aggression.**

The whispers that had started in New Jersey—the ones that told me I was powerless, unworthy, deserving of shame—quieted when I pushed my body to exertion on the court. When I sank a perfect shot, when teammates who'd initially viewed me with suspicion began saying my name with respect.

For a brief time in middle school, life normalized. I had friends. I had skills. I had an identity beyond *"the new kid."* I belonged.

Then came Coach Hazlett—my science teacher, my basketball coach. I thought I'd learned everything I needed about predators from Keith. I was wrong. This was worse. Some monsters don't hide in woods with BB guns. Some wear whistles around their necks and carry clipboards.

The day it happened, I'd strained my thigh during practice—a sharp pull that sent me limping to the sidelines. Coach Hazlett noticed immediately.

"Let me take a look at that," he says, voice dripping with concern. "Come to my office. I'll wrap it for you."

I follow him without question. He's my coach. My science teacher. A man the school had entrusted with our safety.

The office door clicks shut behind us.

"Sit down," he says. "Let's take a look."

I look down at him as he kneels before me.

A receding gray hairline, **slick with sweat**.
A bloated, alcoholic-red face, patched over with **broken capillaries**.
Dandruff flakes from his scalp, landing in his lap, on the floor, on the bench beside me.

The room is quiet. Too quiet.

His breath grows heavy.
Thick. Gurgling.
His **gut heaves in and out.**

I can smell him now.
Sour breath and sweat-stained polyester.

The bandage stretches between his fingers.

His hand moves with practiced ease, sliding up my leg, past the injury, fingers slipping beneath the hem of my shorts, reaching for my groin.

Something's wrong. My eyes dart to the exit. It's right there—steps away. Should I run? Can I? My muscles tense, but hesitation holds me still.

I feel ***trapped.***

He wheezes louder.

He's trying to molest me.

I stand abruptly, blood rushing in my ears.

"I'm fine. It feels better. All good."

My voice sounds foreign, too high, too tight.

I take off out of the locker room like it's on fire. My teammates run drills on the court, oblivious to what **just** transpired. Clarity strikes me: the early morning practices, the mandatory showers, the memo he'd sent to parents insisting we all "get clean" before school.

> *The boys have to take a mandatory shower after practice. Cleanliness is Godliness. -Coach Dave.*

He makes us get up at **5 a.m.** in the freezing-cold Kansas winter to practice early in the morning just so he can watch us shower.

When I got home that afternoon, I told my mom what happened; she called the school.

She got him on the phone and laid it out:
"If you ever try to touch my son again, I'll kill you."

My dad was angry that she called. He thought we should have left it alone. Maybe I was being dramatic. He was worried about the return fire. This call didn't sit well with Hazlett. Of course, he faced no consequences. Instead, he took his anger out on me. I was cut from the basketball team and began failing science—and not because I didn't do the work. In class, he would tilt his chin down, peer over his glasses at me, and shake his head with deliberate slowness—a silent message that needed no translation: *You are the problem. You brought this on yourself.*

Even now, when I think of it, my skin crawls. That slow, deliberate shake of his head—that calculated intimidation, that visual reminder of his power over me.

I got into trouble for this poor grade—the injustice still burns. I tried to explain myself to my parents. I studied. I did the work. Their minds were unable to see the evil staring them in the face. Even after what happened, they found it impossible that a teacher would compromise their ethical obligation to their work over anything. I was grounded and had to do extra work to compensate for my poor grade.

My trust in authority figures.

Shattered.

Telling the truth doesn't matter anymore.

I accept the system is built to protect people like him. It's another demonstration of how **unfair life can be**—how justice isn't always about what's right, but about who can decide what is just. If I only had control. The realization that I couldn't punish his offense enraged me. **I need control.** The whisper in the deep feeding on pure hatred. He was never going to pay for this.

And the worst part? The life I had built, the friends I had made, and the team I had fought to be part of were all taken away. Because I spoke up. And for that, I **paid the price.**

That betrayal didn't fade. It buried itself deep. I told myself I'd never trust another coach, teacher, or so-called leader again. If the system was rigged, why bother playing by the rules?

Hazlett did finally get busted. Twenty years later, he was arrested and sent to prison for trying to lure minors for sex.

Years later, I'd see the same pattern in Hollywood, where people in positions of power preyed on the vulnerable.

I did what any fourteen-year-old boy would do.

I rebelled.

The next development could be filed under the old classic "falling in with the wrong crowd." My teammates on the basketball team didn't want to hang out anymore, and with those friends cut off, I turned to new ones—interested in other activities—activities of a more subversive nature.

The First Drink: A Poison That Felt Like a Cure

"The first time I picked up a bottle, I didn't know **I was shaking hands with the enemy.***"*

The basement smelled like old carpet, Old Spice, and stale cigarettes—the pungent cologne of adolescent rebellion. My new friend had liberated his older brother's six-pack, and we were about to discover what made those swimsuit models in beer commercials smile so provocatively at men holding cans of Pabst Blue Ribbon.

We were outcasts at school, united by our shared disdain for the frauds and tyrants who controlled our daily lives. Two wounded animals who'd found each other in the wilderness.

He looked at me, a conspiracy forming between us. "Want to take the first sip at the same time?"

I nodded, heart racing with anticipation and fear.

"One—two—three!"

The first swallow burned like liquid fire.

I coughed and grimaced. "That burns!"

But the second sip settled more easily. The third went down like water.

Then—warmth. A liquid glow spread from my stomach outward, a chemical embrace that promised everything would be okay.

One beer, and the pain vanished like morning fog. Two beers, and the anxiety that had been my constant companion since New Jersey fell silent for the first time. Three beers and the thoughts that haunted me—the thorns, the locker room, the failing grades—blurred at the edges until they became someone else's memories.

I was drunk. The realization hit me with the force of revelation. I felt good—transcendentally good.

Everything I had been carrying—every wound, rejection, doubt—faded into insignificance. I had found the cure. Forgetting was as easy as twisting a cap, pulling a tab, and pouring liquid oblivion down my throat.

Alcohol didn't loosen me up—it unlocked me. I wasn't broken. I wasn't too much. I wasn't a burden.

I was free.

My friend's face suddenly turned ashen. "I think I'm gonna puke," he mumbled, lurching to his feet—throwing up into a drain on the floor. I laughed. He laughed. We had another. A friendship forged in rebellion and sealed with alcohol.

That first drink at fourteen transformed into many drinks and an extended middle finger to the system. We expanded our repertoire—dirty magazines hidden under mattresses, cigarettes smoked behind the school gym, small acts of defiance that grew bolder with each success. I hadn't had a best friend before, not a real one. Despite our destructive behavior, or perhaps because of it, this friendship felt authentic. It was us against the establishment, two soldiers in a private war.

Over the next year, our ranks swelled as other outcasts joined our cause. We became a band of rebels, each carrying our own wounds, finding solace in collective defiance.

Of course, right as I carved out this precarious sense of belonging, my father announced another move. Microsoft had offered him a position that would catapult our family into wealth. We were leaving Kansas.

The scorn that boiled inside me transcended ordinary teenage anger. This wasn't frustration—it was existential despair. Once again, I had nothing. No stability. No confidants. No faith to cling to.

We were about to go from financially struggling to wealthy overnight.

But here's something nobody tells you: Money doesn't solve problems—it buys you a six-thousand-square-foot mansion with a sports court and hot tub to have them in. The whispers from the deep **don't care about your zip code.**

The Gloom

Seattle greeted me with perpetual twilight—a city drowning in its own tears. The **endless drizzle** felt personal, as if the sky itself mourned what I'd lost. Leaving my rebel friends behind in Kansas tore a vital piece of identity away from me. As a parting gift, they'd handed me a mixtape—a plastic rectangle housing magnetic memories, songs I'd play until the ribbon warped and stretched.

I was a founding member of the resistance against middle-school oligarchs, and now I was being exiled. I'd finally discovered people who understood me, who saw through my defenses without demanding I lower them, it was all ripped away. Again. Loneliness crashed back in with heaviness, darker and more ruthless, amplified by Seattle's constant gray.

I pressed play on that tape, again and again. The Cure. Metallica. New Order. A soundtrack for displacement, an anthem to fill the hollow space where belonging should've been. I couldn't articulate it then, but those songs spoke a language my teenage soul understood instinctively: the poetry of alienation.

Seattle was a foreign country where I didn't speak the language. Cliques had already been formed, territories marked and defended. I was the Midwest transplant dropped into a hostile landscape, where even the rain seemed resentful. So I adapted the only way I knew how—through rebellion refined into an art form.

Every new school meant a fresh battle. Middle-school boys, swimming in testosterone and insecurity, are territorial creatures. I didn't want new friends; I wanted my old ones back. Those who knew me before explanations became necessary.

Instead of trying to connect, I retreated inward, growing roots into myself. My new public school became a stage, and I decided to portray a character nobody would suspect—the slow kid. Hood pulled tight around my face. Voice hesitant and unsure. Occasional outbursts of frustration when called upon. I pretended to be intellectually challenged, a mask so convincing even I sometimes forgot I was wearing it. Yeah. It was a scam. A dark one. But it worked.

"I… I don't know," I'd stammer, eyes lowered—a masterclass in vulnerability. Teachers responded predictably, lowering expectations, offering extra help, even slipping me answers when they thought no one was looking.

It worked better than anticipated. For half a year, I maintained the con, collecting easy grades like souvenirs from a place I never wanted to visit. My performance required isolation; closeness might expose the seams. I allowed myself only one friend—a confidant who understood the game, who laughed quietly at my calculated theatrics.

After each manufactured meltdown in class, I'd glance back and wink. He loved my one-man show and never told anyone. I ate lunch alone, communicated sparingly, perfecting the emotional camouflage.

This wasn't merely playing a role—it was rehearsal for a lifetime of deception. Learning to wear masks. Practicing the art of faking it. A skill that would later serve me well in Hollywood—and nearly destroy me in the process.

Eventually, one teacher noticed my friend's poorly concealed laughter always followed my carefully staged outbursts. Mr. Benson, my math teacher—a bodybuilder with forearms like tree trunks—finally caught on. Math was the hardest subject to fail convincingly; I was genuinely terrible at it.

"Hang back a minute," he said one afternoon, crossing his massive arms.

My heart quickened, my mask slipping. The strings controlling my puppet show were about to be cut.

"Take off the hood."

In that instant, I knew the gig was up. Five simple words severed months of careful illusion.

"You're not slow, are you?"

I swallowed hard, caught between defiance and surrender. Then I nodded. He had me cornered.

"The teachers all know it's an act," he said, voice firm. "Knock it off. Got it?"

Silence.

"Got it?"

"Yeah," I whispered. "Got it."

When word reached my parents, they took me to a renowned specialist, famous for rubber-stamping ADHD. I'd been labeled a troublemaker, and with no one contradicting that label, I wore it like a second skin.

The doctor, a thin man with a pronounced lisp, fidgeted behind his mahogany desk. His fingers drummed an irregular rhythm against his notepad.

"Do you have trouble sitting still in class?" he asked, pen tapping incessantly.

I shifted in my seat, already bored. "Who doesn't?"

He nodded quickly, scribbling notes. *"I see many young men like you. Like us,"* he corrected, smiling conspiratorially. *"It's attention deficit hyperactivity disorder. We're smart and creative but can't sit still or finish things. Sound familiar?"*

"Sure." His symptoms were vague enough to apply to anyone.

Without hesitation, he scribbled furiously on a prescription pad. *"Ritalin. For most, it makes them hyper. But for us? It calms us down. Your brain is wired differently. Coffee makes most people wired, but it helps us focus—even relaxes us."*

He tore off the prescription, handing it to my mother like a sacred text.

"Try this for a month. It'll change his life."

I asked, "Do I take it every day?"

"Yes," he said without looking up.

We left clutching that piece of paper, unaware it would alter my life trajectory. Ritalin didn't slow me down—it electrified me, set my nervous system ablaze. I quickly kept that discovery to myself.

Soon, Mom trusted me to manage my doses.

You can already see where this is going. And if you can't? **You will.**

High School

The diagnosis bought my parents an explanation for why I "was the way I was." The medication got me high. The first few times I used it, I felt a distinct "pick me up." So, why not take two at a time? It was easy to say I lost the bottle—we need to refill it early—and nobody thought of it as an "upper" back then. It was "doctor's orders." I weaponized that prescription for the next eighteen months to my advantage. It snapped me out of hangovers and got me fired up for sports. It became my upper, and alcohol became my downer—a primitive chemical balancing act performed by a teenage boy playing pharmacist with his brain chemistry.

I kept it together enough to avoid major trouble. Maybe it worked. We'll never know.

Deep into my sophomore year, I leaned against a locker between classes. The hallway buzzed with the usual chaos—slamming metal doors, shouted conversations, the squeak of sneakers on linoleum. I was talking with Stacy about weekend plans, something about a party at Mike's place. Everyday high school chatter before the bell rang.

That's when I noticed him in my peripheral vision. A new kid. Samoan. Built like a refrigerator with arms. He cut through the crowd with purpose, eyes locked on me with laser precision. I didn't know him. Had never seen him before. But something in his walk triggered alarms in my head.

Mid-sentence, I turned to square up—instinct kicked in.

Too late.

His fist connected with my nose before I could get my hands up.

CRACK.

Everything went white.

The sound was worse than the pain—my nose compressing inside my skull. Yellow lockers. Stacy's white sweater. All of it—blood-splattered. She screamed, jumping back as if I'd suddenly burst into flames.

The hallway went silent for a split-second, that strange collective intake of breath that happens when violence erupts in an unexpected place.

Then everything accelerated.

Fury flooded my system, a chemical cascade that wiped thought clean. No calculation, pure reaction. I launched at him, my vision narrowed to a tunnel with his face at the end. My first punch caught him on the jaw. His head snapped back, but he was solid, didn't go down. He countered with a hook that grazed my temple, sending stars across my vision.

Someone shouted, "Fight!" and suddenly we were in the center of a rapidly forming circle. Faces blurred at the edges, voices merging into a primordial roar. The crowd pulsed, hungry for blood—any blood, didn't matter whose.

My nose throbbed with each heartbeat. I drove forward with my right shoulder, connecting with his sternum. He staggered back but stayed upright.

"Fight! Fight! Fight! Fight!" the crowd chanted, the syllable becoming a tribal drum.

He lunged, grabbed my shirt and delivered a massive head butt. I stumbled backward, tasting copper, but dug my heels in and tackled him full force. We went down hard, a tangle of limbs and gnashing, momentum carrying us across the slick floor like we were skating on ice.

We were moving too fast to stop. We slammed into the glass windows at the front entrance of the school—the ones that stretched from floor to ceiling. The glass didn't break—**it exploded.**

Time slowed. I felt individual shards scrape my arms, my back. The sound was like a crystalline symphony of destruction.

The impact knocked the wind out of me. For a second, I couldn't breathe, couldn't move. He was underneath me, gasping. We staggered to our feet, ready to continue what gravity had interrupted.

Before I could recover, my friends were there, piling onto him. Three of them pinned him down while he thrashed, cursing.

"Farnsworth! That's enough!" The vice principal grabbed my shoulders and yanked me back with surprising strength.

I was shaking, adrenaline still coursing through me. My legs felt strange, disconnected from my body, as I was marched to the office.

All I could think was: *I didn't start this. I didn't start this. I didn't start this.*

But it didn't matter. It never did. I was sent home with blood crusted around my nostrils, glass cuts stinging on my arms, and another mark on my permanent record.

The calls came in that evening. My mother's voice from the kitchen, tense but controlled.

"It's not necessarily your son's fault," I heard the administrator explain. "This other student is part of a gang member relocation effort from Los Angeles. They're trying to give these kids a fresh start away from their environment."

Translation: They dumped their problem on us.

I was suspended anyway. Three days. The other kid got sent back to California.

Later that evening, the phone rang again. I answered it—"Hey homie," a new voice with a slight accent. "That was a hell of a fight you put up. I wasn't expecting that."

It took me a second to realize it was him—the guy who hours earlier had broken my nose.

"It was nothing against you, man," he continued, sounding almost apologetic. "I wanted to get sent back home. Figured starting something would do it."

The irony wasn't lost on me. I'd been desperate to get back to my Kansas friends, to reclaim what I'd lost. This guy was doing everything he could to get back to the place they'd dragged him from.

"Yeah, well," I said, touching my swollen nose. "Next time, maybe ask for a transfer."

He laughed. I laughed, too.

The fight finally convinced my parents that I needed a "better environment." They decided on private school, like changing the container would somehow fix what was inside.

They sent me to Overlake School in my junior year—prestigious, private, filled with even more privileged, creative lunatics. Bathrooms like five-star hotels doubled as Vicodin dispensaries. Mommy's "migraine pills," conveniently uncounted and freely shared.

I was given a brand new car and started dating the prettiest girl in school—a young man handed everything a young man could dream of.

Still, I struggled. The whispers never quieted.

There was one bright spot in this gilded cage: Professor Paul Hunter. Brilliant. Unhinged. A literary assassin with ink-stained hands and zero tolerance for mediocrity.

Paul Hunter published fine letterpress poetry under his Wood Works imprint, his words appearing in *The Southern Review*, *Prairie Schooner*, and *North American Review*—where real poets proved themselves. Now, somehow, I was in his creative writing class.

He saw me.

Not the con artist, not the screw-up. Just... me. Not in a predatory way like Hazlett. In that rare way great teachers sense something raw in a student and push them harder for it.

We riffed off each other. His sharp humor dueled my sarcasm, and for the first time in years, I participated without faking it. No slow-kid act, no manipulation—words coming to life between us.

He challenged us to rewrite *Romeo and Juliet* in modern dialogue. And for once—I excelled. Shakespeare's rhythm clicked with something primal inside me. The desperation, the flaws, the inevitable tragedy—I understood it all too well.

I heard praise; at times, it became more intoxicating than alcohol. A flash of what I might become if I could outrun my demons. But validation didn't stop rebellion. The drinking didn't stop. New faces, same poison.

Somehow, I juggled it all—All-state athlete, highest goal scorer, and heavy partying—until I couldn't anymore. It caught up to me. It always does.

I drank to feel alive. I drank to disappear.

And I always found another bottle waiting.

Pulled from the Fire

My senior year of high school.
Ah. Memories.

More like nightmares. I have friends.

Wait.

A few.

Wait.

Very few.

Actually, they pretty much all hated me.

But I have the best-looking girlfriend in the whole school and my family is wealthy.

I put all my golden eggs into her pretty basket.

The problem with the scenario?

When something isn't perfect—when you disagree—it could mean… **THE END.**

I couldn't bear the thought.

One night, we had an argument at a party. She left.

I drink—a lot.

The alcohol mixed with testosterone has me reaching for my keys—searching for her in the heart of the Pacific Northwest in the middle of the night.

Rain turns to sleet in Pacific Northwest winters, and **darkness swallows everything.**

I'm drunk. Not party drunk. Not a little buzzed. The kind of drunk where speed isn't speed—it's invincibility, and I am on a mission. I must talk with her wherever she is. Yellow lights become dares. Curves in the road, challenges.

When I drink, I don't get drunk—I disappear. The man behind the wheel isn't me anymore. The booze rewires my body, hijacks my brain, turns me into something else entirely. A heathen. A predator. A passenger in my own skin.

Here's something to consider: **I've never had a car accident sober. Not once.**

The road twists through the trees, wet and gleaming under my high beams. If you've never been to Seattle, picture this: trees everywhere. Not the decorative kind you see in front yards—the kind that have been standing for centuries, towering, unshaken. **The kind that don't move when you hit them.**

One second, I'm gripping the wheel, wipers flashing against the sleet—**the next, impact.**

The car folds like tinfoil around an ancient Douglas fir. My body **snaps forward.** The airbag explodes—**BLACKNESS.**

I'm out cold.

I hear a voice. Is this a dream? Am I hallucinating? No, it's **her voice.**

"Wake up, sweetheart."

It's not a hallucination. It's **real.** A voice I've known since childhood, crisp and clear as church bells—**my grandmother.**

She's been dead for a few years. But here she is.

Stirring me to **consciousness.**

It isn't flesh and blood, but it's **undeniable.**

Presence.

Smoke curls through the car—thick, chemical, burning plastic. **Fire is coming.**

I try to move—**the doors won't budge.** The frame twisted on impact, sealing me inside. I hear the voice again.

"Break the back window. Climb out. Now."

If I don't get out, I'm dead.

I don't hesitate. I turn, brace myself, and **kick the back window out with everything I have.** I crawl through the shattered glass and hit the wet ground on my hands and knees, gasping for air.

And then—boom.

Heat slams into my back as I twist around. **Flames burst through the windshield.** The entire front half of the car ignites.

If I'd hesitated for even five seconds, **I would've burned alive.**

I sit there, rain pounding my face, staring at the inferno. Smoke curls into the night sky, twisting like a living force into the sleet. My heart hammers. My hands tremble.

As I walk through the freezing rain, I formulate a plan. Hide. Avoid a DUI.

A car passes.

I hop in the woods.

Hide.

I stare out from the darkness until the coast is clear.

I repeat this process for the next eight miles.

I stagger up our block as the pain starts to set in.

The mansion is the first house on the right.
It takes a moment to trudge through the grass around the house in cowboy boots.

I look up at the windows—the lights are on—they know.

They've been notified of my "criminal behavior."

Should I go inside? Let my mom know I am ok? She's probably on the phone with my dad. He's away on business again... No, I need another drink. I can't face this music.

I crawl under the deck, where I have more beer stashed. I crack one open.

Guzzle.

Could I escape to another country? Canada's close—Mexico? Anywhere but here. Wait. I don't have any money. I don't even have a car. Did I really hear my grandmother's voice tonight?

GUZZLE.

The adrenaline wears off. I slump over.

Out cold.

Birds chirp.

My eyelids are frozen shut.

Light flows in through the lattice.

Reality rushes me with the choppy memory of last night.

I crawl out from underneath the deck trembling, brush myself off, and make my way inside.

My mom is **frantic.**

I want to blend into the wallpaper and slide past.

No such luck.

I spin an unbelievable story about passing out in the woods, maybe a concussion, waking up disoriented. They buy it—or pretend to. No DUI. No charges. Another near-miss that teaches me nothing.

You'd think something like that would've made me "wake up."

You'd think that hearing my dead grandmother's voice pulling me from the fire would've made me look for God.

But it didn't.

I never even considered it.

Instead?

I ran.

Straight **back to the bottle.**

I hadn't thought about that night or my grandmother's voice until years later. I swept these events under the rug. Looking at them meant taking responsibility, and I had lied. I remember how much our house had changed when money was flowing. Money became a God. The general thought was everything should be perfect now that we have money. But it wasn't. Not for me. I recognize how my parents, who grew up with so little, couldn't understand why I wasn't happy. They had given me everything. Everything but attention and true guidance. So I kept seeking it—through outlandish acts of self-destruction. I'd love to tell you it got better after this catastrophic event—but the spiral downward was only the beginning, and soon I'd face more serious legal issues than I ever imagined.

The Gun Incident

The car was covered by my parents' insurance and I quickly had a new set of wheels. No consequence. Everybody bought my story about passing out in the woods, but trouble kept finding me. Or I kept finding it, and it always started with girls and drinking. No more than eight months later, before graduating from high school, I made a mistake that came with a real price tag attached.

My freedom.

That night began like any other. Partying. The usual.

I drop my girlfriend off at her house, the engine idling as she steps out. A moment later, her brother and his friend roll up, their car lurching to a stop—drunk, loud, total idiots.

And holding a shotgun.

They think it's funny—pointing it at my car, waving it around, laughing like lunatics. They toss it onto the seat of their car and walk off into the night.

I sit there, watching them disappear in the mist toward the house. My girlfriend is already inside. I get out and peer into their car.

The air is wet and cold, clinging to my skin. The shotgun sits there, an **omen** in the dark.

My chest tightens.

A voice **slithers through my mind**...

They were laughing at you. Pointing it at you. Take it.

A dog barks in the distance, sharp and jarring.

My body jerks. Before I even know what I'm doing, I grab the gun and hurl it into the woods.

Problem solved.

They won't be pointing that at me anymore.

At least, that's what I tell myself.

The next day, the cops call my parents. I was the last person near the car. They know that.

My mom and dad—believers in the system—urge me to talk to them.

"I guess you better go talk to them," they say. "It'll all work out."

Naively, I believe them.

They don't know any better.
They aren't the kind of people who have cops knocking.

Until me.

I walk into the station thinking honesty will clear everything up.

The investigator greets me with a warm smile.

"Have a seat. This won't take long. Do you want something to drink?"

His voice is calm. Friendly. Disarming.

"We're not here to bust you," he assures me. "We need to know what happened. This isn't some O.J. Simpson case. They want the gun back, and everything will be settled."

Taking him at his word, I explain everything.

What I don't know—what no one told me—is that the shotgun belongs to a retired cop.

The moment I admit to taking it, the warmth disappears.

His **eyes harden.**

Cuffs click around my wrists.

And just like that, my life changes.

Just like that, truth becomes a weapon.

Just like that, honesty gets me locked up.

Just like that, I learn the system doesn't care about what's right—only about what it can prove.

"You're under arrest."

They charge me with felony possession of a firearm—the harshest penalty they can throw at me.

I sit there in handcuffs, my mind racing.

How did doing the right thing go so wrong?

My parents' words echo in my head.

It'll all work out.

Yeah. Sure.

If this is "working out," I want no part of it.

Cuffed and helpless, I realize something brutal: the truth isn't always your ally. Sometimes, honesty chains you faster than any lie ever could.

King County Jail

Before they take me downtown, I ask to use the restroom.

"Hold it."

I figure, fine. This won't take long.

I'm wrong. They aren't taking me to a local holding cell. They're taking me straight to King County Jail. Downtown. The weight of that creeps in on me as we drive.

I lean forward as far as my cuffs allow.

"Hey, man... I don't even understand why I was arrested. I told them what happened. They can go get the gun and give it back."

The cop glances at me in the rearview mirror, face unreadable.

Then he says something that makes me feel like an idiot.

"I'm gonna give you a piece of advice: Never talk to the police."

I look at him in the rearview. "What?"

"They can lie to you, kid," he says. "They can tell you whatever they want to get you to admit to a crime."

I feel **dumb.**

You idiot. You never should have said a word to anyone! They had nothing.

I walked into that station and handed them everything they needed on a silver platter.

My bladder is on the verge of exploding.

I ask again to use the restroom. Desperation creeping in.

"I can't stop," he says.

I hold it as long as I can.

In humiliating defeat, I let go.

I feel the warmth pool underneath me. By the time we pull up, the seat is soaked—and so is my dignity.

The cop doesn't say anything.

He doesn't have to.

Sitting cuffed in the back of that car reinforced my disdain for the system. Honesty had officially become a liability. My trust in authority was officially dead. Yet, even then, I refused to take responsibility for my actions. It was easier to blame anyone else.

That whisper urging me to steal the gun—it would take me years to uncover whose voice it was.

Jail, Elvis, and Bad Decisions

One minute, you're a teenager with your **whole life ahead of you.**
The next? Concrete walls.

Fluorescent lights.

Freedom gone.

Here I was.
LOCKED UP.
Baby-faced.
I'm sitting in a holding cell with pee-soaked jeans waiting to be processed.

It's no bigger than a closet.
The smell hits first—
Sweat. Body odor. Cheap booze. Bad decisions.

It's just me, an older Asian guy who doesn't speak a word of English, and a seven-foot lumberjack ginger psychopath pacing the room—a caged animal.

Boots slam against concrete.
Breath heavy with whiskey and disdain.

Then—

The ginger lumberjack stops pacing...

He leans down inches away from the poor man's ear sitting next to me.

He starts belting out a song.

"Wise men say, only fools rush in..."

An Elvis impersonation not worthy of a Vegas dive bar. He sings it over and over again.

For hours.

I sit frozen on the cold metal bench, staring at the chipped paint on the walls.

What have I done?
How did I end up here?

The me from back then would've **blamed bad luck.**
A **misunderstanding.**
A **series of unfortunate events.**

But the truth?

I'd been heading toward this moment for the last four years.

Drinking.
Fighting.

A runaway train with no brakes.

And the tracks?
They always end in **two places**—

Jail.

Or a coffin.

And somewhere, somehow, a part of me knew it.

I wasn't falling into this moment—I was being **pulled toward it.**

The ginger lumberjack finally stops singing.

Relief. For five seconds.

Takes down his pants.

And sits on the toilet.

A Joker-sized grin spreads across his face.

I look away, painfully anticipating what comes next.

The door unlocks and swings open.
"Matt Farnsworth. Come with me."

They did not have to repeat it.

After booking me, they handed me a red jumpsuit with a hole in the crotch. At least it wasn't filled with urine. They threw me in with hardened criminals—guys awaiting trial for murder.

A man in the hallway paces back and forth, back and forth.

"I didn't push her off the cliff, she fell. She wasn't stabbed. They said she was stabbed!"

The place **reeks of psychosis.**

No one explains the rules.

They walk me to a massive open space called **The Gladiator Floor**.

No cells. No bars. No privacy.

Just rows of bunk beds lining paint chipped cinderblock walls.

The noise eats away at my soul—a chaotic mix of shouting, laughter, and threats. A row of windows faces the towering watch station in the center of the room, where guards watch from behind thick glass. The back wall has no windows at all—no view of the outside world.

No hope.

Did I mention I decided to go in and speak to the cops on a Friday evening? That means I'm stuck until the courts open Monday. No bail. No phone call. This is my home for the next 48 hours.

They don't assign bunks. You pick one and pray no one challenges you.

I find an open bunk against the back wall.

I sit down.

Keep my head low.

Try to **disappear.**

The Intimidation

Don't make eye contact.

Don't look weak. Don't appear a threat.

Blend in.

I think I'm doing a good job of it.

Until **I'm not.**

From across the room, a massive Black dude locks eyes with me. Six-foot-five, 300 pounds of muscle and menace, and he has his **sights set on me.**

He stands slowly, his frame towering over the chaos around him. Every step is deliberate. Measured. A lion approaching a wounded gazelle.

My pulse skyrockets.

He stops inches from me, kneels down so we're eye-level, and holds my gaze.

Inches away from my face—so close I can smell stale breath.

"Hey," he says, voice low and cold. "I know you. You're that white boy who likes to ride around screaming the N-word."

Every muscle in my body locks up.

I feel the room shift. Conversations quiet. Other inmates watch.

I swallow hard. "I... I think you've got the wrong guy." My voice is steady, but inside? Pure **TERROR.**

He doesn't blink.

"You telling me I don't know what I'm talking about?" his tone sharpens, slicing through the air like a blade.

If I back down now, I'm done. If I push too hard, I'm done.

I have seconds to decide.

I take a slow breath. "No, man," I say, calm but firm. "I don't think I know you, and I don't think you know what you're talking about."

Silence stretches between us.

He doesn't blink.

A long pause.

Then he steps back—**he laughs.**

A deep, booming belly laugh that shakes the air around us.

I don't move. Don't react. I sit there, **bracing for impact.**

Then, as suddenly as it started, he stops laughing. His face goes stone cold again.

He leans back in. Points at me.

Then he walks away.

I let out a breath I didn't realize I was holding.

My heart is hammering in my ears as I lean back against the cold wall, trying to steady myself.

My hands **unclench.**

That was a test.

And I barely passed.

The Gladiator Floor in Action

Jail isn't built for peace.

It runs on chaos, violence, and fear. Fights break out hourly. Sometimes, the guards break them up. Sometimes, they watch. Free entertainment.

That first night, **I don't sleep.**

You don't know when it's morning.

I sit up on the cold slab they call a bed, my body still sore from the tension of the night before. I'm grateful I've made it through the night without having my face handed to me.

I have no idea what's coming next.

The toothbrush they give me is a joke.

A flimsy plastic stick with toothpaste already inside it.

But it's one small piece of normalcy, so I use it.

I walk over to the row of sinks. Head low. Trying to stay invisible.

That's when I see them.

Three men. Reflected in the mirror. Their movements slow, deliberate. My stomach twists. Predators. And I'm the prey.

Before I can react, they're on me.

Fists from **every direction**.

Blows hammering my ribs, my face, my gut.

I swing wildly, but I'm outnumbered, overpowered, and drowning in their attack.

The floor comes up fast. My body hits cold, **unforgiving concrete.**

My ears are ringing. My mouth—full of blood.

Then—**they leave.**

I lie there, gasping for air.

Heave.
Pain.

Heave.
Pain.

My ribs—stinging with every breath I try to catch.

I attempt to sit up, but pain shoots through my body—pure fire.

No one helps.

Laughter echoes in my ears.

My vision—blurry, regaining focus.

In a moment, I can see again.

Men standing near the doorway watching me suffer.

Enjoying it.

Outdated tile walls. The stink of bleach and urine floods back in, searing my nostrils.

I'm still here.

A thought flickers in my mind—thank God they didn't do more.

But it isn't gratitude. It's sarcasm.

As I lie there on that grimy floor, blood flowing down my face, pain stabbing through every breath, I curse God.

"How could You let this happen?"

"How could You leave me here?"

Anger boils up inside me.

There is no God, I think.

Because if there was, He sure as hell isn't here.

Some people have their moment of reckoning in times like this.

Not me.

I don't wake up.

I dig in **DEEPER**.

Double down on my defiance.

My rebellion from God isn't new—but now, **it's absolute.**

Graduating to Work Release

When I returned to school, the gossip mill had been churning.
They were pressing charges to the **fullest** extent.

The retired cop was furious about his gun being taken, and he wanted charges pressed.

No let-up on the throttle.
No **mercy.**
They were out for blood.

I was always the one **who got caught.**

At the time, I called it bad luck.
A curse.
Another unfair consequence for a life that never seemed to cut me a break.

But...
It was a pattern. A cycle.

A warning **I refused to see.**

That summer, while my classmates were planning on starting college and celebrating, I was sitting in a courtroom, waiting for my sentence. **I pleaded guilty.** I had already admitted to the crime. My dad sat silently in the back as the judge handed it down: thirty days in the work-release jail **after I graduated high school.**

By the Fourth of July, I was in my cell, staring out a tiny window as fireworks lit up Queen Anne Hill. A few miles away, people were living their lives. Drinking. Laughing. **Moving forward.**

My girlfriend—history.

And me?

I was trapped with men who **had lost everything.**

The first lesson you learn in jail? **Sleep facing the bars.**

I learned that when an inmate got **strangled to death** in his sleep—someone had wound a sheet through the bars and used the bars as leverage to strangle him. I hadn't even been there a week.

After that, I made it a habit: feet toward the bars, **always watching.**

At **eighteen years old,** I thought this was my punishment.

I thought this was the moment I'd finally had enough.

I was **wrong.**

The lesson keeps coming back, louder each time, **until you listen.**

The Visit

While I'm locked up, my dad brings my brother for a visit.

At first, I think it's kindness—support, even.

Maybe it is. But it's also something else—a homemade scared-straight program.

He turns to my brother, his voice low and firm: **"Don't ever do this to yourself."**

I freeze, humiliation hot on my face.

I'm his son in trouble, but now I'm something else, too:

A cautionary tale.

A walking, breathing example of failure for my little brother to study.

Part of me gets it.

You can only run so long.
You can only dodge the truth so many times.

Eventually, the mirror finds you.
Eventually, you have to face the void.

But right now?

I'm blind.

Family always has opinions—how we should live, what we should do, how we should think. Their fears, their failures, their baggage—it all gets dumped on you.

But at this moment, I can't see clearly. I'm too busy searching desperately for someone—anyone—to give me answers. Answers from people as lost as I am.

*"That indecisiveness—that inability to trust my true God-given inner voice— would keep me trapped for decades. **It was the beginning of the fall.**"*

The Cycle Continues

When I get out, I try to put it all behind me. I tell myself I'll be different—better somehow.

But it doesn't last.

Days blur into weeks, months. I bus tables during the day, but the nights? They're reserved for drinking. I tell myself I'll get it right this time, but depression digs its claws into me deeper than ever. Doctors prescribe SSRIs, hoping they'll lift the fog. Instead, they mix with the booze, creating a chemical cocktail that turns my brain into mush.

Most days, I drift. Most nights, **I drown.**

My parents say they want me to have independence, but the truth is simpler—they want me out of the house. I don't blame them. I'm a burden, a ticking time bomb. They know it; I know it. So, I end up in a lonely apartment downtown, the silence deafening, the loneliness constant. So I find girls to date.

I see the pattern clearly now:
Every crash, every spiral, every crisis—it always comes back to women. My entire sense of worth hinges on whether these relationships succeed. Usually, they don't.

Each breakup becomes more proof I'm worthless, unwanted. It feeds the cycle, deepens the despair.

But I'm not ready to see that yet.

I want control so badly I need to drink to kill the feeling, numb the hurt. Those childhood wounds the enemy left me with have never healed. They've never even been addressed. Instead, I seek validation in women. I define myself by these relationships. If she's unhappy, it's the end of the world. If she leaves, it's catastrophic. I take drastic action at the slightest hint of trouble—so naturally, I cause trouble. Problems give me excuses to drink, to relive my trauma, to create my own earthly purgatory. I become a master at this.

The Midnight Drive

She lives in Olympia.
This new girl I'm dating.

I don't even remember how we met.
But suddenly, I'm in love with her.
She's everything. Or at least that's what I tell myself tonight.

I'm in my apartment, wasted.

Completely smashed.
When I drink, the voices in my head start talking.
Wild theories about how it's all going to end.

I am in **another blackout.**

I need to see her.
Now.

Olympia is an hour away from downtown Seattle.
An hour I don't have any business driving—especially drunk.
But logic's not running this show anymore—alcohol is.

I'm not fighting it tonight.

It's midnight, and suddenly driving an hour south sounds perfectly reasonable.
No logic. No second thoughts.
Reckless, **blind impulse.**

I don't even make it out of my building without disaster.
The parking garage gate blocks my way—so I smash through it.

Metal screeches, hinges snap, but I don't stop.
Don't look back. How bad is the damage? Don't care.

You see, I am on a life-and-death mission now.

Somehow, I'm on I-5 South.
Somehow, I make it past Tacoma—45 minutes into the drive—before reality catches up to me.

I don't remember losing control.
One second, I'm driving. The next—I'm tearing through a military base fence at full speed.
The car jolts to a violent stop, steam pouring from the hood, smoke in the air.

Before I can think, I'm surrounded.
Military Police swarm from every direction, shouting, guns drawn.

But I don't surrender.
Instead, **I fight.**
Drunken punches thrown at trained soldiers.

They tackle me. Hard. Drag me into the barracks.
Sit me down roughly in a chair while I spit slurred insults at them before I pass out.

Hours later, my dad arrives in the early morning hours, forced to deal with the chaos I've created.
Again.

The drive home is brutal.

My emotional state is unhinged. Between the medication and the alcohol, I'm in a dissociative state. I unravel emotionally. My dad comforts me. This is bigger than a simple car accident.

Another Lesson Ignored

They charge me with DUI and property damage—serious enough that I should land in jail, especially with my record.

But my dad has money. Connections. Influence.
We hire the best lawyer money can buy.

We fight the charges, exploiting a loophole because the accident happened on federal property, which is unusual.
Something about my "Miranda rights" not being read.

Somehow, it works.

A couple of court dates.
A few pieces of paper signed.

Simple as that—I'm back on the street.

Another bullet dodged.

That should have **killed me.**
Another lesson ignored.

That should have **woken me up.**
Another chance wasted.

That should have **been acknowledged.**

I wish I could say this wakes me up.

That it snaps me awake.
But you already know—**it doesn't.**

Reflection

I'm sitting in my recliner writing this, the leather cool beneath my arms, staring at my cat named Ted whining at me to play with him. The sound of his impatient meow cuts through the peaceful quiet of my Tennessee home. It's 2025. Hang on, I need to put my glasses on to read along with you what I have written. The glasses—a new permanent reminder that I'm now approaching fifty years old.

I apologize for putting you through all that earlier. It's painful to read it out loud. Reliving these painful memories puts a knot in my throat and a pit in my stomach. I could pray that it weren't necessary for me to bear my soul and spirit raw, but that prayer has already been answered, and that is the reason you are reading this book.

I'm curious—what do you feel about what you've just read? Do you see the pattern? The enemy was attacking my family long before I came along. Generational curses, deeply entrenched, a silent poison, coursing through our family tree's roots. It's chilling to realize how that unseen toxin influenced every choice I made, every belief I held about love and worthiness. Every bottle I reached for. Every line I crossed. Every relationship I sabotaged.

There is a reason why I couldn't see God in all of this. I couldn't see God in a miracle that saved my life. In my own grandmother's voice pulling from the carnage. The enemy's toxic curse had blinded me—as effective as physical blindness, but spiritual in nature.

2 Corinthians 4:4 says, *"The god of this world has blinded the minds of unbelievers, to keep them from seeing the light of the gospel of the glory of Christ."*

The abuse that was dealt out by my grandfather posing as a pastor was demonic. There is no other label. A child forced to listen to sermons about God, preached by the same father who violated every word he spoke behind closed doors. The enemy couldn't have crafted a better scenario to turn religion into a hypocritical joke and drive a family away from God. The oath of divine order had been blasphemed in a way that only a miracle could resurrect it. It drove my family in a straight line away from God. Blinding us. That trauma became a curse unknowingly passed down—silently, invisibly, poisoning generations.

It would not be until decades later, married with my own children, I learned the full truth. My mother, drowning in alcohol one night, finally broke her silence. She admitted what her father had done. That he had started abusing her as young as eight years old and would not stop until she was old enough to fend him off. She had spent our lifetime pretending, inviting her parents into our home, smiling through family gatherings, suppressing the truth. After she finally spoke the truth, we never saw my grandparents again.

I became furious over the unfairness of the situation. It weighed on me like stones stacked on my chest. My grandfather was still preaching. Occasionally, moving from one small church to another. Who else was he still preying on?

One night, not long after we had found out what had happened, my mind fluttered with images of the abuse. I am a writer and filmmaker after all. What I hear becomes a visual representation of events displayed like a storyline I stitch together in my mind. I am not an idle man. My tendency at that time was immediate action. I called my grandfather. Told him I knew exactly what he had done. Told him he would rot in hell. He denied everything. "We were good to her," he said. His voice was stern but he was clearly lying—not about to divulge his demonic sins. I hung up irate and guilty. My impulsivity exposed the demon—this vile curse. The old phrase *be careful of a wolf in sheep's clothing* came to mind as I sat there decompressing—still shaking with disgust. There is an inherent evil in people who use religion to veil their true intentions.

This phone call exposed the darkness, and word spread quickly—Soon, my mother's siblings learned about the accusations. Yet even after their niece—my cousin, the daughter of my mother's own brother—confessed she'd endured the identical abuse, at the hands of the same man, they turned their backs, denying it all. Not by coincidence, she too—my cousin—battled addiction and alcoholism for many years.

The parallels are not lost on me. My cousin. My mother. Me. Three generations carrying the same wounds, seeking the same escapes. The same bottles. The same numbing agents. Different bodies, same prison. The enemy thrives in secrecy and denial, creating wounds that become legacies, pain passed down like heirlooms.

I didn't understand then that when darkness is brought into the light—even painfully—it's the beginning of God's rescue plan. The truth was exposed, and truth is the very thing that sets us free **(John 8:32)**. But like all shocking events that happen in our world, it takes time to untangle—to understand all the details of what led to the event that caused the upheaval in the first place.

The enemy recognized me as his next target. I had exposed the secret keeping us sick. Which is why I am the one fighting the enemy now on the front lines of our family. Back then, he not only made a plan to punish me for years as I blindly listened to him, but he would also lead me to temptation after gorgeous temptation, offering me fame, fortune, and power. I had no weapons to fight back with because he was smart enough to use religion to steer me away from the one weapon that I could use to defeat him.

If you are in Christ, you are marked as God's own **(Ephesians 1:13),** *and Satan has no legal claim over you.* He blinded me from God and the Gospel. Before the battle began he raided our arsenal and removed the only weapon I could use to defeat him. A weapon I was told was useless. I believe God is sovereign and that no curse or spiritual attack can reach you unless God allows it for a greater purpose **(Romans 8:28).** That is why I am here. Speaking with you now.

A deep void was created by the demon that corrupted my mother's spiritual being. She could only connect emotionally with us boys up to a certain age. Her adult emotions had been stunted at the time the curse was passed down. She possessed all the faculties to care for us at very young ages. Dote on us and give us love, but as my brother and I became men I believe she found it hard to express her feelings and continue to be affectionate. Being affectionate with an adult male child of her own made her uncomfortable. Understandably. Who could blame her? This has changed as she has healed.

Nonetheless, this cultivated a sense of emotional abandonment in me. Instead of seeking love and affection from someone who had been stripped of their ability to give it, I sought it out in the women I dated. The pattern was formed and the cycle began. The curse's web grew larger. I rebelled against my family and became an outcast.

The enemy's strategy was brilliant in its simplicity: Take a family wound, make it unspeakable, and watch as the confusion and pain create distance. Distance creates loneliness. Loneliness creates vulnerability. Vulnerability without God creates addiction. Addiction destroys. The curse completes its cycle.

The enemy grins when families are destroyed by sin. You know who first rebelled against God? Not Adam. Not Eve. Lucifer. Before there was sin on earth, there was sin in heaven.

Ezekiel 28:17 says, *"Your heart was proud because of your beauty; you corrupted your wisdom for the sake of your splendor."*

Lucifer wasn't lacking anything. He had it all—beauty, power, privilege. But it wasn't enough. Back then, how was I any different? Why didn't I simply "wake up"?

Looking back, it's easy to ask that question. But at the time? It never felt like a choice.

My parents felt that money would solve their problems. They were searching for something different. My dad thought he could fix everything that happened by being successful and giving my mom everything she ever asked for. The problem—nobody knew what was wrong. This very evil curse could have been a driving factor in my parents' separation when I was a child, which only deepened the emotional damage, allowing the enemy to gain an even stronger foothold in our lives.

Self-sabotage gave my parents a reason to pay attention to me. I became proud of my ability to create chaos and gain attention. And I continued to seek their approval any way I could get it. But ultimately, the blame for my behavior is on me. I own that now. I was a weak kid with a weak mind and no resolve. Weakened even further by my own inability to accept my mistakes and correct the path I was on. I thought I was fighting a system aligned against me, but what I couldn't see was that I was really fighting my own flesh and foolish pride. Do I blame a curse on my family's initial foundational corruption? Yes, I do. But I also know that darkness feeds on darkness, and back then, that's the only thing I consumed.

Ever seen the movie *Cool Hand Luke?* It's about a man named Luke, brilliantly played by Paul Newman—a stubborn prisoner who refuses to conform to the rules of a harsh Florida prison camp. Throughout the film, Luke repeatedly defies authority, no matter the cost. The more the guards punish him, the more Luke resists. Eventually, the warden delivers the now-famous line: "What we've got here is failure to communicate. Some men you just can't reach. So you get what we had here last week—which is the way he wants it. Well, he gets it."

Luke wasn't ignorant or unaware; he was proud, defiant, and trapped in his own rebellion. The harder life pushed against him, the harder he pushed back, blind to how his pride only brought him deeper pain. He was unreachable—not because others didn't try, but because he chose not to listen.

That was me.

I was stubborn. Every consequence I suffered felt like validation of my rebellion. Like Luke, I kept pushing back, refusing to communicate, refusing to see the truth staring me square in the face.

In the end, Luke's stubbornness cost him everything. And as you are about to find out, for many years, mine did too. I lost relationships. Lost opportunities. Nearly lost my life. All because I couldn't see that my defiance wasn't freedom—it was another chain in the curse that had bound my family for generations.

Maybe you recognize your own patterns in Luke's story—or mine. We choose defiance, convinced of its strength, only to realize too late that we've been fighting ourselves all along. Are you, like I was, fighting battles that only lead you deeper into pain? Could letting go of your stubborn defiance set you free? I see now: defiance wasn't strength. It was chains holding me captive.

This generational curse would eventually be broken—not through my strength or wisdom, but through something much more powerful. The journey to that freedom wasn't quick or easy. It required confronting truths I'd spent a lifetime avoiding. It demanded forgiveness I didn't think was possible. It meant seeing the enemy for what he truly was.

But I'm getting ahead of myself. That redemption—hard-earned, miraculous, powerful—is still ahead. For now, there's more darkness we must face, together.

Now, I have to go play with Ted before he tears down my podcast studio. He doesn't know it yet, but he's been one of the gentlest reminders that life—even after all the pain—can be simple, quiet, and sacred.

Speaking of facing reality, let's dig deeper.

The War I Couldn't See

My battle started before I was born.

The enemy slithered in.

I didn't see the war I was in.
I didn't see the **enemy I was facing.**
I didn't see the chains I was dragging behind me.

I'm writing this from the other side—scarred, sober, staring down the truth. Back then? I was too drunk on my own lies to hear them. I thought survival was enough.

I was **dead wrong.**

Denial is a **slow IV drip of self-administered poison.**

For years, I told myself the darkness wasn't real. **Evil didn't exist.**

But if that were true, then why couldn't I escape?

No matter what I achieved. No matter what I built. No matter how many times I swore I'd change.

It always came back because the darkness **was real.**

And the longer I denied it, the more power it had over me.

That's what **step one** really is.
Not only looking into the void.
But first, **admitting it EXISTS.**

The darkness isn't some abstract metaphor.
It is a living, breathing force that convinced me to do its dirty work.

That's why this first step isn't optional—it's where **the fight begins.**

You have two choices:

Keep the IV in. **STAY NUMB.** Stay comfortable. Keep lying to yourself. Keep **losing.**

or

Rip it out. Feel the pain. Face the fire. Start **fighting for your life.**

There is **no third option.**

Truth is where step one begins.

BLUEPRINT STEP 1: FACE THE VOID
(Own Your Reality—No More Lies)

"You cannot rebuild what you refuse to admit is broken."

WAR STRATEGY:

Here's your first mission. No excuses. **No hesitation.** Before you can win, you must admit where you're losing. Most people die having never faced who they really are. They hide from their failures, mask their weaknesses, and lie to themselves daily. **You will not be most people.** You will face the void.

ACTION ORDERS:

1. Write 3 Brutal Truths

- Where are you right now?
- What patterns are keeping you stuck?
- What excuses have you been using?

No fluff. No spin. Only cold, unfiltered facts. Write them down. Face them. **Own them.**

2. Write Your Current Eulogy

If you died today, what would people honestly say?

- *"He had potential, but wasted it."*
- *"She was a talker, not a doer."*
- *"He was always going to change—but never did."*

Read it back to yourself. Does it make you proud? Does it make you sick? The truth should do both.

3. Rewrite Your Future Eulogy

Your past is **not** your identity. Your mistakes are **not** your name.

- Who do you want to be?
- What legacy would you want to leave?
- What would make your life matter?

Write it out and keep it visible. Reference it when self-doubt creeps in.

WAR CRY:

Most people avoid the void—the darkness we all inherently contain. That's why most people **never change.** You are here because you were called to something greater.

The void isn't your enemy. The void is your training ground.

Most people run. You won't. You are **not most people.**

BLUEPRINT RECAP:
BEFORE: *(The Eulogy That Almost Was)*

"Matt Farnsworth was a guy who always had potential. He could've done something great if he had only gotten out of his own way. He looked for comfort in everything but Christ. He was talented, but he never fully committed. He wanted success, but he wanted shortcuts more. He left behind people who loved him, but he always kept them at a distance. He had all the tools. All the gifts. But fear kept him small. Pride kept him stuck. He could have broken free—but he never did. He left the world exactly as he found it: unchanged."

AFTER: *(The Eulogy I'm Writing Now)*

"Matt Farnsworth was a man who refused to die with potential still inside him. He rebuilt from nothing, forging strength from scars and wisdom from wounds. He didn't simply overcome—he became unbreakable. He was a warrior, a leader, a man of faith. He didn't only fight his demons—he set fire to their kingdom. He left behind a legacy of strength, redemption, and purpose. He didn't only change his life—he changed the lives of others. And when he met his Maker, he arrived empty—having given every last gift away to the world."

VICTORY INDICATORS:

You Know You're Succeeding When:

- You can name your failures without making excuses
- You feel uncomfortable, but keep moving forward anyway
- You've stopped blaming others for your situation
- You catch yourself in a lie and correct it immediately
- You review your "current eulogy" and genuinely want something different
- Your conversations include phrases like "I was wrong" or "That was my fault"
- You feel the weight lifting as you acknowledge your reality

RED FLAGS:
- You find yourself saying "but" after admitting mistakes
- You create elaborate justifications for your situation
- You shift blame to others or circumstances
- You avoid writing your truths because they're "too painful"
- You read this chapter and immediately skip to the next without doing the work

REALITY CHECK:

Facing the void is brutal. It's supposed to be. When you write your brutal truths and current eulogy, you might feel sick to your stomach. Your mind will fight you, offering excuses and distractions to avoid the pain of reality. That resistance is normal—it's your old self fighting to survive. Some new warriors break down when they first face their truth. Others get angry. Some need to walk away and come back. Whatever happens, remember: discomfort is the currency of progress. The more it hurts to face, the more you need to face it. This isn't about punishing yourself—it's about freeing yourself to become who you were meant to be.

WAR ORDER (FINAL COMMAND):

Close this book. Grab a pen. **Do the work.**
1. **Write your three brutal truths.**
2. **Write your current eulogy.**
3. **Rewrite your future eulogy.**

And when you're done, look in the mirror and ask yourself one thing:

"Am I finally ready to stop lying to myself?"

*"Fight. Because if you don't take control of your future—**the enemy will.**"*

CHAPTER 2

Pretending to Be Normal

*"Facing brutal truths isn't easy. But it was nothing compared to the years I spent **perfecting the art of denial**."*

My parents wanted me to go to college. Fresh off my numerous run-ins with the law, I had zero leverage. I'd have to ride this one out if I wanted their continued support. So I did what they asked. I got into Seattle Pacific University, a Christian school, though I had no interest in the Christian perspective they offered. The girls at the University were far too nice and well put together for my taste. On the surface, it appeared I was succeeding—3.8 GPA, good at what I put my mind to. But I was an **impostor** among all of these wholesome people who worked hard and cared about humanity. The structure, the expectations, the feeling of being trapped in a system I didn't understand or respect—it all felt **suffocating**. I remember going to chapel and feeling angry I had to sit there. I only signed up for this to get my parents off my back.

Part of what drove me into acting was blowing out my knee playing soccer. With athletics suddenly off the table, the frustration was palpable. I needed a release.

During one of my quarterly meetings with my college counselor, he suggested I take an acting class. *"Channel that energy somewhere,"* he said. He was right.

The class spoke to me in a way nothing had since that poetry class in high school. Something about inhabiting someone else's feelings felt like freedom. I wasn't acting—I was escaping.

I started watching movies obsessively: *On the Waterfront, Rebel Without a Cause, and The Seventh Veil*. I submerged myself in Orson Welles and Federico Fellini movies. I became a student of film.

I went to current movies to study acting. I remember sitting in a theater watching *Jerry Maguire* when it came out, beer smuggled in my jacket. A little buzzed watching Tom Cruise on screen, I wasn't impressed. I was calculating.

If this guy could do it, why couldn't I?

I dove in deeper, signing up at the Strasberg Institute downtown, a private acting group. Acting came easily to me. I had a tremendous intensity. Probably all of that suppressed emotion boiling under the surface. We had a student who was ninety-three years old in class. This was her first acting class. She had always wanted to be an actress and she was finally giving it a shot. She inspired me. When one of my acting classmates wanted to head to LA, it took me all of thirty seconds to make up my mind to go with him. I'm not going to wait until I'm ninety-three years old to give this a shot, I thought.

When I dropped out of college, I believed moving far away and starting fresh would fix everything. I wanted out. I thought leaving the area would help me. And it did. For a while. I thought I was running toward salvation, but it was a temporary distraction.

We broke the news to our parents, packed up, and headed to LA. They weren't exactly thrilled about us moving there alone at twenty-one.

Los Angeles doesn't greet you—it swallows you whole; the so-called **"City of Angels"** is an oxymoron, a glittering land where Lucifer rules. I thought I was **escaping darkness.** Truth? I was driving straight into its heart—dragging a tiny remnant of my past behind me in a U-Haul. Traffic snarled, people rushed, and the smog turned the sky the color of old bruises. But all **I saw was gold.**

In LA, you get processed by the demons themselves. Every wannabe star, every desperate dreamer—all inventory in the Devil's warehouse.

We didn't have a home when we landed in LA, so we ended up in a run-down motel in Santa Monica.

Our first taste of liberation. You could see the Pacific Ocean from our window, endless blue stretching toward tomorrow. The waves that felt like hope to me were dragging my friend under. That night I found him curled up on the bed, crying for his parents. That's how this city works—it doesn't break you, it makes you watch yourself shatter.

The same walls that felt like opportunity to me were **squeezing the life out of him.**

A month later, the dust settled. He found a place in Culver City and I landed a studio apartment off Pico. The locals called it "the slums of Beverly Hills." The bathroom was straight out of a horror movie—pink tile from the 70s, rust stains, mold that looked alive. That year, the rains hit hard. El Niño didn't bring rain—it brought judgment. My ceiling became God's art gallery, displaying everything I was running from in brown-stained Rorschach tests.

Every crack in the wall, every leak—I turned it all into some hero's origin story. Every flaw was character development. The biggest agents were breathing the same Beverly Hills smog. I could taste success like copper in my mouth.

Here's another lesson I didn't learn until much later: **Demons don't disappear** when you change your surroundings. They follow you, lurking under the surface, working on you.

They grow stronger in the dark. Pills, distractions, validation—they're numbing agents. They let the demon sit quietly until it's ready to claw its way into your life. At that time, I wasn't drinking. I had a new purpose. A new goal, but Hollywood isn't an industry—it's Satan's ideal hunting ground. He imports people desperate for validation and keeps them hooked on promises of **fame**, fortune, and meaning.

I was sprinting toward oblivion with my eyes closed. I thought I was chasing success. I was **chasing the Devil's carrot.** And the worst part?

I didn't even know **I was starving.**

The Fog of Ambition

Determination can be a good thing.
The same **obsessive drive** that fuels addiction can be leveraged as motivation to generate success.

I pounded the pavement in LA, knocking on doors of low-level agents in sleazy offices.

"I've prepared a monologue," I'd say. *"You'll love it—give me five minutes."*

One of my go-to pieces was from **Eugene O'Neill's *Long Day's Journey into Night.***

"The fog was where I wanted to be... Everything looked and sounded unreal. Nothing was what it is."

I delivered the lines **with conviction.**

"I wanted to be alone with myself in another world where truth is untrue, and life can hide from itself. As if I had drowned long ago. As if I was a ghost belonging to the fog, and the fog was the ghost of the sea."

The fog. The addiction. The numbness.

"Who wants to see life as it is if they can help it?"

That was the real trap.
I wasn't chasing success.
I was **chasing escape.**

That monologue got me in the door.

The Lure of Fame

The monologue brought me success quickly—bigger agents, bigger opportunities, a recurring role on a national TV show, and various independent films. Life was moving fast, and when I chased earthly pleasures, it always seemed to go well—at first. The doors kept opening, but so did the bottle. The pressure to perform had me searching for a **release.**

Up in Seattle, my dad's career had paid off. Microsoft stock options and executive-level success created a safety net I didn't deserve but gladly used. Between my parents' growing prosperity and my newfound success, I managed to secure a house in the Hollywood Hills, banking on future earnings that hadn't yet materialized. I was living the Los Angeles dream on borrowed confidence and borrowed cash.

Los Feliz became my trophy—an up-and-coming hipster paradise nestled between Hollywood and Silver Lake, where creatives chased fame, status, and the illusion of success. The Devil rewards those who play by his rules, but he never gives without taking back even more. And he was coming for me.

I stand at the window of my new house, glass in hand, the city spread before me like a fallen constellation.

Los Angeles at night doesn't sleep—**it transforms.**

Downtown's skyscrapers pierce the darkness, man-made stars burning against the black canvas. The Hollywood sign floats in the distance, letters half-dissolved in darkness, a promise whispered rather than shouted.

From here, the city's chaos arranges itself into perfect order. All my pain, all my struggle, all that desperate clawing—invisible now. It's light. It's beauty. It's possibility.

The warm night air slips through the open window, carrying Radiohead's melancholy from the Greek Theater below. I couldn't have imagined it—Thom Yorke's voice really climbing these hills tonight, finding me exactly where I stand.

I take it **as a sign.**

Not a warning, but a **benediction.**

This city. This house. This moment. It feels like the answer I've been chasing since Seattle. Since jail. That broken kid who didn't belong anywhere finally found a place that makes him feel worthy.

I look out over the glittering landscape, conviction settling into my bones. This is going to be it—the place where everything finally comes together, where all the pain finally makes sense.

I decide to worship at this altar of light and ambition. Los Angeles becomes **my religion**, fame **my salvation**, success **my redemption.**

This view. This house. This city.

They **become my God.**

This is finally going to give me the calm and serenity I've been searching for my entire life.

I am going to make it.

I am home.

The First Hit

Christina Fulton lives next door—Nicolas Cage's ex. Her house is so close I can practically reach out and touch it from my bedroom window.

She is blonde and nearly perfectly made. There's always some guy pulling up in an expensive car.

Then there's Weston, her child with Cage.

He's ten years old. Weston isn't just another kid of Hollywood royalty—he's different. Wild one moment, withdrawn the next. He carries an intensity that keeps people at a distance, always teetering on the edge of **snapping.**

I see it clearly when his mom dotes on him, no matter how bad his outbursts get. His father is absent. Their house feels less like a home and more like a never-ending drama scene.

Weston Cage has already learned to wear dysfunction as a **badge of honor.**

I don't realize it yet, but he won't be a predictable neighbor.

He'll be **a problem.**

One night, a month into living here, Christina knocks on my door.

"Want to check out The Well?"

The Well is darker than a typical bar—moody red lights, Indie music humming low in the background, exposed brick walls soaked in secrets.

Christina seems to know everyone.

Especially the bartender.

I watch as he slides something into her hand during our first drink.

A few rounds in, she grabs my arm, her grip urgent.

"Come with me," she says.

We duck into the bathroom.

The lock clicks behind us.

She flashes a gorgeous smile.

I have no idea the enemy is standing in front of me, so I open the door willingly.

She pulls out a bullet—a metal device.

Twists the chamber.

White powder falls into place.

Cocaine.

This is what they do.

This is what success feels like.

Here I am—about to do coke with the sexy blonde from *The Doors movie*.

The first hit is like swallowing a live wire.

Heat tears through my skull.

My nostrils blaze.

My pulse hammers—pure electricity.

Then—**clarity.**

Sharp—impeccable vision.

I'm not high.

I'm **INVINCIBLE.**

It sears through me. Suddenly, everything snaps into focus.

The music grows louder.

Christina is magnetic.

The bathroom keeps secrets.

The night comes alive.

The demons' revolving door in my life swings wide open.

RED FLAG MOMENT: The first high isn't a gift—it's a trade. The Devil never gives without taking something in return. What he offers feels like paradise, but the price tag is hidden, and it is steep.

The crash wasn't slow.

No sleep.

I pace.

Pace.

PACE until morning.

Watch the spectacular sunrise over the hills, cloaked in utter **darkness.**

Invincibility? Over.

My skin crawls, peeling off my bones.

Every nerve ending exposed—raw, **biting.**

The voice from the deep rises to meet me.

You need more.

My thoughts become more morbid—erratic, frantic.

A misfiring engine.

My brain isn't asking for it.

It's **DEMANDING** it.

Even as my body rejects the drug.

The fog doesn't creep in—

It consumes me.

But I **don't have more.**

I try to focus.

I can't.

I look in the mirror.

Horrific images flash in my mind—death, destruction, cloaked figures.

My jaw clenches so tight I fear my teeth might snap.

I turn on the shower.

Close the glass door.

Cold water hits me.

A shock to the system.

It does **nothing.**

Purgatory engulfs me.

I slide down into the corner of the shower.

My body covers the drain.

Water pools around me.

Up to my chin.

I can't move.

The door rips open.

Water floods out onto the tile.

My friend stands there, watching me spill onto the floor.

I mutter, "I'm never doing that again."

The high is over.

But the nightmare?

It's just getting started.

Within twenty-four hours, I'm asking Christina **where she got it.**

The Dealer

Through Christina, I met Phil—the coke dealer with a mansion in the hills.

She took me to one of his parties a week after that first hit. Money flowed as freely as the drinks. Ryan Phillippe was there with Reese Witherspoon. Other A-listers I'd only seen in magazines.

Phil handed me his number that night.

I had my own connection now.

Here's what they don't tell you about cocaine:

It doesn't only get you high—it hijacks your **SOUL.**

You don't sleep.

You can't sleep.

And things start to slip when your auditions start at 9 a.m. after being up all night with demons dancing in your head.

You are no longer doing coke at night.

Now it's your morning coffee.

The Bulletproof Monk Audition

After my new morning coffee bump in my car, I'm sitting in a waiting room, loaded, my heart racing, my leg bouncing.

An attractive young woman is staring at me.

"You look just like my ex-boyfriend," she says.

I smirk. "Really? Is he ugly like me?"

She laughed. "No, he's handsome. His name is Brad Renfro."

Brad Renfro. The child actor from *A Time to Kill*. He'll overdose years later in 2008.

She leans in closer, her voice low.

"Wanna guess what tattoo I have on my butt cheek?"

I blink. "No clue."

She grins. "It says, 'Daddy.'"

Typical LA small talk.

Before I can process that I'm talking to Bijou Phillips, the door swings open.

"Matt Farnsworth."

The casting assistant waves my headshot.

I shove the cocaine deeper into my pocket and stumble into the room.

The casting director's eyes lock onto mine, keen and unrelenting. He sees straight through me.

"Ready when you are," he says.

Pure **panic.**

"Man, I don't know what's happening," I blurt. "I need to get out of here."

He frowns. "That's not one of the lines."

"I'm not saying the lines," I laugh nervously. "I'm not in character."

I flee.

I bolt out of the Santa Monica casting office.

Somehow... I make it to my car. Somehow... I'm driving onto the 10 freeway.

But not driving.

Gridlock.

Not normal LA traffic.

Complete **standstill.**

The demons aren't knocking anymore.

They're throwing a rave in my head.

The air feels too thin, too thick—all at once.

My skin isn't tight, it's foreign.

Is this my body? Am I inside it, or watching it from somewhere else?

The freeway stretches longer than it should—too far. The cars don't feel still—they feel **staged.**

I turn up the radio. Static.

Turn it again. **STATIC.**

Cars **EVERYWHERE**.

HONKING.

TRAPPED.

So I do what any coked-out lunatic would do.

I run.

Leave my car in the middle of the freeway and start jogging through Santa Monica.

Not thinking. Running.

From what?

I don't know.

Movement will later become my salvation in recovery.

But right then?

It was another way to run from my mistakes.

The next day, I had to get a friend to help me find my car.

It had been towed.

The Parties That Looked Like Heaven

The cocaine connections opened doors.

Literally.

Through Christina, I got invited to Nicolas Cage's Halloween parties.

His house was a massive gated black and crimson brick castle. The front door lights, torches. As you stroll up the driveway of his Bel Air mansion, you pass Dennis Hopper and James Caan as if they're regular people. Patricia Arquette greets you at the door.

Inside, firebreathers dance between sword swallowers while exotic snakes slither past your feet. In the private movie theater, James Hetfield from Metallica chats about horror films.

Nothing was real.

But that's the thing about LA.

It never is.

This became my life: Auditions by day—when I could keep it together.

A blur of parties, pills, and powder by night. The higher I climbed socially, the deeper I sank personally. Every line of coke, every A-list handshake, every wild night—another step into the fog.

The parties at sunset were a hallucination of success—concrete jungle, movie stars in G-wagons, the illusion of "making it."

LA baptizes you in darkness. The enemy never rushes. He doesn't force his way in. He doesn't need to.

He waits.

At first, he's subtle. An idea, a nudge, a thought so small you don't even recognize it.

You shake it off. You call it nothing. A coincidence. A fleeting impulse.

Then he lingers.

He waits for the nights you're exhausted.

He waits for the moments you let your guard down.

He waits for you to start justifying what you swore you'd never do.

And when you do—

He steps closer.

He plants the doubt.

He turns up the volume.

Because the enemy doesn't strike when you're strong.

He strikes when you think you're safe.

The Bad Neighbor

One day, that darkness followed me home. I had been out traversing LA all day. From Paramount Studios to CBS Radford. I was exhausted. I could never have expected what I saw when I got home. Blood dripping from my dogs' mouths.

Dark streaks of fresh blood strewn across the floor. One cowering in the corner, the other shaking next to me. The back door stood wide open.

A violation. **A warning.**

Then—I feel someone behind me.

I turn. Weston Cage.

Standing there in the open doorway.

Eyes empty as winter graves.

Not blank. **Hollow.**

"If you tell anyone, I'll kill you."

Not a threat. A prophecy.

He'd broken in. He attacked my dogs with a wooden stick used to secure the windows.

But it wasn't the violence that startled me—it was the void behind his eyes.

He meant what he said.

Soulless. Satan's fingerprints all over him.

I obviously called Christina and told her what had happened. There was a meltdown.

When I first moved in, they tried to get me to sign an NDA. Standard celebrity procedure. *You're too close. You see too much. You hear too much.*

Sign here and shut up.

I refused.

The next day, Nicolas Cage pulled up in a Lamborghini, apologizing. I promised silence. What good would tabloids do?

The dysfunction was generational, carved into their DNA.

I buried that memory. Or thought I did.

For years, Weston was a name I tried to forget.

But then, in 2023, his name found me again.

I would end up on the Santa Monica Pier at a movie premiere party.

And there was Weston at the very same party.

He had a role in a Jean-Claude Van Damme B-movie. Hollywood always has space for famous names.

Talent **optional.**

Weston was now a massive man.

Overweight.

"Hey, Weston. I used to play with you outside your house in Los Feliz."

Recognition flickered. We chatted. Weston smiled trying to control the narrative. Pretending he had conquered his demons. I wanted to believe him. But Hollywood is built on illusion. And illusions don't last long.

His Instagram later told the truth. I scrolled through it.

Manic posts. Love-bombing. Grandiosity.

A social media fun house of mirrors for a broken soul.

The headline hit no more than a year later.

TMZ: "Weston Cage Arrested for Brutally Beating His Mother, Christina."

I felt no shock. Only gratitude.

That could've been my kid. Another Hollywood casualty. Another generational curse.

The city demands sacrifices. Look at the pattern: Travolta. Newman. Stallone. Redford. Madsen. Coppola. All lost firstborn sons. Dead. Francis Ford Coppola is Nicolas Cage's uncle for those of you that did not know that.

If you want to dive into that rabbit hole, you'll find much more.

Coincidence?

Ask Bob Dylan about his bargain with "The Chief Commander."

"What was your bargain?" the interviewer asked.

"To get where I am now."

"Should I ask who you made the bargain with?"

"With the chief commander... on this earth and in a world we can't see."

Fame isn't the prize.

It's **the bait.**

The bargain always has a cost.

I saw that cost close up—with Weston. With myself. With everyone who stayed too long in the fire.

I escaped by grace alone.

But something darker was still coming.

The Devil wasn't done with me yet.

His lies weren't shared in private—they were blasted from every billboard, sold in every theater, wrapped in a hundred different shades of spiritual enlightenment.

Every morning in Los Angeles, someone's offering salvation.

Crystals. Meditation. Ancient wisdom recycled and marked up 1000%.

The spirituality buffet never closes.

These people think they're ascending.

Every new age practice, every channeling session—it's all "spiritual growth."

I watched it happen.

Star after star, creating their self-righteous concocted version of heaven.

Madonna diving into Kabbalah. Cruise with Scientology. Everyone finding their "truth."

Everyone **staying lost.**

Hollywood is the ultimate seller of the wide road.

You know the one Jesus talked about:

Matthew 7:13 says, *"For the gate is wide and the way is easy that leads to destruction, and those who enter by it are many."*

Here's what they don't tell you:

Satan loves religion.

Loves spirituality.

He'll let you worship anything—crystals, yourself, your success.

Because all of that worships him.

Anything but **Christ.**

The enemy's franchise spans every city.

Every industry. Every income level.

Different bait. Same trap.

He doesn't need you famous.

He needs you **BLIND.**

Back then, I thought Weston was the problem—another disturbing incident in Hollywood. But now, looking deeper, I realize Weston was only a symptom of a much larger battle. Let me explain clearly what I now see and why it matters to you, too.

Reflection

Hello again—my glasses are on, and reading this alongside you took me straight back to Los Feliz, where I was blind to the battle I was living in. Back then, I thought the drugs—the fast life—were all part of achieving success in Hollywood. But now? I see it clearly. I see the war. The deception. The idols I worshiped, and the lies that whispered my name. And I see how easily the enemy kept me numb.

There's a profound difference between what's soulish and truly spiritual—and most of us can't see it clearly without divine help. This distinction isn't rudimentary theological theory—it's the battlefield where your destiny is decided. Scripture says,

"For the word of God is living and active, sharper than any two-edged sword, piercing to the division of soul and spirit, of joints and marrow, discerning the thoughts and intentions of the heart." **(Hebrews 4:12)**

Think of it this way: your soul is your mind, will, and emotions—the parts of you that interact with the world. Your spirit is the part of you designed to commune with God. When your spirit is dormant, your soul takes control—and the enemy knows exactly how to manipulate a soul disconnected from its spiritual anchor.

It's like driving a car with no GPS. Your soul's got the gas pedal. The Devil's got the directions. He's taking you straight to hell—**a beautiful drive.** Meanwhile, the part of you meant to be en route to God—those directions—are a paperback map that's slid between the seats, and you haven't thought about it in years.

Maybe it flashes through your mind when you avoid a horrible accident or see a tragedy outside the car window, but that flash fades like a candle blown out. And the enemy? He doesn't even have to hijack you. He redirects your attention when you feel lost and start fumbling for that map. He whispers in your ear, flips your favorite song on, sends you that DM you've been waiting for, and you instantly ditch searching for that map.

That's what happened to me. I was emotionally driven, validation-starved, high on affirmation, and low on discernment. I confused being moved with being led. And I paid for it.

In college, I majored in religious studies. Yes, that's right—me, studying theology, fascinated by the Gospel. I excelled in those classes. But here's the critical mistake I couldn't see then: I engaged God's truth only with my soul—my intellect, my emotions, my will—while my spirit remained dormant, unawakened.

I was on a path toward discovering my true calling. But the enemy saw my progress and quickly offered a distraction—acting, fame, false worship, and counterfeit gods. **James 3:15 warns clearly about wisdom that** *"does not descend from above, but is earthly, soulish, demonic."* My religious knowledge wasn't transforming me because it never pierced beyond my soul into my spirit. The division never occurred.

This purposefully placed distraction is a dangerous first step many young people unknowingly take into darkness. They become *"soulish, having not the Spirit,"* **as Jude 19 describes.** They separate themselves, convinced they're pursuing some unique or elite path—when they're simply following their ungodly desires masked as ambition urged on by the enemy. This step is the blindfold the enemy slides over your eyes.

Celebrity worship still captivates our culture today. Yet movie stars felt larger than life in the late '90s and early 2000s. Before social media, they were our YouTube stars, influencers, and cultural gods—untouchable, unreachable icons we only glimpsed through magazine covers and red carpets.

Back then, I genuinely believed that if I could become famous and wealthy, all my problems would vanish—I would've *"made it."* Some of you may be too young to remember Blockbuster Video, but there was a time when watching a movie meant going to the theater or renting it afterward. That world captivated me. Being so important that people would drive, pick up a movie you starred in, and take it home to watch—or even better, pay to see you on the big screen—that felt like salvation.

I vividly recall sitting in the famous Cinerama Dome on Sunset Boulevard at the premiere of *Fight Club*. The massive screen forced your eyes to scan side to side to take it all in. Onscreen, actors Brad Pitt and Edward Norton seemed more than human—they were gods. I wanted that unshakable certainty, that freedom from insecurities haunting me daily—insecurities I thought fame and applause could silence forever. I truly believed their lives were perfect. Their confident swagger on screen mirrored what I wanted to become, professionally and personally. I admired that bravado.

This is the very essence of soulish thinking—earthly wisdom appealing to our need for validation, status, and admiration. It bypasses the spirit completely, feeding directly into the soul's appetites. The more I pursued fame, the deeper my spirit slumbered.

Looking back now, I'm stunned at how easily celebrity worship blurred the line between fiction and reality for me. I convinced myself that fame made these actors immune to suffering. Of course, now I know the truth: Brad Pitt has openly shared his struggles with alcoholism. Edward Norton has discussed battles with anxiety. The flawless lives I envied were as fictional as the characters they played.

Here's the truth I eventually learned by fully immersing myself in the Gospel, yet initially failed to apply to my own life:

"For as we have many members in one body and all the members do not have the same function, so we, being many, are one body in Christ, and individually members one of another." **(Romans 12:4–5)**

I was trying to be something I wasn't created to be—like a hand attempting to be a foot, stumbling clumsily in shoes it was never meant to fit into.

So why did the enemy want me chasing these idols so fiercely? Because he knew something I didn't: idols aren't merely golden calves or ancient statues. They're anything—fame, wealth, validation, even our talents—we elevate above God. Hollywood isn't mere entertainment; it's a system designed to turn humans into objects of worship, subtly teaching us to glorify created things instead of the Creator Himself.

The Gospel confronts idol worship directly. When Jesus says, *"No one can serve two masters"* **(Matthew 6:24)**, He's addressing the heart of idolatry. Every idol demands worship that belongs only to God. Every idol promises fulfillment, but it can never deliver. Every idol ultimately leads to emptiness because we were created to worship only One who can satisfy the deepest longings of our hearts.

He maintains influence as long as the enemy can keep us operating from our souls—our intellect, emotions, and will—rather than our spirits. A soul without spiritual guidance is like a powerful car without a driver—impressive but directionless and ultimately dangerous.

After my accident, God granted me a gift—the ability to tell stories that help others see and fight this spiritual battle in their own lives. Sometimes, I can simply look at someone and sense what's happening in their walk. This isn't something I pursued—it was thrust upon me, like the ministry of redemption I now speak of. God's charismatic gifts aren't about our natural abilities; they're expressions of

His grace, enabling us to fulfill our true purpose.

The tragedy of idols is that they promise everything—success, happiness, validation—but leave us empty-handed. It took me decades to recognize this. What I once saw as the perfect life now strikes me as painfully empty, a hollow existence beneath bright lights and makeup. Real salvation never comes from a movie screen—it comes from Jesus, the One who sees beyond the spotlight, meets us in our brokenness, and fills the emptiness idols create.

The real reason I struggled with faith was that I was pursuing the wrong calling. Had I been living the purpose for which God created me, I would've found all the faith I needed. Instead, as Paul puts it, I was sentimental rather than sober about who I was and what God called me to do.

Maybe you've chased idols, too, believing they'll offer happiness or freedom. Pause now and honestly reflect:

What idols are you clinging to? Do they deliver on their promises or leave you as empty as they left me? What would your life look like if your spirit, not only your soul, was fully awakened?

Here's why idols held such power over me:

My soul **eagerly cooperated** with what the world offered.

In the Bible, what's translated as *"sensual"* in the King James is *"soulish"* in Greek. I wasn't spiritual—I was **soulish**. That kind of wisdom is deceptive. It looks deep. It feels elite. It whispers, *"You're special. You're chosen. You're above them."* But it's counterfeit. It's demonic.

True wisdom comes from above. When the Holy Spirit fills you, He **unites with your spirit**, not your soul. And once that happens, everything shifts. Your spirit governs your soul. Your soul stops chasing idols. I once had knowledge, but no life. Now I have both. God's Word pierced me—cut soul from spirit—and showed me the difference between what feels spiritual and what truly is spiritual.

The same Hollywood that seduced my soul... now stands as the **backdrop for His glory.** The enemy's plan backfired.

What he meant for my destruction, God used for my restoration. This is true spiritual warfare—when God's Spirit finally unites with ours, governing our soul, directing our body, we become dangerous to darkness.

This is where idols lose power. This is where counterfeits are exposed by the authentic. And this, my friend, is where your journey can take a divine turn too.

The same God who awakened my dormant spirit stands ready to awaken yours. But you must choose Him. I had to learn the hard way—there's only one door to truth. It's not knowledge. It's not charisma. It's not hustle. It's Jesus. Paul said in **1 Corinthians 2:2,** *"I determined to know nothing among you except Jesus Christ* and Him crucified." That's the only door that leads to life. I'd tried to climb in through every window—intellect, image, addiction. But it wasn't until I walked through that door that I found freedom.

Pray with me:

"God, forgive me for chasing empty idols. Awaken my spirit, transform my soul, and set my heart on eternal things. Today, I reject counterfeit promises and choose what is authentic—I choose You. Reveal my true purpose, replacing worldly wisdom with Your eternal truth. Amen."

Because when your spirit awakens, nothing else compares.

Welcome to the battle. Welcome to freedom.

The Gospel As A Weapon

I've got my Bible in my hands right now—same as every morning.

Which brings me to the weapon I needed back then:

Ephesians 6:17 says: *"Take the helmet of salvation and the sword of the Spirit, which is the word of God."*

Wait.

Some of you reading this book aren't Christians. Some of you are, but the Bible is more of a decoration on your nightstand than a weapon.

The Bible is the most-read book in human history. If you're the kind of person drawn to this book I've written, it's not a stretch to think you've either read the Bible or might be willing to.

The real question is: **Why haven't you?**

Why do people **run to every book but this one?**

They'll read self-help books by "manifestation coaches."
They'll binge podcasts on success habits, morning routines, and **how to hack their dopamine levels.**
They'll pay ten thousand dollars to sit in a conference room and listen to a man in a blazer talk about **unlocking their full potential.**

But **one book**—the one that has shaped nations, toppled empires, freed the enslaved, and built civilizations—that book? Nah.

Too **UNCOMFORTABLE.**
Too **RESTRICTIVE.**
Too **UNBELIEVABLE.**

They'll read about **spiritual energy and** *"the universe"* all day, but open the Bible? Nope. Can't have that. That's **too real.**

But what if—just what if—you **picked it up**?

Not as a religious act.
Not to impress anyone.
Not to tick a spiritual box.

But because **you're in a war**, and you're fighting **unarmed.**

Most people are engaged in daily spiritual battles with **zero weapons.**

They try to fight off demons with **willpower.**
They try to heal deep wounds with **grind culture and productivity hacks.**
They try to battle generational curses with **affirmations and mindfulness apps.**

And **they wonder why they keep losing.**

Listen—when Satan himself showed up to tempt Jesus, **Jesus didn't debate.**
He didn't negotiate.
He didn't *"manifest positive energy."*
He didn't visualize success.

He **fasted.**

He quoted Scripture.
He **resisted.**

Matthew 4:4 says: *"Man shall not live by bread alone, but by every word that proceeds from the mouth of God."*

That's how you fight. That's how you win.

And yet, so many people trying to *"change their lives"* have never even opened the one book that could **transform them.**

Let me put it this way—if you're trying to take back your life, why wouldn't you read the one book that has led billions of people out of **slavery, addiction, failure, and hopelessness?**

What does it hurt?

If you're so willing to read **everything else,** test this one too.

Start with the Gospel of John.
Find a version that's easy to read.
And give it **30 days.**

Because the truth is—the Holy Spirit will open your mind when you're ready.

And once He does?

It changes **EVERYTHING.**

Blinded To See

The apostle Paul **got it.**

I was no different from Paul. Like him, I needed to be knocked down before I could see.

Do you know who he was?

Before Damascus, he was **the original blind man.**

Saul, who would later become Paul, was a Pharisee—a religious leader. And he was **killing Christians.**

Killing them.

Because he **thought Jesus was a fraud.**

Then, Jesus **knocked him down** and truly **opened his eyes.**

"Now as he went on his way, he approached Damascus, and suddenly a light from heaven shone around him. And falling to the ground, he heard a voice saying to him, 'Saul, Saul, why are you persecuting me?" **(Acts 9:3–4)**

"Saul rose from the ground, and although his eyes were opened, he saw nothing. So they led him by the hand and brought him into Damascus. And for three days he was without sight, and neither ate nor drank." **(Acts 9:8–9)**

That encounter **changed everything.**

Paul became one of the greatest voices for Christ, warning people about the traps of the world, the flesh, and the Devil.

I was **no different.**

I thought I was **climbing.**

I was plummeting into eternal torment.

I thought I was **chasing light.**

I was running headfirst into the abyss.

The mansions. The parties. Idolatry. The endless **search for meaning—**

More elaborate chains.

The wide road promises everything.
Delivers nothing.
Costs you **everything.**

Truth finds some people quietly, during everyday moments.
God taps their shoulder, and they turn gently, saying, *"Yes, God? What would you have me do?"*

Me?
I needed a demon in my basement.
A burning car.
A broken neck.
And soon—as you'll discover—a prison sentence hanging over my head.

Some people hear God in a gentle breeze kissing their cheek.

I required **a Category 5 hurricane.**

That's the thing about **spiritual deafness**—

A red flashing light with a siren does not go off when **God begins speaking to you.**

It is **not obvious.**

It is in the subtle hints. The events you can't explain.

The moments you **brush off.**

And when you **keep ignoring Him?**

That's when things **get ugly.**

That's when He lets you find out exactly what earthly pestilence you've been **dancing with.**

The enemy never sleeps.

He's **watching too.**

He doesn't need a Hollywood contract or a drug dealer's business card.
All he needs is **your participation.**

He is the Prince of the power of the **air.**

The AIR we breathe.
We accept his **blasphemy** because we have been—
Groomed by his world.

We **laugh** at the mockery.
We **buy tickets** to his shows.
We consume his lies like hotcakes on Shrove Tuesday.

Why?

Because it's easy—until it isn't.

Until your life hangs by a thread.

And even then, some welcome it.

That's how twisted he makes us.

That's how cruel his deception is.

And I?

I was his most **compliant fool.**

I repeated his lies so often,

I mistook them for my own voice.

I repeated his **lies** so often,
I mistook them for my own thoughts.

That's how he wins.
Not with **force**—
But with **numbness.**

He doesn't **shout** these lies.
He plants them **openly.**

He torments—
And so do his **minions.**

Then he lets you **repeat them to yourself.**
He destroys you **one thought at a time.**

Because the **harshest prison** isn't made of steel.
It's built inside your head.

The voice that sabotaged every good thing before it materialized.
I thought that was me.

It convinced me I was **broken.**
It convinced me I was **weak.**
Then God's Word revealed the truth:

Those voices weren't mine.

They never were.

And until you can hear that voice inside your head, you are—
Defenseless.

I spent years locked in a prison I paid to build.

But the **TRUTH** set me **FREE**.

Now that you understand who the real enemy is—

Let's learn how to **RECOGNIZE his tactics.**

BLUEPRINT STEP 2: IDENTIFY THE ENEMY'S VOICE

(Inventory Your Reality)

"The first step to reclaiming your mind is learning which thoughts are weapons aimed at your soul."

WAR STRATEGY:

Your mission is clear: Identify the exact moment the enemy plants a thought designed to sabotage your purpose. He doesn't shout; he whispers subtle doubts that sound exactly like your own voice—thoughts that sever the critical connection between your soul (mind, will, emotions) and your spirit (your eternal identity in God). By recognizing and rejecting these lies immediately, you protect that connection, reinforcing your mind against future attacks. The moment you clearly distinguish the enemy's weaponized thoughts from your true spiritual identity, you take back control.

Your ability to walk boldly in your purpose depends entirely on this skill. If you master recognizing the enemy's weapons—every destructive thought designed to rob you of hope, identity, and purpose—then you're already winning the war.

Your soul is the battlefield—your mind, your emotions, your will.

It's time to march forward.

ACTION ORDERS:

1. Track Your Self-Talk Tape

Your mind constantly plays recordings—messages programmed into you long before you knew better.

- What's the first thing you think when you wake up?
- What's the last thing you think before sleep?
- Do you hear yourself speaking internally?
- Who wrote these messages—you or someone else?

Identify who programmed these thoughts: Family. Friends. Teachers. Society. Coaches. The enemy hides behind familiar voices.

2. Trace Each Lie to Its Source

The enemy doesn't need new lies—he recycles old ones that worked before.

- Where do these thoughts come from?
- When did you start believing them?
- Do you really believe them?
- Do you agree with them?

A lie doesn't become real unless you accept it. **Name it. Reject it. Replace it.**

3. Rewrite Your Internal Talk Tape with Truth

If a thought doesn't align with what God says about you—it's a lie.

THE ENEMY'S LIES VS. GOD'S TRUTH:

Lie #1: *"You'll never change."*
 Truth: *"Therefore, if anyone is in Christ, he is a new creation. The old has passed away; behold, the new has come."* **(2 Corinthians 5:17)**

Lie #2: *"You're too weak to overcome this."*
 Truth: *"My grace is sufficient for you, for My power is made perfect in weakness."* **(2 Corinthians 12:9)**

Lie #3: *"You're not good enough."*
 Truth: *"You are fearfully and wonderfully made."* **(Psalm 139:14)**

Lie #4: *"You don't deserve a second chance."*
 Truth: *"While we were still sinners, Christ died for us."* **(Romans 5:8)**

Lie #5: *"You'll always be an addict."*
 Truth: *"For freedom, Christ has set us free; stand firm, then, and do not submit again to slavery."* **(Galatians 5:1)**

How to fight back:

- Write down every lie you tell yourself—**every single one**.
- Cross each out. Physically. With a red pen.
- Replace each with God's truth from Scripture.
- Speak truth aloud daily until the lies fade.

When lies return—don't debate them—**replace them immediately.**

WAR CRY:

The enemy will **tell you who you are** until you start **fighting back**. He has been programming your defeat through your own thoughts since you took your first breath. No more. Your mind isn't neutral territory—it's the war zone. If he controls your thoughts, he controls your life.

Stop his lies the moment they appear. Refuse to let his words define you. Speak truth, even before you believe it.

Take back your mind. **Now.**

BLUEPRINT RECAP:

BEFORE: *(The Thoughts That Controlled Me)*

"You're not that smart. Other people know better than you. People don't like me. I'm different from everyone else. Don't even try, you'll fail. You're an idiot. Life is pointless. May as well drink. At least I can escape for a while. When you die nothing happens. There is no God. Heaven is a fairy tale. I'm glad I'm not as gullible as the people who believe in a magical Jew named Jesus."

AFTER: *(How I Rewrote Them)*

"The enemy called you an addict. God calls you redeemed. You're a new creation in Christ. Your identity isn't defined by your failures but by God's grace. Every day sober is another victory. Every challenge overcome is strength being built. Your past doesn't determine your future—your choices today do. You're not perfect, but you're forgiven. You're not play-

ing a role—you're becoming who you were always meant to be. You're a warrior in progress, a father finding his strength, a husband growing in love, a man walking in purpose. Your struggle qualified you to help others. Your testimony is your weapon. Your scars prove you survived. Your wounds became wisdom. Your past isn't your prison—it's your weapon. And the enemy? He should have killed you when he had the chance."

VICTORY INDICATORS:

You Know You're Succeeding When:
- You recognize your internal voice
- You can identify which thoughts are yours and which are the enemy's
- You automatically counter lies with truth
- You stop internalizing criticism
- The time between hearing a lie and rejecting it gets shorter
- You catch yourself before speaking destructive words
- You notice patterns when negative thoughts appear

RED FLAGS:
- You agree with thoughts that diminish your worth or purpose
- You can't distinguish between conviction (from God) and condemnation (from the enemy)
- You repeat the same negative self-talk daily without challenging it
- You believe thoughts that contradict Scripture
- You accept defeat as your identity

REALITY CHECK:

This battle won't be won overnight. Your mind has been programmed for years—expect resistance when you start reprogramming it. The enemy won't surrender territory easily. Some days, the lies will feel overwhelming, almost impossible to reject. **Good.** That resistance confirms you're reclaiming ground the enemy doesn't want to surrender. The harder the pushback, the more important the territory. When you stumble—and you will stumble—get back up immediately. Warriors aren't defined by never falling; they're defined by how quickly they rise and keep fighting.

WAR ORDER (FINAL COMMAND):

Write down every limiting belief that's controlled you. List them all. Cross each one out in RED. Then rewrite them with TRUTH.

Example:

- "I'm not strong enough" → "I am unbreakable."
- "I'll always be an addict" → "For freedom, Christ has set me free." **(Galatians 5:1)**
- "I'm not good enough" → "I am fearfully and wonderfully made." **(Psalm 139:14)**

Do this **today**. Not tomorrow. The war isn't outside. It's inside. You hear the voices. The doubts. The lies.

"You're not good enough. You'll always be this way. Today, we kill that voice inside that wants you weak."

CHAPTER 3

The Demon in the Basement

The Rituals

Those voices? I knew them intimately. They were more than whispers—they'd become companions.

But some nights, they weren't whispers at all.

It was a Tuesday night. I remember because Tuesdays in LA were slower. No parties worth attending. An empty evening in the hills.

My house was silent except for the occasional clink of ice in my scotch whiskey glass. The usual crowd of parasites and party-seekers had found somewhere else to orbit.

I saw an ad on TV for the LA Philharmonic. The Philharmonic presents: *The Works of Niccolò Paganini.*

Something about the name seized me. **Paganini.** I had never heard of him before, never listened to classical music willingly. I felt an almost magnetic pull.

Without thinking twice, I bought a ticket. One seat. **Just for me.**

I remember walking into that concert hall alone. The space was cavernous, with sweeping curves and polished wood. The lights dimmed to a deep red, making the stage glow like an **altar.**

Why was I here? What was a party guy from the Hollywood Hills doing at a classical concert?

I sank into my seat, program in hand, as the orchestra took the stage. The first notes of Paganini's "Le Streghe" (also known as "The Witches") pierced the silence. It was abrupt.

Aggressive.

Powerful.

Classical **whiplash.**

The music wasn't simply beautiful—it was unsettling. The solo violinist's fingers flew across the strings at impossible speeds. It wasn't the violinist's effortless conquering of technical impossibilities that hinted at occult forces—it was the bow striking the violin strings. It was violent. Like it made them **"cry,"** producing sounds that seemed beyond human ability.

I sat transfixed, a strange sensation washing over me—something like recognition. It was as if the music was speaking directly to some taboo, unnamed part of myself.

During intermission, I read the program notes about how people believed Paganini had sold his soul to the devil for his supernatural abilities, how he would write his music in cemeteries for inspiration. How crowds would cross themselves when he played. He was a womanizer and a drunkard. Eventually contracting syphilis, he was forced to retire. At the time of his death, he refused last rites thinking he could not die. The Catholic Church had denied him burial in consecrated ground because of his rejection of last rites. I found the story entertaining and alluring, ignoring the tragedy, focusing on the artistic gift, and desiring that kind of creative **ability for myself.** I even found myself believing that I needed to be tortured and debauched to have success. I assumed that alcohol and drugs were essential ingredients of creative genius. The masters I admired all lived such **tortured** lives—their pain seemingly fueling their brilliance. Without any thought of the afterlife, salvation never crossed my mind. I was seduced by the lie that to create something meaningful, I had to **suffer.** That authentic art demanded self-destruction.

My inexplicable attraction to this concert—to the music of a man they called The Devil's Violinist—was no accident.

The enemy was calling to me. And I was answering, without even knowing his name.

Soon, I would be called to more **dark visions** that would erode my soul further. But looking back, I see now—there was much more to the **seductive** notes of Paganini's violin score filling my ears. The invitation had been extended, and **I accepted.**

The Black Mass Was Coming For Me

Los Angeles **wasn't a city anymore.**

It was a ritual. And rituals **require sacrifices.**

After the incident with Christina's unwell child, we parted ways, and even though we weren't dating, it was still another woman gone from my life—**one with connections.**

Christina's brother, David, moved in with her, and I thought:

This will keep the connection open. He's my age and new to LA.

I quickly **discovered** he was as big a party animal as I was. I found a new enabler.

A **seven-foot giant.** A man who **commanded rooms** by walking in. A man who never had to fight, because no one was stupid enough to challenge him.

Together, **we tore through LA.**

Blocks beneath my house in the hills lay **a playground of drunken depravity.**

We became hunters in the LA nightscape—two predators working in tandem. We'd spot women across the bar, and David's imposing presence would clear a path. His seven-foot frame made bouncers step aside, and VIP sections opened up. We had access everywhere. My house became a revolving door. Faces blurred together—names forgotten by morning. I started keeping a bowl of toothbrushes in the guest bathroom—different colors for the strangers who might wake up there. A detail that amused my friends but should have horrified me. Some nights I'd find myself in a woman's bed with no memory of how I got there. Other mornings, I'd wake to find strange women in mine. The conquests meant nothing—temporary distractions for the growing pain inside. More often than not I was too intoxicated to act on the impulses that put me in these situations. I was becoming what I'd always sworn I wouldn't—a man who used people—a man who treated women as objects to be collected and discarded. The pattern accelerated after each party. More drugs. Stronger drinks. **Riskier behavior.** I wasn't only participating in the Hollywood debauchery anymore—I was hosting it. Leading it. I was to become a sacrifice.

The parties were endless.
The freeloaders never left.
The consequences **blurred into the background.**

The demon was...

Thriving.

Selling Your Soul: The Tigerland Deal

The casting room **buzzed with artificial energy.**

Actors pacing. Rehearsing lines.
Assistants chattering.
The hum of the overhead lights.

But **something felt off.**

The **shadows stretched longer.**

The **air pressed heavier.**

I'd been here before—**four callbacks deep** for *Tigerland,* a gritty war movie that could change everything.

Joel Schumacher—the director **loved me.**

The role was **practically mine.**

Then came **the call.**

A Tuesday.

My agent's voice **slick with enthusiasm.**

"Congratulations! You got the part."

For eight seconds, I tasted victory.

Eight seconds of pure validation.

Eight seconds of thinking I had made it on merit alone.

Then came **the poison, wrapped in casual words.**

"We need you to hang out with Joel."

Those words rang in my ears like a warning.

I didn't need to ask what it meant.

Everyone knew.

The entire industry whispered about it.

But **whispers don't save you** when the offer is made to you directly.

Joel Schumacher—**a man with a reputation for bedding thousands of men.**

One of Hollywood's worst-kept secrets.

He had launched **many careers from the casting couch.**

The equation was simple:

Your body for stardom.

Compromises.

Each one leading you **deeper into darkness.**

First, it's *"just drinks."*
Then, it's *"just dinner."*
Then, it's *"just this one time."*

Before you know it, you're not selling your talent—**you're selling your soul.**

My agent's voice buzzed in my ear, **detached and robotic.**

"It's how the game is played, Matt. Everyone does it. You want this, don't you?"

I looked around **my empty house.**

Last night's party was strewn about.

Mocking me.

A broken glass on the floor looking back up at me with contempt. An empty whiskey bottle tipped over on the counter.

This wasn't the life I had dreamed of **when I came to Hollywood.**

Was I willing to **destroy what little was left of myself** for a chance at something more?

"No," I told my agent.

The word felt... **heavy.**

Barely audible.

But it carried the weight of **a decision that would alter my life.**

"I won't do it. I couldn't do it."

And just like that... **the enemy's offer was rejected.**

The Devil Doesn't Forgive Rejection

The role went to **Colin Farrell.**

If you poke around the internet, you'll find that Kevin Spacey **"discovered"** Colin Farrell after a performance in a play in London.

Spacey introduced him to the **right agents.**

Made the **right calls.**

That's **how it works.**

It's **not about talent.**

It's about **who owns you.**

I'm not saying there was **a transaction there for fame.**

But that connection **still makes my skin crawl.**

Kevin Spacey's reputation for preying on young men was, and still is, out there.

The stories I heard were **so dark I can't even pen them here.**

That **vile place—wrapped in external beauty—demanded one thing:**
Submission.

Play the game.
Roll over.
And **you can have your fame.**

Saying **no** to *Tigerland* came with **consequences.**

The **calls slowed.**

The **meetings dried up.**

The Devil doesn't forgive **rejection.**

He **rewrites the script.**

He makes you **pay.**

I sank **deeper** into the parties, the cocaine, and the lies.

I became **hollow** inside.

The demon **grew.**

Patient.

Watching me wounded.

Stalking me.

Calculating.

Starving.

While I stumbled in the dark looking for a light switch to success.

Not knowing I am standing, defenseless, in front of **a man-eating lion—**

Jaws open, breath hot, waiting to **rip the flesh from my bones.**

I didn't know that refusing the enemy's deal wasn't the end. It was only the beginning of an even darker confrontation.

Darkness Descended

The coyotes gather on the ridge against Griffith Park.

A ridge that shouldn't exist—born from destruction when a house slipped from its foundation like flesh from bone.

No one rebuilt. The land reclaimed its territory.

And now? It belongs to the wild.

I hear them first—their voices.

A **cackling chorus.**

A primal symphony echoing through concrete canyons.

Laughter from another world.

I have to see.

The curtain slides beneath my fingers.

Sunset paints the ridge in blood orange and gold fire, and there they stand—twenty, maybe more. Families with their babies preparing for the nocturnal night.

HUNTERS.

ALIVE in a way humans have forgotten.

The coyotes vanish as quickly as they appeared. Ghost predators returning to the night shadows.

In this part of LA, the night soundtrack includes death—a cat's scream jolting you awake almost every other night.

Scientists once collected coyote scat from these hills, analyzing remains and isotopes. Their discovery? These aren't wilderness hunters anymore. They've evolved. Adapted. Between sixty and seventy-five percent of their diet comes from our world—our garbage, our ornamental fruit, our pets.

Cat remains appear in twenty percent of urban coyote scat.

Out here, where the city bleeds into wilderness, it's eat or be eaten.

I lay back down, trying to **relax.**

For the first time in months, the house isn't throbbing with music, yelling, or the sound of bottles clinking against countertops. Quiet. Heavy. Watchful.

I flip through the channels, but all I see is static and shadows—as if the TV knows something I don't.

I'll never forget the feeling—something on top of me as I doze off. Pressure.

Moments before I fall asleep, a memory flickers in my mind—something I haven't consciously considered in a long time.

A time when my neighbor Christina had walked through my house with me. She'd wanted to see the remodel. I showed her around.

As we went downstairs, the **temperature dropped.**

Christina shuddered, wrapping her arms around herself.

"Do you know what happened down here?"

I froze, shaking my head.

"There was an old man who lived here. He died upstairs, but it's not him you should be worried about. It's the guy who took care of him. He lived down here. He was into some... dark things. Witchcraft. He used to chant at night, lighting candles and talking to himself. He was evil."

At the time, I laughed it off, told her the whole house had been remodeled. "Nothing to worry about."

But now, alone in that oppressive silence, her words haunt me.

> **RED FLAG MOMENT:** The occult doesn't ask for permission—it only needs an open door. Culture numbs you to its evil, but ignoring it doesn't make it go away. It allows darkness to move freely in your life.

I try to shake it off, chalking it up to a vivid memory triggered by exhaustion.

But deep down, I feel it: **something isn't right.**

There is darkness in this beautiful house.

They don't call Lucifer the Morning Star for nothing. He is beautiful, alluring, and utterly deceptive.

But I have **made him angry.**

And this time, he is not sending my agent to make me an offer.

My eyes blur, and **I'm out.**

The Darkness Takes Form

I wake up in the guest room downstairs, though I don't remember going there.

The sheets are crisp, untouched.

The air—unnaturally cold.

My head feels heavy, but my senses are razor-sharp, as if someone has dialed up the contrast in the room.

I sit straight up.

That's when I see it.

Not a shadow—shadows behave.

Shadows obey light.

This doesn't.

A black faceless mass in front of me.

It moves, slick and unnatural, slipping through the air, warping everything it touches.

The dim light from the curtains bends around it—like even light is afraid to get too close.

Time stops.

My heart pounds against my ribs as the thing draws closer.

This isn't fear—this is primal, the kind of terror that lives in your DNA, a terror not taught, but known.

The kind of dread only the enemy can conjure.

I want to move, to scream, to do anything, but suddenly, my body won't respond.

Frozen.

I sit paralyzed, staring at this formless thing that seems to stare back, though it has no eyes, no features.

The silence is absolute, broken only by my own ragged breathing.

The second it moves closer, **my chest caves in.**

Something is stepping on me.

The air thickens—tar in my lungs.

My lungs fight, pulling in nothing.

SUFFOCATION.

A weight presses down on my shoulders, heavier, heavier.

Hands. Many hands. Holding me down.

That's when I know: it isn't alone.

There are more.

Watching. Waiting. Enjoying this.

A voice slithers into my mind—low, familiar. My voice.

"It's okay, man. Let go."

I know it isn't me, but it sounds like me—an echo of me.

Then, another voice. A different one. A growl, crawling up my spine.

"You've always belonged to us."

The bed sinks beneath an invisible weight. I hear fabric stretching, feel cold indentations pressing closer. A whisper drips like venom: "You think He wants you?" The sound curls around my mind, injecting stabbing painful jabs as it moves.

My own retreating voice answers back: *"No one's coming."*

It's gaining ground.

A Glimpse of God

Amidst the terror, a fleeting thought surfaces: God.

Have you ever been so terrified that you cried out for God or said, *"Jesus?"*

I can't move. I can't scream.

But deep in the pit of my mind, one thought forms—Jesus.

The mass **recoils.** Like a snake.

So I force it again.

"JESUS."

A screech rips through my skull—something jagged, **TEARING THROUGH BONE.**

The weight on my chest doubles—triples.

It is fighting back.

*"**Jesus**—help me!"*

The pressure in my head snaps.

The mass reels back as if struck.

It hates that name.

The air itself splits—ruptured, violent.

And for the first time, I can breathe.

As the sun bleeds through the curtains, the black mass shrivels.

It doesn't disappear.

It flees.

Like a roach when the lights come on.

It isn't faith. Not yet.

It isn't a prayer. Not yet.

It isn't devotion or belief or surrender. Not yet.

It was a reflex.

A frightened man reaching, grasping, clawing for something—**anything.**

Jesus.

One word. One breath.

And the darkness ran.

One word made it cower.

A cry of pure truth that pure evil could not overcome.

For a few heartbeats, hope filled my chest.

But I still wasn't ready to face what surrendering to that name truly meant:

To cherish the work He did on the cross.

Reflection

I'm sitting at my desk in Tennessee again—coffee hot beside me, glasses perched on my nose—reflecting on something that's taken me nearly twenty-four years to fully grasp.

Reading about that night—the black mass, the chaos, the torment—I still get chills thinking: How could I have been so ignorant? It's astonishing how hindsight reveals our blindness.

For years, I rationalized that night away. Alcohol withdrawal. Sleep deprivation. Hallucination. The truth became clear only after fully stepping into the Gospel and understanding spiritual warfare. Back then, I was in such intense, unrecognized spiritual warfare that my soul became an easy target. The drugs, alcohol, and people I surrounded myself with were gateways—they appeared to relieve the burdens they secretly enhanced. Demons can—and do—take human form. I saw it daily in Hollywood. What I witnessed hours before that terrifying experience placed me directly in evil's crosshairs.

Here's something I didn't mention earlier. On the very day of that demonic invasion, I'd attended a film screening featuring my neighbor, Christina. Despite everything that had happened, we maintained a professional relationship. The film opened with Christina performing a graphic demon-conjuring scene, drenched in occult imagery. In one disturbing scene, the lead actor slit his wrists, draining blood into a cup over a cocaine-shaped pentagram before snorting it. The narrative revolved around dark rituals, sexuality, and a mysterious visitor impregnating a woman while witches eagerly awaited. The camera lingered perversely in these scenes, as if it were leering at me.

During the screening, I felt a strange heaviness—a weight pressing down that I dismissed as fatigue or the theater's stale air. Other audience members laughed and applauded, completely unaffected. But something in me recoiled even as I forced myself to smile, to play the part of the supportive neighbor. Looking back, that wasn't just discomfort—it was my spirit, though dormant, attempting to sound an alarm my soul ignored.

What do I know now that I didn't back then? What has the Gospel taught me?

Here's a verse worth memorizing:

"The eye is the lamp of the body. So, if your eye is healthy, your whole body will be full of light, but if your eye is bad, your whole body will be full of darkness." **(Matthew 6:22-23)**

This isn't metaphorical—it's literal. What enters through your eyes doesn't stay contained in your mind. It seeps into your soul, colors your emotions, shapes your will, and ultimately influences your spirit. Images carry power. They're not basic pixels on a screen or light patterns on your retina. They're seeds planted in your innermost being.

With all I've learned, I'll never watch something like that again. Movies like these aren't harmless entertainment—they're invitations. When I see previews filled with demonic themes, I no longer brush them off. They are carefully disguised doorways, traps set to lure us into darkness while convincing us it's harmless fun.

Los Angeles and Hollywood's entertainment industry are unquestionably evil. I say this from experience. I've been behind the scenes—inside major studios, screen-tested for films, met celebrities in their homes, and seen the true darkness behind their glamorous façades. Most of them were miserable. The enemy owned them.

Later in this story, you'll discover that I'm the creator of a popular horror movie. Recently, there was talk of remaking it. I could've cashed in, stepped back into that world, and played the game again.

But I won't.

Because I know the price. I know what I carried home with me after making that film. It nearly killed me. Money, fame, prestige—none of it is worth reopening that spiritual door and risking the freedom I've fought so hard to regain.

But let me get back to that night after the screening. I remember driving along Hollywood Boulevard in a sickening fog. The chant from the film echoed in my mind, the images burned into my psyche, completely unaware I'd brought pure evil home with me. I laughed it off. Ignorance is bliss until the "impossible" stares you in the face, becoming undeniably "possible."

"This wisdom descendeth not from above, but is earthly, sensual, devilish." **(James 3:15)**

The writing of the film I witnessed did not come from above. The inspiration came sideways. It was earthly, soulish—demonic. Looking at the film industry, I'm reminded: *"For where envying and strife is, there is confusion and every evil work."* **(James 3:16)**

Ambition creates envy. Hollywood is built on envy, which causes strife. And the result? Chaos and evil personified. Have you ever watched a show and been shocked by a scene you saw? Your favorite Netflix show suddenly throws a moment that causes you to feel a disconnect in your spirit? This infiltration is purposeful, and there is a direct correlation between what you're witnessing and the enemy's agenda. These moments aren't accidental—these are calculated insertions designed to desensitize you, to normalize what should repulse you.

"...in which you once walked, following the course of this world, following the prince of the power of the air—the spirit that is now at work in the sons of disobedience." **(Ephesians 2:2)**

How do we survive on earth? We breathe air. The enemy—the prince of the power of the air—owns this world, and the media we consume daily allows him direct access. He's clever and strategic. Think about it: if you were cast out of Heaven and took control of the Earth, what would you do to harm the God who cast you out? You'd slowly corrupt His creation, watching humanity decompose in admiration of your handiwork. You'd flood them with free pornography accessible to children, empower leaders hostile to the Gospel, feed them foods that make them sick, then prescribe medication with endless complications. You'd incite them to turn against each other.

The enemy doesn't need to possess you to destroy you. He needs to influence what you consider normal, acceptable, even entertaining. This is warfare at its most sophisticated—not with swords and guns, but with stories and images that reshape your perception of reality.

I want to ask you something critical:

Are you protecting yourself?

What are you allowing through your eyes today that could destroy your marriage tomorrow? What images, words, or entertainment are eroding your soul? Everything you watch, hear, or scroll through either strengthens your spiritual armor or cracks it open.

The battle isn't hypothetical—it's happening right now, in living rooms, on smartphones, and through headphones. The most dangerous battlefield isn't some distant land—it's the six inches between your ears.

Sitting here in 2025, looking back, I can see what happened so you might avoid it. The enemy didn't simply tempt me; he sent a recruiter. Attractive, familiar—my neighbor already under his spell, guiding me step-by-step into darkness. Spiritual warfare always operates this way: first seduction away from purpose, then gradual descent into pleasure, and finally, enslavement.

I'm not asking you to become a monk. I'm urging you to be conscious. To recognize that your attention is a battlefield. To understand that what appears to be harmless entertainment could be the enemy's Trojan horse.

Maybe you don't believe in spiritual warfare. Maybe this all seems like superstition. I thought so too. But remember Christina? She warned me about the evil in my basement while actively performing demonic rituals onscreen. She believed she was good. Satan blurs the lines, offering excuses for our actions while letting us condemn others for doing the same.

So, let me ask you this:

What would it hurt to consider this possibility? To acknowledge that what your eyes see and your ears hear deeply influences your soul? At worst, you'll have consumed less garbage. At best, you'll have shielded yourself from evil targeting you daily.

Many health-conscious people carefully filter what goes into their bodies—organic food, filtered water, supplements—while carelessly consuming any content that entertains them, regardless of what spiritual toxins it might contain. Yet the irony in my own story is apparent: I was poisoning both body and soul simultaneously. The alcohol that was destroying my health and the visual poison was corrupting my spirit. Both were killing me, on different timelines and in various ways. Pure Holy Spirit wisdom has a distinctive mark. It is pure. It does not compromise on morals, ethics, or the truth.

Right now, as you read these words, the enemy's invitation is extended to you, just as it was to me. What will you let in today—light that brings everlasting life, or darkness that seeks to devour?

I spilled my coffee everywhere—no metaphor intended. Keep reading—I'll clean this up and meet you in the next chapter.

Writing My Narrative

If I can control the story, I can control my destiny.

That's the lie I tell myself.

If Hollywood doesn't want me unless I do the unspeakable, I'll carve my own path. **I'll win on my terms.**

See the problem here? **"My terms."**
Always **"my terms."**

I still hadn't fully grasped it yet. I still thought victory meant proving myself—achieving greatness by sheer force of will. But that was precisely the trap. Even when rejecting darkness, I still played the enemy's game: pride disguised as determination.

The idea to write a movie hit me during a trip back to Centerville, Iowa, with my dad after my aunt's death. The town I remember visiting as a kid—pure Americana—small diners, family-owned shops, kids riding their bikes home before sunset—is now a faded Rockwell painting, colors drowned in rust and regret.

Storefronts sit abandoned, houses reduced to burnt-out husks, and the people?

Their kids drive around the town square, scooping the loop—hollow-eyed.

They aren't living—**they're possessed.**

Meth has devoured this place.

The contrast is stark, impossible to ignore—a story demanding to be told.

I pour myself into writing—a fictional script built from everything I'm witnessing. I channel every ounce of anger, grief, and clarity into these pages. Writing isn't an outlet. It's redemption—a way to transform darkness into something meaningful.

The writing pulls me away from drinking. The fog lifts slightly. My audition performance gains momentum. I start working again, clawing my way back toward the dream Hollywood seemed determined to deny me.

Auditions pick up. Hope flickers back to life. And the biggest offers I've ever received come in.

The Crossroads

Two massive opportunities hit at once. The first? **A lead role in TNT's *Witchblade*.** I finally book a lead role in a major television series.

Thirty episodes. **$60,000 per episode.** With that kind of money I could **invest overnight,** finally have security, and carve out my own space in Hollywood.

But before I can sign, another call comes in—the exact same day. **George Lucas's team wants me to fly up to Skywalker Ranch.** Two weeks earlier, my manager had sent a tape to the casting agent of the new *Star Wars* movie being made. Lucas saw it and wanted to meet me.

Not for a regular audition. For Anakin Skywalker.

This isn't some cattle-call casting. Lucas doesn't fly just anyone to Skywalker Ranch. This is the kind of opportunity they **gossip about in Hollywood**—the kind that only happens to **DiCaprio-level** actors.

The idea of stepping into a legacy like *Star Wars* is intoxicating.

But.

The *Witchblade* producers need an answer.

Now. If I hesitate, the offer could be **off the table.** But Lucas's team? They aren't bending either. No flexibility. No guarantees. **One shot.**

Do I take the sure thing? A TV deal. A locked-in future.

Or do I bet it all on *Star Wars*? A legacy. A chance at **immortality.**

I choose *Star Wars*. How could I not?

The Steinbeck Room and the Fallout

I'll never forget that night at Skywalker Ranch—the *John Steinbeck Room*—high ceilings, the air thick with history. The following day I sit across from George Lucas himself. The man is so tiny in stature that his feet don't even touch the ground when he sits in his chair. Childlike. Yet the weight of his presence is immense.

For a moment, I let myself believe:

I've made it.

But dreams turn to dust fast in this business.

The role goes to Hayden Christensen. I watch from the sidelines as *Star Wars* catapults him into global fame. And *Witchblade*? Thirty episodes, $60,000 per episode—vanished overnight. I'm not merely losing roles. I'm losing time. Losing traction. Losing myself.

Years later, I discovered that Lucas had told the casting director he wished he'd hired me.

He thought the movie would've been better with me in it.

Talk about a slap in the face.

Am I failing?

Or is **God protecting me?**

That particular *Star Wars* film has become **one of the franchise's most criticized.**

Hayden's career **never fully recovers.**

Curses often come disguised as blessings.

But sometimes, blessings come with **a curse attached.**

CHAPTER 4

Addicted to Misery

I didn't understand yet that every missed opportunity—everything I thought was a *"curse"*—was, at times, meant for protection.

At the time, each setback felt like another nail hammered into a coffin I was constructing for myself.

As you can imagine, the setbacks destroy my already **fragile ego.**

The crushing disappointments of my Hollywood dreams don't push me back into serious addiction.

I do.

See what I did there? I took back ownership—something I'll learn to do much later.

But not yet.

At this stage, I am drinking again **daily.**

The kind of drinking that turns days into smudged watercolors, where mornings and evenings bleed into one another and time becomes a theory rather than a reality.

I don't take it on the chin and keep moving.

I take the losses **personally.**

For most of my life, I've blamed external circumstances—

Bad luck.

Setbacks.

Other people.

But here's the truth:

Disappointment isn't what destroys you.

It's how you respond to it that does.

The pain is catching up, its footsteps growing louder behind me with each passing year. **The life I've built is crumbling beneath me.**

No matter how fast I run—

The demons always know exactly where to find me.

They never left.

And they know exactly where to set the next trap.

I keep auditioning. The show must go on, even when the audience has left and the theater is crumbling.

I land a role opposite Katherine Heigl in an independent film.

A downgrade? Maybe.

But at least it's momentum—forward motion. It's something to tell my parents when they call and ask how I'm doing—something that sounds like success even when it tastes like compromise.

I was handed a **distraction.**

A fork in my story.

After we finished shooting the film, they added one additional day to the shoot.

The distraction arrives in the form of a blonde woman—twenty-one, fresh meat on the LA scene. Not an actress, a "dancer"—those quotation marks doing heavy lifting.

They doll her up, ensuring she stands out. Hair too blonde to be natural.

She does. She stands out.

I still remember my line with her that day:

"I like my girls better when they're alive."

After the shoot, we head to The Dresden, a place soaked in old Hollywood charm—

Dim lights. Smoke in the air. Marty & Elaine, the quirky lounge duo, crooning jazz tunes so bad they're good. The kind of place where Bogart might have nursed a scotch, where secrets are traded over martinis, where Hollywood's golden age lingers in the velvet curtains.

She leans in close, her hand on my arm, wild yellow eyes locking onto mine with sniper-like intensity.

"God, you're amazing," she whispers. "I've never met anyone like you."

The attention is intoxicating.

It feels like my first hit of cocaine—softer, sweeter, but **equally lethal.**

And then it becomes cocaine right there in my basement—the same basement where, months earlier, a demon tried to take my soul. We hardly slept that night. The drugs, the attention, the validation—it's all one intoxicating blend. She has an answer that soothes all my aches and pains. Every word she spoke felt tailor-made, each sentence another thread weaving a web I couldn't see. Hours passed like minutes. By dawn, I was convinced she was different—special—perhaps **even meant for me.**

In my drug-induced state, I call my mother that morning. With irrational excitement, I rambled on about this incredible woman I'd met. How she understood me, how connected I felt. My mother listened cautiously, hearing the chemical euphoria in my voice, the desperation poorly disguised as joy.

Looking back, I understand how vulnerable I was—how crushed my ego was from recent setbacks, how starved for validation I had become. In my fragile state, I was a mark, easy prey for something dark disguised as exactly what I craved—a wounded animal stumbling into a hunter's sights.

In my broken state, still reeling from lost opportunities, I cling to this feeling, to her. She knows precisely what I need to hear.

I'm being played.

Spiritual Warfare in Disguise

There are things so embarrassing, so humiliating, that even admitting I put up with them pains my soul.

So many red flags you could stack them and reach heaven.

And still—I went **all in** with her.

I was her mark.

And in my brokenness?

I let her charm entrance me.

This woman, fresh from Union New Jersey—

Rewrote my entire script.

That one drink turned into two.

Then, into a constant party.

She was fun, unpredictable, and knew how to distract me. A magician pulling rabbits from hats while picking my pocket.

She didn't love me. She loved what I could provide—the house in the hills, the parties, the connections. I was a ladder to climb, a door to walk through, a name to drop in the right circles.

And I didn't love her either.

I loved **being needed.**

And that?

That's a dangerous dynamic.

Discomfort is the currency of progress.

The more discomfort you can endure without running to a vice, the more you grow.

She was my **new vice.** A human crutch that kept me limping rather than healing. A painkiller that numbed the symptoms while the disease progressed.

And her grip?

It crushed me—slowly, **completely.**

The White-Knuckled Nightmare

"Your comfort zone is your prison. The longer you stay, ***the harder it'll be to escape."***

She was my white-knuckled nightmare.

What is white-knuckling?

It's frustration compounded—you hold your fists **clenched** so tight your knuckles turn white.

Because letting go feels like losing.

We weren't building a life together.

We were collapsing in slow motion.

That's the thing about toxic relationships:

The comfort of shared chaos owns you.

Addiction bonds you.

The dysfunction starts to feel like home. The fighting becomes familiar territory. The making up—your favorite drug. The cycle becomes the only rhythm you know how to dance to.

She told me everything I needed to hear—

Not because it was true.

Because it served her agenda.

She was a master of this.

The youngest of six, doted on, told she was the greatest thing in the world.

She carried herself with a brazen confidence that made you believe her. Every gesture she made, every word she spoke, carried the weight of **absolute conviction.**

And for some reason, with all I had going for me, I bought a ticket to her one-woman show.

Have you ever been sold something that promised to be amazing—**only** to find out it didn't work at all?

For me, that was my ex.

She wasn't anyone in Hollywood. No agent. No connections.

This wasn't a career move relationship.

I wasn't looking to climb the ladder.

I wasn't looking for power.

I was looking for **comfort.**

And she gave me that.

But not honestly.

We didn't work.

Facing the truth meant upheaval.

And I wasn't ready for that.

She was peace, sex, and love under false pretense. A forgery so convincing I framed it and hung it on my wall.

And I was too exhausted to question it.

I convinced myself I could build a future on a foundation of lies.

I was perfecting the art of **failing.**

But there's another truth I was too afraid to face:

You can't heal until you're honest.

And honesty was the one currency we never traded in.

The Spiritual Chessboard

A few months in, she got pregnant as I was finishing funding my new film *IOWA*.
She'd sworn she was on birth control.
She wasn't.

A **calculated move** to cement her role in my life.

I was trapped.

Happiness? No.
Joy. **No.**

That would come later.

At that moment, I was furious.

Because **I know.**

She **played me.**
"My lease is almost up with my roommate, and we have to move out. I can go back to New Jersey and live with my mom and dad," she said. She was cunning, baffling, and had already calculated my response.

"Of course not. You can move in with me."

She knew my commitment would be to doing the right thing.

Step up and be a father.

She knew she had me trapped.

I felt like a wolf caught in metal **jaws clamped around my leg.**
But those jaws weren't holding me back—
They were holding me **in place** until I could see clearly.

I stayed because of honor—because I wouldn't abandon my child.

And the prison I perceived at the time?

Would eventually **save me.**

I begrudgingly—**with a fake smile**—accepted her moving in and she became a permanent fixture in my house in the hills.

Reflection

I'm in the middle of a grueling workout. That's what I do in the morning in my home gym. The medicine to take care of my temple. The barbell feels heavier today—maybe because I'm lifting more than just iron. I'm lifting memories between sets, and some storylines weigh more than others. With each rep, the past pushes back against my muscles, demanding to be acknowledged before it will release its hold.

Flashes of that toxic relationship rarely arise anymore, but writing this has me courting old demons between deadlifts. I have to drop the weight and catch my breath—not from physical exertion but from the sudden clarity about my role in the ensuing chaos you're about to read in the subsequent chapters. The metal clanks against the rack, the sound echoing through the room like a bell of truth I can no longer ignore.

Back then, I placed every failure squarely at her feet. She was my excuse, my scapegoat. If I didn't succeed, it was her fault—her drama, her demands, her dysfunction. The late-night arguments, the tear-stained accusations, the slammed doors—all her doing, never mine. I genuinely believed she was safe and right for me, ironic as that sounds now. If you ever re-read this book, and I hope you do, you'll see she was anything but safe. If there was an apple in a garden, she'd be the first to take a bite and then blame the guy standing next to her. But here's the harder truth I avoided for decades: I knew exactly what I was choosing.

The problem wasn't simply her. It was me. I wasn't genuinely loving, compassionate, or supportive—the kind of partner she deserved or anyone deserves. Instead, I thrived on selfishness. We were locked in a cycle of mutual sabotage. We weren't toxic together—we were toxic for each other. We handcuffed each other to mediocrity, both using the other as an excuse to avoid our true potential. Without me, she'd probably be back in New Jersey, chasing her dreams on a simpler, likely happier path. Without her, maybe I would have faced my monster sooner. "But what if's" are not a part of God's design, are they? He doesn't make mistakes.

The relationship wasn't failing; it was functioning exactly as designed—keeping us both comfortably miserable, safely stagnant, predictably broken. A very long lesson.

The revelation that took me decades to see: While I was chasing Hollywood's empty promises, God was orchestrating something bigger. My son wasn't an accident or a trap—he was God's anchor, keeping me from drifting into deeper waters.

I believed her pregnancy would hinder my career. That it would change everything. It did. I could not see that these "mistakes" were escape hatches. Every perceived "failure" was a wall God built between me and my own destruction. What I saw as setbacks were the hands of a Father slamming the jaws of a beast closed before it could swallow me whole.

The big roles I was so close to getting? That would have been a paint-by-numbers pathway back to drugs and elitism. My dad often says, "You would have ended up dead." Looking back, I know my dad was right. But there's something even worse than death: **condemnation**—living and dying separated from God.

God allowed these experiences to guide me toward accountability and humility. I had to learn firsthand that true freedom doesn't come from blaming others, nor does safety come from hiding behind excuses. Instead, real freedom begins when we honestly recognize our part in our own downfall and acknowledge our need to seek God. I couldn't see His hand guiding me then, gently (and sometimes forcefully) trying to break through my stubborn blindness. He wasn't absent; He was patiently waiting for me to recognize the truth about myself, my choices, and the enemy's deception.

This is the beauty of God's redemptive work: He doesn't save us from others—He saves us from ourselves. He doesn't change our circumstances—He changes our hearts. The same relationship that I once viewed as my greatest burden became the very catalyst God used to bring me to my knees. What the enemy meant for destruction, God transformed into the beginning of my redemption.

Maybe you're facing something similar right now. Maybe you've spent years blaming others, circumstances, or even spiritual darkness for your struggles. Take a deep breath and honestly ask yourself—are you overlooking your own role in your chaos? Is it possible that the thing you're running from, the truth you're resisting, is what God wants you to confront?

The most dangerous lie isn't the one someone else tells you—it's the one you tell yourself. Are you ready to see clearly now, like I should have back then?

Your greatest pain, your deepest wound, your most toxic relationship—these aren't problems to escape. They're invitations to transformation. The question isn't whether God can use them—it's whether you'll let Him.

Understanding my role in that toxic relationship was the first layer of truth God revealed later in my story. What came next was even more complicated—years of fighting off addiction. There is a silver lining in this maze of madness—an incredible redemption worth every dead end turn. Stay with me; the path gets clearer ahead.

Exposed

Now, my days consisted of taking care of a newly pregnant woman.

A dramatic shift in my carefree bachelor lifestyle. I wake to the sound of throwing up and my time is spent finding food to manage her cravings. She had no money—no job, and so I became a sort of caretaker overnight and, she became a dependent.

I would say leech but this is the mother of my children. The drinking and friends petered out over the course of a month. It's her and I and a baby on the way.

With my alcohol faucet suddenly shut off, the habit revealed itself as something darker—a creature. **A living unseen being.** Now, stripped of my crutches, it has nowhere left to hide.

Removing the chemical doesn't fix you. **It exposes you.**

The spirit of addiction wears many masks, but the cage it locks you in is always the same.

It amplifies the whisper from the deep until that whisper becomes the only voice you hear, drowning out reason, drowning out hope, **drowning out God.**

I'm not running toward anything.

I'm still running away.

What am I still running from?

The truth.

That I'm not in control.

The drinking stops with the pregnancy, and real life hits—tearing me in half.

Take away the chemical cushion, and suddenly, you're **raw nerve endings in human form.**

Every emotion hits like a sledgehammer. Every thought screams for attention—**like nails scraping down a chalkboard.**

The creature I have been feeding? It's still there, staring back at me in the mirror—hungrier than ever.

I grit through those first weeks of sobriety. A man hanging off a cliff by his pinky.

No booze. No coke. No anti-anxiety meds. No escape.

The darkness inside me—**exposed.**

Stripped of my coping mechanisms, I am confronted with my ugly, unfiltered **REALITY.**

It's an exorcism—not the Hollywood kind. The real kind.

But before you can cast out a demon, **you have to name it.** You have to **look it in the eye** and acknowledge what you're fighting.

And for the first time, I see it.

My demon.

It stares back at me. Behind my eyes. Looming. Patient. Persistent.

Drooling with a salacious appetite for destruction.

But I do not know its name.

So, it remains.

The straight edge is where you find yourself. The real you. The one you've been masking in bottles, smoke, and excuses.

But when two addicts try to get sober together? It isn't survival. It's two **drowning people** trying to save each other.

The problem.

I was the one throwing her a rope while I drowned.

Neither one of us knows how to swim in sobriety's deep end. So, we do what addicts do.

We find a new way to drown.

> **RED FLAG MOMENT:** Sobriety without true surrender isn't freedom—it's swapping one chain for another. The enemy doesn't care what numbs you, as long as you stay numb.

Enter the **weed** dealer.

Hollywood's **favorite pharmacist.**

Without alcohol, I last a week.

Weed is considered *"no big deal"* even though it's illegal at that time.

It's called being California sober. Weed doesn't count.

And I **need something.**

I call a friend of a friend, and the deal is done.

The dealer makes house calls to **Harrison Ford and Steven Spielberg** before stopping by our place.

He shows up a day later with the supply and a menu to order from, like you're ordering a smoothie.

The same **weakness,** wearing a **different mask.**

I tell myself I have peace. But real peace doesn't come in pre-rolled ounces. It doesn't come in thick clouds of THC. It doesn't come in the numbness. That's not peace.

That's purgatory. It's a padded cell for the soul, and I'm locking the door from the inside.

The darkness is still there, but moving slower, **speaking softer.**

Every hit from the bong is **another brick in the wall.**

Every exhale **pushes me further** from the truth I don't want to face.

Remember, the enemy doesn't need you to fall fast.

He's patient.

He needs you to **stay numb.**

The Death of a Film in Real Time

In 2003, I finished writing *IOWA*, my passion project. With a lot of help, the film got the green light.

Back to Centerville, Iowa in late spring—cornfields stretched out for miles, swallowing the horizon. Life moved slow—except for us.

Making movies isn't glamorous—it's trench work. You need a team, an army ready to fight for your vision. I made a choice that would complicate things: I gave my girlfriend the starring female role and producer credit. Christina Ricci and other big-name stars had expressed interest in the same role. Their involvement could've given the film commercial credibility and wider distribution, but I went a different direction. **I own that bad decision.**

When you're making a film, people circle like sharks smelling blood in the water, pretending to help but waiting to pick your bones clean. The crew extract as much petty cash as possible before jumping ship to a new set—especially in the indie film world. We shot on film, which wasn't cheap. Being a union production added another layer of complexity—guaranteed daily rates meant higher budgets, and we were forced to hire industry veterans who knew exactly how to milk every opportunity.

She was nine weeks pregnant when we started shooting, which overwhelmed everything. She was sick, exhausted, and half-present. My attention went to directing, but I was also consumed with managing her emotions. My nerves were on the fritz. What do I know about being a father? I was twenty-seven years old and scared to bits, hanging on by a thread. I wore every hat imaginable—producing, directing, acting, juggling endless fires—and filming in rural Iowa added even more pressure. Her performance struggled amid all this, and so did the film. Business isn't about feelings, but sometimes feelings get involved in business.

Could I have salvaged it? Maybe. Built enough hype? Possibly. Elevated it to the next level? Not with her attached. I had cast someone based on emotion rather than logic. Would it have been better with a star in the role? For sales, of course.

After production wrapped on *IOWA*, we returned to LA, exhausted. Shortly after, my son was born. Fatherhood opened emotional roads that were once dead ends, powerful and undeniable. **Our bond was immediate.** Some men have a hard time adjusting to a baby; I wasn't one of them. I changed diapers, did 2 a.m. feedings, comforted him through colic, and found strength in the bond we shared. This changed me. The miracle of becoming a parent evoked questioning in me about the essence of life. It calmed a part of the darkness in me. Subdued it. He brought light into my world—purpose beyond the facade I was working so hard to build.

I continued editing the film, piecing together my vision frame by frame. Editing was tedious, painstaking, and slow-going, but that year went by in a flash. You know that exhaustion of being a new parent—the kind that makes you forget what happened ten minutes ago? That's exactly where I was.

Still, I finally completed the film and began submitting it to festivals and distributors, hoping for recognition. Lo and behold, the Tribeca Film Festival picked it up.

This was it—I was finally on my way. Tribeca! The **validation** I'd been waiting for. My girlfriend had another surprise: she was pregnant again. Another accident—that's what she called it. Not that I wasn't an active participant.

We traveled to Tribeca. Sitting in the theater, watching my ex's face fill the screen, the full weight of my emotional casting decision hit home. Tribeca was supposed to be my moment of vindication; instead, **it was humiliation.** I watched critics shift uncomfortably, buyers discreetly checking their phones, each glance a quiet dagger in my hopes. The film was gritty, unpolished, deeply raw, and without a recognizable lead, virtually impossible to sell. I had built my house on quicksand. Critics largely panned it. There were a few bright spots: *The Village Voice* likened my directing to David Lynch, and *The New York Times* dropped Tarantino's name in reference to my style. But beyond those glimmers of praise, the film sank quietly into obscurity.

Yet, even from that sinking foundation, something remarkable happened.

In researching *IOWA*, I'd met a woman severely burned—over seventy percent of her body—in a rolling meth lab explosion. I'd started filming her tragic, compelling story, and that footage evolved into an award-winning documentary, *Dying for Meth*. Suddenly, I was nominated for major awards alongside giants like CBS and NBC. Endorsed by organizations like the National Association of Counties, Boys and Girls Clubs of America, and even the Department of Justice, I spoke to crowds of thousands. At one point, I addressed more than three thousand elected officials—men and women capable of **creating real change**—sharing my experiences, shining a harsh light into the darkness of addiction.

For the first time, my voice wasn't echoing in empty theaters. It was resonating through conference halls filled with people who could truly make a difference. All the chaos I had chased began to have purpose. All the disappointments now had meaning.

And just when I thought the saga of *IOWA* was behind me, just when I thought that chapter had finally closed, Hollywood surprised me again.

My phone rang.

It was Michael Cooper from William Morris—one of the biggest agents in the industry.

"We saw your performance in Iowa. Undeniable," he said. "We can build on this."

Suddenly, the doors I'd thought permanently closed began swinging open once again.

But the enemy doesn't quit. He **changes the bait**.

And that's how I found myself at the Chateau Marmont, where careers are made—or **destroyed**.

The Sliding Doors Moment

Suddenly, the same industry that has ignored me is calling. I've done it. I've clawed my way up without selling my soul. No casting couch. No compromises. Finally, Hollywood is taking me seriously.

The Chateau Marmont isn't a hotel. Perched like an icon on Sunset Boulevard. It's a **test**. A Hollywood gate disguised as a bar. **John Belushi** died here. **Helmut Newton** crashed his Cadillac leaving here. **Lindsay Lohan** practically lived here until they threw her out.

The place breathes temptation through its Spanish colonial pores. Walk through those doors, and you're stepping onto the Devil's home court.

I'm here meeting **this agent**—the power brokers of Hollywood.

Sitting across from one another, he looks me in the eye. Holds the gaze for a beat. "We're going to show you the power of William Morris."

Then he walks away.

Leaving me there. **With the setup.**

Directly behind him, I see her.

Naomi Watts.

Fresh off her breakup with Heath Ledger. Radiating the kind of star power that turns heads and ruins lives.

She waves me over with a smile that could launch any career.

This wasn't a meeting. It's an initiation.

You want to know what temptation looks like?

The Devil doesn't show up with horns and a pitchfork. He shows up as everything you've ever wanted.

The enemy doesn't like rejection.

He waits. He's patient. He lets you think you've won.

Then he comes back with something better. A sweeter deal. **A new offer.**

This is his counteroffer. Gift-wrapped and sitting two tables away.

I look at Naomi—then I look at the door opening in front of me: **Fame. Wealth. Power.** All mine for the taking.

One small compromise. One little bite of that apple.

I can easily **do this.** It would be a pleasure. This is a much softer deal than the Joel Schumacher offer.

But **something stops me.**

Not hesitation. **Not morality.** Something **stronger than me.**

A force **yanks me back, like hands on my shoulders.**

My feet aren't **mine anymore.**

The weight of **regret presses** against my chest.

The demons watch as I turn—**not victorious, not righteous. Gone.**

One second, I'm sitting at the table with everything I thought I ever wanted. The next, I'm walking the streets above the Chateau, empty-handed.

Defeated.

I've turned down an entire kingdom and have nothing to show for it.

But I **keep walking.**

Hollywood Punishes Disobedience

Each step toward the car feels like carrying a cross.

I want to **turn back.**

I stop and think about it.

But something keeps pulling me away from that place. Now I know it was the Holy Spirit saving me.

But back then. It **STINGS.**

The city lights spread out below me like a **neon graveyard of broken dreams.**

Right down there, Naomi Watts is probably already moving on to the next option.

The machine never stops.

I die a little that night.

My children become the force driving me toward **the greater good.**

Something inside me knows—it tells me—the enemy wants **my son** as payment for success.

Many people who do not understand the **way evil works** would see my decision as foolish. I can understand that. Naomi and I share the same manager—the one who makes the calls, the one who arranges this power move meeting, sliding the pieces into place. My new agent has co-signed the setup. This is their way of saying: Welcome to the big leagues. You better be ready to play now.

A man offered **a key to Hollywood success** and refuses to take it.

Un-heard of.

The enemy is displeased with my choice.

When I get home that night, I don't tell the woman waiting for me, pregnant with our second child, aware that in Hollywood's eyes, I'm the one getting the calls, the meetings, the opportunities. This already bothers her more than anything else I would tell her that night.

Reflection

It's late afternoon here in Tennessee. Upstairs, my wife is preparing breakfast for dinner—the kind of warm, comforting ritual I never imagined myself appreciating when I stood beneath the bright lights of the Chateau Marmont all those years ago. Funny, isn't it? Life has a way of redirecting our desires.

Suppose you'd told the version of me walking away from Naomi Watts and Hollywood's glittering promises that I'd one day find happiness debating homesteading in the South. In that case, I'd have laughed you off Sunset Boulevard.

The most significant change for me at that time was my children. Not long after that Naomi Watts encounter, my daughter was born. My children quickly became my greatest passion—rivaling, then surpassing, my love for filmmaking. I took them everywhere—every restaurant, every park, every amusement park, and zoo in Southern California. My favorite moments weren't callbacks or red carpets; they were spent chasing my kids around the house, acting like a giant baby monster intent on kissing them. Even now, their laughter fills my soul when I ask if they remember me acting like a giant baby.

Back then, I genuinely thought fame, wealth, and influence would "set my kids for life." I couldn't yet see I was already giving them something infinitely more valuable—my time, my presence, my genuine love. They didn't care about money or fame. They needed a father who chose integrity over compromise, even when it hurt.

What I called "failure" at the Chateau—turning down Hollywood's golden offer—was actually God's protective mercy. That night, there must have been some shred of spirit still inside me guiding me away from damnation. The offer was too good, too tempting. The enemy had dangled precisely what he knew I wanted most, offering a piece of his earthly kingdom for the price of a soul.

Was there a shred of light in me that pulled me away? No. It was the bright, burning light of two children waiting for me at home. God used their light to steer me away from everything I'd spent years chasing. That is how powerful God's grace can be. My children awakened a sensitivity in my hardened heart, activating two vital qualities: attention and humility. They captured my full attention.

"And he shall turn the heart of the fathers to the children, and the heart of the children to their fathers..." **(Malachi 4:6 KJV)**

I wasn't ready to incline my ear to God yet, but He turned my heart toward my children first. Just as Malachi prophesied, God softened the heart of a father through the presence of his children. That's how grace works—it meets you where you are, then turns you where you need to go. God was gently bending my stubborn heart toward humility for the first time, giving me something larger than myself to protect. They have always been my throughline—the precise scalpel cutting through the calloused layers of my soul, allowing the spirit finally to emerge. It would take years and moments of cataclysmic despair for me to fully acknowledge the gift, to genuinely incline my ear to His voice.

My children didn't need Hollywood money or fame. They needed a father who remained true to himself, who would be present, and who would teach them that character matters more than compromise. Here lies God's beautiful irony: it wasn't them who needed me most—it was I who needed them.

She wanted to get married—felt it was the right thing to do. At the time, I believed honoring that request was another way of doing the "right" thing for my children. So I did. **I married her.**

Maybe you're wrestling with hard choices in your life, reflecting on roads not taken or what *"could have been."* Consider this carefully: Could those seemingly missed opportunities be hidden acts of protective mercy? Is it possible God has already positioned you exactly where you're meant to be?

Give it some thought—but right now, my wife is calling me to dinner. Sorry to send you back into more Hollywood betrayal, but that's the path I walked.

Betrayal: *Chapter 27* and Jared Leto

Hollywood **doesn't forget disobedience.**
And it doesn't forgive it, either.
But my agent wasn't done with me yet.

After walking away from *"the offer"* at the Chateau, he still put me out for **some smaller independent films**—trying to salvage something.

One of those films?
Chapter 27.

This Hollywood lesson in betrayal came with a project about John Lennon's killer.

Nobody had adapted that story into a movie.

It had the potential to be a **career-defining role.**

The director didn't want a big name.
He wanted someone fresh—someone who could **disappear** into the character.

And he **wanted me.**

I **gained weight** for the role.
Bought glasses identical to Mark David Chapman's.

Checked into a **seedy motel** and filmed myself in character.

I became him.

The director called.
"You got it, man. You're the guy."

Yes! A **lifeline.**
A chance to prove myself.

Then **Hollywood's politics kicked in.**

My agent **sold me out.**

You see, I had turned down his offer at the Chateau, and he was going to make me suffer for it.

He pulled the producers into a meeting and pushed for **Jared Leto** instead.

He convinced them that Jared's name would bring more attention to the project.

He wasn't wrong.

But this wasn't about the movie.
This was about **my agent's career.**

Jared was a rising star.
Landing him made **my agent** look like a genius.

The director called me again.
I'll never forget his words.

"Your agent sold you out for Jared Leto."

"I fought for you. I told them you were the guy."

"Jared's good... but you were perfect."

"I'm pretty sure this deal made Jared your agent's new client."

That phone call **stung.**

But this is show business—not show friends. A smile to your face and shiv down your spine.

I thanked the director, but inside, I was **reeling.**

Betrayed. Discarded.

A **pawn** in someone else's game.

This wasn't just losing a role. That was the moment I knew I was done chasing **Hollywood's approval.**

The Devil's Playground

Hollywood has played its hand. The system isn't built for guys like me—at least, not unless I'm willing to play along. But I'm not about to disappear.

If they won't let me through the front door, I'll find another way in.

Despite everything, *IOWA* still has some legs; it's still making waves. That's when the past comes knocking. Through industry connections, it put me in front of someone unexpected—Mark Cuban's brother.

We're talking about his company acquiring my film.
Small studios are circling.

They own a company called Magnet Releasing.
For a moment, I think I'm on my way.

Again.

They're going to make an offer.

Then, Cuban's brother leans in and says something odd.

"You should try horror."

Horror?

At first, it didn't make sense.

I was an **actor** and a **serious filmmaker.**

I realize he's passing on releasing *IOWA*, but he was sure I could make a *"killing"* in the **Horror genre.**

Horror wasn't **art.** Horror was **cheap thrills and blood spatter.**

But then he broke it down:

"Horror is a profitable genre in film."
"It has a dedicated fanbase."
"And it's recession-proof. People always pay to be scared."

His **words get inside my head.**

Horror is a business.

I see dollar signs. If Hollywood refuses to pay me unless I cave in, maybe I can cash in with my writing skills.

And I'm desperate for my next big move.
I've already been to the top of the mountain and watched the ground collapse beneath me.

The ***Witchblade*** deal? Lost.
The ***Star Wars*** audition? Extinct.
The **William Morris push?** Dead.
The **Chapter 27 betrayal?** Still ringing.

And horror—the genre Hollywood treats like a back-alley drug deal—is a way to make something fast. Something profitable. Something they **can't ignore.**

So I do it.

I write a horror film. A brutal, bloody slasher.
The Orphan Killer.
I bet everything on it.

I ask my family and friends for money.
I convince them this move will change everything.
That this is my comeback.

And my girlfriend?
She wants in too.

She has to be the lead.

Another compromise.
Another pattern repeating.

This isn't a film.
It's the same cycle, dressed in different clothes.

But putting her in the film means I don't have to pay an actress.
And horror doesn't require serious acting chops.
Run, scream, hide.
She fits the role.

She does well.

The industry has used me.
My agent has betrayed me.
And now?

I'm playing the same game.

Compromising to make money.

Blood and Echoes

3 a.m.

I am standing in the dark in an abandoned hospital.

The door behind me in the morgue is **kicked open.**

BAM!

A beam of a flashlight cuts through the dark.

A walkie-talkie crackles.

"Matt, we need you on set."

We're making a **movie.**
It's only a **movie.**

But standing here in this **morgue,**
surrounded by **empty drawers waiting to be filled,**
I know better.

This **isn't a movie.**

It's a dark **door I'm opening.**

And those kinds of doors, once opened, **work both ways.**

Some things **follow you home.**

I hit the set. The fake movie blood is about to flow. This scene was particularly brutal. The main character was trying to escape out a window. The Orphan Killer was coming up behind her without her knowing. Just before the hand reaches out and touches her shoulder, we realize it's a nun. It's not The Orphan Killer. The nun knows that there is a killer in the building. She's mortified. She starts screaming. The lead character slaps her across the face, trying to get her to calm down.

"You have to be quiet, or he's going to find us."

Too late. The camera on my shoulder catches The Orphan Killer entering the frame. He swings the ax with ferocious velocity. Tearing into the nun. Blood flies everywhere. And cut.

"Check the gate. Did we get that? Yeah, we got it."

Then, the sound guy approached me. The blood drained from his face as well.

"I think we got it, but I heard something weird in the dialogue. I made a note. We don't need to do it again."

The Church's Secret

Evil loves irony. Remember that.

We are on a new set. Another location with its own secrets. This time, an **ancient Catholic church** in Elizabeth, New Jersey—where the stone walls are about to reveal a dirty secret.

The priest gives us his blessing—**for a price.**

"Film wherever you want," he says, his collar too tight around his neck.

But...

"Stay off that balcony."

Here's something about forbidden places:

They **call you.**
Like Eve and the apple.
Like every locked door in every horror movie.

The Devil doesn't need to work hard when curiosity does **his job for him.**

So I **wait.**

Until the priest leaves. Until the chapel is silent, except for crew footsteps echoing off sacred stone.

Then I climb.

Each step creaks—

What I find up there haunts me to this day.

Once you read this you can't...

Un-read it.

A mattress. **Small. STAINED.**

A VHS camera on a tripod—**an unblinking eye.**

Scattered tapes on the floor. **Labels scratched off.** Their contents, obvious.

This **isn't** a saint's balcony.

It's **a predator's nest.**

I will never erase this moment from my mind.

For a second, I want to be *The Orphan Killer.*
Want to grab the ax from set and **bring real justice.**

But I'm not wearing a mask.

I'm not playing a role.

I'm a man, standing in filth, staring at the evidence of **real evil** hiding behind a collar and a cross.

Then—chaos.

A confrontation erupts in the chapel.

He knows.

Maybe a nun confides in him. Maybe guilt makes him paranoid. But suddenly, he's there, **spittle flying** from his lips, screaming for us to leave his church.

His church.

As if he owns the right to **desecrate it.**

We're thrown out. A **million dollars of equipment** locked inside with a monster.

It takes until **morning** to negotiate its release—**like paying ransom to a kidnapper.**

But here's the Devil's best trick:

He showed me real evil wearing the **clergy's clothing.**

Made me believe I was righteous in my **RIDICULE.**

Justified in my blasphemy.

The Orphan Killer wasn't a movie anymore.

It was **VINDICATION.**

I was certain I was exposing **darkness.**

But it led me **deeper into the shadows.**

When you play in the dark too long, **the dark starts playing back.**

The darkness has no emotion.

It has no remorse.

It is your worst nightmare.

That's how the enemy works.

He shows you true evil—then convinces you to fight it with more.

Makes you believe **darkness is the cure for darkness.**

And I fell for it.

HARD.

The Darkness Comes Through

This all leads to me taking my slice of digital hell back to Satan's workshop in Los Angeles. I don't know I'm unlocking Pandora's box. I'm about to discover how the occult can reach through the veil.

Remember that scene in the abandoned children's trauma unit where my sound guy said he heard something? It's about to break through the spiritual void and enter my world.

One night, alone in my editing suite, headphones on, I hear it—a child's voice, faint but unmistakable under that dialogue: *We need help.* Or maybe it's *You're going to hell.* Either way, it sends me into a different dimension of **fear.**

Ice shoots through my veins. My heart pounds as I rip off the headphones, frozen, spiraling. I spin around, half-expecting to find someone—or something—to be standing behind me. Nothing is there. Nothing visible, anyway. I grab my things and bolt, barely able to breathe.

Driving home, my hands grip the wheel so tight the leather bends. I tilt my rearview mirror down, again, half-expecting to see something—or someone—sitting in the backseat.

Fear? Exhaustion? Rationalizations race through my head, but in my gut I know better. This isn't film editing—it's disturbing something ancient. Something spiritual.

I remember Robert Brown, my editor on *IOWA*, telling me about working on *The Amityville Horror*—the terrifying true story of a young man who murdered his entire family. While cutting that film, his office suddenly felt freezing, like an icebox. He had to wrap himself in a blanket to keep working. It happened every day he editing the film, no matter what he set the thermostat to.

At the time, I laughed off his story as Hollywood marketing.

I'm not **laughing now.**

The streets of LA morph—darker, more sinister, as if the city itself has become a living, breathing manifestation of everything I'm trying to escape. Is it paranoia, or is it real? And if it's real—who sent that voice?

I'm not exposing darkness; I'm playing with it. Dancing with it. Inviting it in for a nightcap.

Maybe God is planting a seed of awareness, nudging me awake with spiritual defibrillator paddles. Or maybe it's the enemy, sowing confusion, planting doubts, trying to pull me deeper into the abyss.

Sometimes darkness touches us—not to harm, but to reveal. Discomfort wakes us up. Whispers from the void make us finally seek truth.

But the enemy uses darkness differently. He wants us curious, fascinated—seduced, like a predator luring prey into shadows.

That night, I make two mistakes at once: dismissing the spiritual reality while simultaneously glorifying darkness. I'm blind to the battle already raging—a battle for my soul, fought in editing bays and midnight drives down empty streets.

Who plants that seed?

Is it God, illuminating the stakes, giving me a glimpse of reality to wake me from spiritual slumber?

Did I just hear a cry from the fiery lake?

Or is it the enemy, attempting to frighten me into retreat, deeper numbness, greater distance from the truth?

Maybe both. Because what the enemy means for destruction, God transforms into opportunity.

Even in our darkest hours, seeds of redemption, awakening, and truth can take root.

That night, the voice terrified me.

But fear can be the beginning of wisdom. And darkness? Sometimes, it's where the brightest work begins.

Creation isn't merely art—it's spiritual warfare. I'm shaping something that can affect others in ways I can't predict. I need to know what source I'm deriving my creative power from.

Am I stirring up light or stirring up darkness?

Without clarity, we might open doors we are not prepared to walk through.

And that night, I was **dangerously close to stepping through one.**

C.S. Lewis captured my mistake perfectly in *The Screwtape Letters*:

"There are two equal and opposite errors into which we can fall about the devils. One is to disbelieve in their existence. The other is to believe, and to feel an excessive and unhealthy interest in them."

The Devil's Double-Edge

It does not stop me. I built a legend.

Marcus Miller isn't just another horror character—he's a figure that brings violent redemption for those who've been wronged. A digital wildfire waiting to ignite. My goal isn't merely to sell a movie; it's to strategically create something bigger—a movement. Something people feel compelled to belong to.

Marcus Miller—*The Orphan Killer.*
Had a mom.
Had a dad.
Watched em die.
And then went mad.

A rhyme. A creed I write. A scripture for the digital cult I'm deliberately constructing.

It starts with a plan: go viral. Facebook is brand new then—no algorithms, no ad costs, no restrictions. Everything I post reaches thousands instantly. So I lean in, hard.

We dress our lead actor head-to-toe in fake blood and his iconic mask, capturing thousands of unsettling photos in carefully chosen locations: the abandoned LA Zoo in Griffith Park, my own doorstep with Marcus Miller ringing the bell wielding an axe, or downtown LA chasing my wife through empty streets.

Then come the captions—disturbingly simple and direct:

> *I'm right outside your door.*
> *I ♥ Death.*
> *I kill people.*

These stark images, paired with eerie, provocative text, take social media over. Horror fans devour it—they want to be scared, and this feels dangerously real.

The impact is immediate. Within a week, Marcus Miller's Facebook page exploded from a few followers to fifty thousand. Then half a million. Then a million. Horror communities eat it up, tagging friends, sharing, spreading fear across the digital universe. Marcus Miller isn't a character anymore—he's an entity, stalking screens and imaginations.

Fans aren't passively watching—they're participating. Marcus Miller becomes their digital idol, a dark figure uniting outcasts, misfits, and horror devotees. They aren't just an audience—they're disciples.

I'm not simply marketing a horror movie. I'm orchestrating an experience, creating a community built on terror, excitement, and belonging.

But I made a critical mistake. I release a Blu-ray disc for people to buy. I include subtitles in six languages. The instant it's released, the piracy begins.

Free downloads pile up.

BitTorrent is the LimeWire of the indie film scene back in 2010.
Three million people pirate the movie. Then eight million. Then ten. The numbers keep climbing, and with them, Marcus Miller's legend grows.
BitTorrent themselves call me:
"Who are you? Your film is being downloaded in six different languages on our platform."

The piracy stealing my money is buying me something else—notoriety. Every illegal download is a brick in Marcus Miller's monument. The more people steal it, the more famous it becomes.

Major festivals notice. Sitges. San Sebastián. The Vatican of horror cinema comes calling because I've already built a congregation. They don't discover *The Orphan Killer*—they're catching up to it.

In Spain, three balconies of screaming fans chant, *"Marcus! Marcus!"* like they're summoning something.

David stalks through packed theaters in full costume, never speaking—just embodying the nightmare we've built. The press **can't get enough.** We are plastered on the front page of every newspaper in Spain.

Germany and Austria ban the film outright—too extreme, they say. That only makes it more valuable.

Only the most infamous slashers—like *The Texas Chainsaw Massacre*—get banned in Germany. Underground copies trade like contraband.

Even amid the screaming crowds, I feel it—**that strange nothingness.** Like something's speaking to me in the quiet moments I try to avoid.

Success that feeds on itself while eating me alive. Popularity that grows while my bank account shrinks.

I'm living in the silence before a scream. The pause before the fall. The Devil has me celebrating on a cliff's edge, too drunk on false victory to feel the ground crumbling beneath my feet.

Everything I touch turns to gold, but I can't pay my rent. My movie is watched around the globe, yet I'm drowning in debt. The more famous *The Orphan Killer* becomes, the more **hollow I feel.**

When you build your life in darkness, **the light becomes unbearable.** The noise outside is deafening, but inside? Silence. The kind that eats at you. The kind that lets whispers creep in.

Ten million downloads.
Ten million invitations to darkness.
Ten million steps toward the bottom I need to hit before I can finally look up.

The Devil gives you exactly what you ask for—then makes you choke on it.

What happens when your greatest success becomes your perfect destruction?

Long Beach is about to show me.

CHAPTER 5

One Shot of Tequila

When Demons Win

"You don't just wake up one day and decide to destroy yourself.
It happens in small, daily agreements."

I thought moving to Long Beach was a fresh start, a chance to escape the chaos of LA. But sometimes what feels like escape is actually the enemy setting you up for the final blow. We're now living in Long Beach, CA. Sublime's *"What I Got"* bleeds from every bar's speakers into the Belmont Shore night. The irony isn't lost on me—I have what I got, but I **don't love it.**

Second Avenue stretches before me like a gauntlet of temptation. Nine bars within stumbling distance. High-end boutiques nestled between watering holes like pearls on a hangman's noose. This is Long Beach's version of paradise—where the ghetto meets the gold coast, where million-dollar homes share alleys with crack dealers. It isn't just base temptation—it's a loaded gun, cocked and pointed at my head. I live in the middle of **my own execution,** and I pretend not to notice.

We land here because LA has become too expensive. *The Orphan Killer*'s fame doesn't pay the rent. Ten million downloads don't mean a thing when you can't afford groceries. I skate by with help.

Our house sits one block off the main strip. At night, bass vibrations pulse through the walls like a demonic heartbeat. The perfect environment for an alcoholic trying to stay sober—like building a recovering pyromaniac's house out of matchsticks. While the movie is going viral, my wife finds her own kind of viral darkness. Instagram becomes her house of worship, and her new high priest is a skinny Canadian roofer who spends his nights photoshopping her into elaborate fantasies. He creates digital works of art using the images she posts of herself. One day, he turns her into a goddess; another day, a mermaid. And she loves it. One of his featured images is one she hasn't shown me—he photoshops himself into an image with her, a couple in a gothic embrace. That's what I found when I checked out his account. It is also filled with pentagrams, a digital homage to

Satan himself. He isn't just an online admirer—he's a practicing Satanist after my wife.

The infection of darkness spreads. My wife's sister dives into the occult, suddenly claiming she can see into past lives and begins doing readings. These *"past-life"* readings become Instagram prophecies, each one pulling my wife deeper into delusion.

During one of their sessions, her sister looks at my wife with dead-serious eyes and says, *"He killed you in a past life. He's evil,"* referring to me. Then, because why stop at one delusion, she tells my wife she's Marilyn Monroe reincarnated.

This is what I'm living with. This is what **my children are living with.**

I'm desperate. The financial collapse of 2008 has left everyone reeling, including my family. Retirement funds have evaporated. Security is absent. Yet, here I am, asking them to invest in a sequel to the movie.

It's not only a bad financial decision; it's a moral compromise. My heart isn't in the project, and deep down, I know it won't work. I'm a total slave to her desire to be famous.

How has she gained such control? The same way water carves canyons—gradually, persistently, one compromise at a time. I've exchanged my boundaries for peace and traded my instincts for approval. When you're constantly managing someone else's emotional weather, you eventually forget your own forecast. Each time I say "yes" to avoid conflict, I give away another piece of my decision-making power. By the time I realize what's happened, she's directing more than just roles in my films.

Never let another person dictate your reality. They'll construct one that eats you from the inside out.

I remember talking to my dad, pitching the idea to him like it was a sure thing. "The first one was a success—we didn't know how to monetize it," I say, trying to sound confident. "This could be even bigger if we do it right." I'm not wrong; it does have millions of fans. But you have to make a good movie.

He believes in me—wants to believe in me—but I can hear doubt in his voice. I ignore it. Addicts are masters at convincing others—and themselves—that everything is fine, even when everything is crumbling. The money he gives me isn't cash; it's trust.

And I'm about to **blow through it.**

The Queen Mary's Warning

I don't see the setup when my wife suggests I stay on the haunted Queen Mary to *"find inspiration"* while writing *The Orphan Killer 2* screenplay. I'm blind to what's happening behind the scenes of this living nightmare—how she's orchestrating this moment, this trip, this *"time away."*

It is already...

Too late.

My writer friend from London decides to fly in to help flesh out the script. He's a good guy, looking for adventure—no idea he's stepping into a spiritual war zone.

I book us a remote cabin on the northside of the ship facing the open ocean—isolated, rustic, cinematic. The kind of place you think will inspire creativity, but it ends up revealing everything you're trying to bury.

We brought hash. Figured it'd help—open things up, soften the edges.

We eat it as soon as we get inside.

Second night, 2 a.m.

The hash **hits wrong.**

This wasn't a bad trip.

This was an invitation.

Paranoia floods my system like venom.
Every shadow stretches too long. Every sound feels like a voice.
The hull of the house creaks like a ship in a storm—like it's alive. Like it's breathing.

But I can't...

I can't breathe.

My friend is talking, but his words feel fake, manufactured. He isn't real. None of this is real. The hallway stretches ahead, narrowing into an impossible perspective. I'm not moving, yet I'm falling—falling into something I can't see.

I need to get out. But where?

The Queen Mary has become a floating coffin. There is **no escape.**

My heart slams against my ribs like a wild animal clawing its way out. I feel like I'm dying. I'm dying right here, **right now.**

I turn, tripping over myself.

"We need to go."

My friend blinks at me, confused. But his face is shifting, morphing into demonic masks.

He's laughing at me. Isn't he?

My breath comes short. "We need to go. Now."

He laughs again. "Relax, mate. Everything is cool." His voice echoes.

A shift in the air. Like something has been waiting for this exact moment to step through the cracks of my currently altered reality.

And that's when the strangers appear.

Right on cue.

Right when I'm weakest.

"Wanna see something wild?" they ask.

Demons always know when to make their move.

They offer to break into one of the ship's most haunted rooms—a sealed-off cabin where a woman was found strangled in the 1950s. Nobody works in that room anymore. Paranormal events frighten them: papers thrown across the room, employees feeling like they are being choked.

Pitch black. Cell phone flashlights illuminate the pitch black room.

I step into the bathroom of that haunted cabin alone. Flashes appear in the mirror—spheres without cause. Voices in the next room murmur about the murder, about the woman's final moments. I feel something watching me, waiting. The air becomes stagnant again. Dead. I want to leave, but I'm frozen.

That night, while I sleep, it comes.

"Matt, wake up! **WAKE UP,** MATE!"

My friend's voice is distant, desperate. But I can't surface. The black mass is back—the same one from years ago—pinning me to the bed. I thrash against it, fighting something I can't see but feel with every cell in my body.

The next morning, my friend sits on the edge of his bed staring at me, white as a corpse. "There was this dark cloud hovering over you," he says, shaking. "You were fighting it. I screamed at you, but you wouldn't wake up."

The demon attacked me at my weakest. That's its purpose—to torment, terrorize, and take what's already broken and shatter it completely.

I tell my friend to pack his stuff, and jump ship.

When I pull up to the house, something immediately feels off. The car door is ajar, like it's been broken into. Nothing adds up. Inside, the stench of stale alcohol smacks me, thick and cutting. Everything looks intact, but something is seriously wrong. I walk to the side door of the house. Unlocked. I make my way to our bedroom. I slowly open the door and it creaks open.

Inside, she lies sprawled across the bed, hair perfect, makeup flawless—as if she's stepped out of a photoshoot. She looks too good. Too polished. She jumps up, smiling.

Has someone been with my wife? My head spins.

My gut screams the truth. This time, I hear it clearly: *She's not yours anymore.*

Not that she ever was.

But I say **nothing.** I don't trust myself enough to believe what I'm seeing. I don't trust my instincts. It's easier to...

sweep this under the rug.

The pain is overwhelming. I need an old friend—one to comfort me, to give me the warm hug I desperately crave.

Hello, darkness, my old friend.

> **RED FLAG MOMENT:** A relapse doesn't start with the first drink. It starts with the excuses, the rationalizations, the tiny compromises. You don't fall—you walk toward the edge, one small step at a time.

The Shot Of Tequila

"The weak man sacrifices his future for his present. The warrior sacrifices his present for his future. One lives for comfort. ***The other builds a legacy.****"*

After that time away on the Queen Mary my wife brings alcohol back into our home. She says she wants to drink again. Says she's tired—tired of being sober, tired of being bored. She tells me she's "the party girl," and proud of it. I don't argue. I watch her drinking at home and out at dinners. She taunts me. But I didn't start drinking immediately.

That doesn't happen until we're almost finished shooting *The Orphan Killer* sequel.
Yes, it's funded with a shoestring budget. My passion for it has faded, along with any illusion the film might succeed. I'm going through the motions now,

directing scenes I no longer believe in. The monster inside me claws at the walls again, searching for an exit—or maybe an entrance.

That first shot of tequila comes late one night, at a bar a block from my house, right after I leave the set.

Panama Joe's.

It's the kind of place where darkness doesn't just fall—it rises from the floorboards, seeping into the wood, the walls, the patrons hunched over sticky counters.

The first shot is waiting for me. **It always was.**

The whisper from the deep is overwhelming now. Not a whisper anymore—a roar, drowning out every other voice in my head.

A waitress walks by, a tray of tequila shots balanced on her fingertips, flashing the kind of smile that belongs in a beer ad. The golden clear liquid catches the dim bar light, winking at me like an old friend—one I haven't seen in eleven years, yet somehow never forgot.

I reach and grab a shot.

I throw it back.

No hesitation. No thought. No **resistance.**

Eleven years without a drink—ends in one swallow.

The enemy never rushes.
He waits.

And tonight?
He wins.

I can still taste it. The warmth down my esophagus. The half-second twitch that hit my face. My youth came flooding back. That moment wasn't about alcohol—it was the old me crawling out of the grave.

One shot becomes two. Two become four. The night blurs into a series of increasingly poor decisions, each easier than the last. The muscle memory of destruction never truly fades; it just waits patiently for permission to return.

I let it in... lie by lie. First her lies, then my own. The lie that I can be around alcohol and stay strong. The lie that her drinking won't affect me. The lie that my marriage is worth saving at any cost. The lie that I can control the monster once I let it out.

Now I'm back—standing at the edge, staring down into the abyss, realizing too late I've been digging this hole for a long, long time. And the only way **forward is down.**

The Beginning of the End

A few months later. Christmas morning. Sunlight streams through half-drawn blinds, highlighting the scattered wrapping paper across our living room floor. I'm hungover but pushing through it. The kids are ecstatic about their new bikes—gleaming red and blue frames, training wheels ready to hit the pavement. Their excitement is the one pure thing in this house.

I search for her, finally finding her sitting alone in our son's bedroom. She's pressed against the wall, knees pulled to her chest, face illuminated by the blue glow of her phone screen. She doesn't look up when I enter.

"Let's go," I say, jingling the car keys. "The kids want to learn to ride their new bikes down at the beach path."

She glances up, for a second. Her eyes are distant, like she's already somewhere else.

"You take them," she says, thumbs still tapping on the screen. "I'm not feeling well."

"It's Christmas," I say.

She doesn't respond. Just keeps scrolling, tapping, disappearing into whatever world exists inside that phone—a world that clearly matters more than the one right in front of her.

"Merry Christmas," I mutter bitterly, turning away.

I take the kids myself. They laugh and wobble down the beach path, training wheels clattering against the concrete. I should be present, should be savoring their joy, their accomplishment. Instead, I'm trapped in that image of her—back against the wall, face bathed in digital light, completely disconnected from us.

It gnaws at my gut. Something feels profoundly wrong. I want to go back, rip the phone from her hands, demand to know what's more important than watching our children learn to ride bikes on Christmas morning. But I don't. I've become an expert at swallowing my instincts, at burying the warning bells under sand.

The slow erosion of our marriage wasn't sudden. It was a shoreline losing ground to the tide, one grain at a time. First, it was the bars outside our front door beckoning both of us. Then the subtle shifts—her phone disappearing into her purse before bed, password changes, the way she angled her screen away when I entered a room. A pattern I refused to see.

The real danger wasn't outside my house—it was inside it. My marriage has become a theater of lies, a carefully orchestrated performance where we both pretend everything is normal while the foundation crumbles beneath us.

Every night after that, she sits in our daughter's room for hours, the door closed just enough to hide whay she is doing. Our daughter's bedroom light stays on.

"She's afraid," she explains when I question her. "I'm comforting her."

But our daughter's face in the morning shows no signs of fear or night terrors. What I'm witnessing isn't maternal comfort—it's the methodical construction of lies, one secret text at a time. She's communicating with someone—someone who clearly matters more than we do.

I know something's wrong.

I feel it with absolute clarity:

Evil.

Pure evil—permeating everything.

It hangs in our house like invisible smoke, seeping into the walls, the furniture, our lungs. I can taste it. Can feel it wrapping around us, tightening its grip day by day.

Yet I stay. I swallow the bile rising in my throat each time I watch her retreat to that room, phone in hand. I convince myself things will improve if I just try harder, if I just ignore the signs a little longer.

This is what addiction does—not only to your body, but to your perception. It blinds you to the obvious. It makes you complicit in your own destruction. And sometimes, the most dangerous addiction isn't to a substance. It's the person **sleeping beside you.**

The Setup for the Fall

After that first shot at Panama Joe's, everything accelerates. One drink becomes many. Many becomes daily.

The Devil doesn't need to work hard once I start drinking.

More intimate images of them photoshopped together start appearing in her Instagram feed. I complain about the Canadian Roofer. I tell her it's enough—he's crossing the line. She's on her device nearly every waking moment. **She agrees.**

Then comes her masterstroke.

"I need to go to New Jersey," she says one night, her voice honey-sweet with manipulation.

"Visit my parents. Take the kids. Everything's been so crazy with social media—I need to decompress. I'm going to an all-women's spa to detox from it."

She gets her hair done. Nails perfected. Plays the part of the devoted wife trying to save her marriage.

"I love you," she says. "We'll figure this out."

"Maybe it's good," I reply. "I'll go see my family. Get some quality time." I'm drowning in cognitive dissonance—that psychological chokehold where the truth is screaming in my face, but I smother it because acknowledging it means facing what comes next.

I know what's happening. I feel it in my gut. But my mind twists it into comforting delusions.

This is healthy.
This is what married couples do to work things out.

The sickest part?

Her intimacy with me never changes.
She never slows down her desire for me.
She spends the night **professing her love for me.**

I don't feel the knife she's slowly **stabbing between my ribs.**

That's how good she's become at real-life performances.

She hugs me tight before she leaves, claiming her undying love.

She sees my trepidation.
She moves in close, grabs the sides of my face, and looks me square in the eyes.

"I love you so much. You and I are soulmates. I'm going to detox from all this and come back as a new wife. I promise this is for the best."

For a split second, doubt claws at me—is this genuine? But her sincerity is flawless, and my desperation wants to believe the lie.

The kids pack their bags. She packs her lies.

The next morning, she's gone. A car service. A smile. A wave.

She texts me pictures of herself and the kids smiling with her family.

And me?

I pack my denial.

I head to Scottsdale, Arizona, where my parents stay in the winter—convincing myself this is normal.

> **RED FLAG MOMENT:** When routines change, when patterns break, something is up. Do not ignore it. Own it. Talk about it. Because if you don't, it doesn't go away. It festers. It spreads. It deteriorates into **something far worse.** Silence isn't protection—it's an accomplice.

The Affair

The downward spiral is in full effect.
 I pester my dad and brother with questions:

"Why do you think she wanted to go there alone?"
"Why couldn't she just stop on her own?"
"It's no big deal, right?"
"She'll detox and come back amazing, right?"
"Right?"

The theater where we sit, waiting for *American Sniper* to start, isn't showing previews.
 It's about to premiere—the end of my marriage.

And somewhere in Florida—not New Jersey—my wife is already living the next chapter of her life.
With the Canadian roofer named Devin.

But this isn't betrayal.
This is mercy.

My own self-induced crucifixion is about to begin.
Slow.
Merciless.

Mandatory to reveal my many sins.

I open *Find My iPhone in* the theater.
I'm not looking for the end of my marriage.
I'm not expecting anything, right?
Right?

It's an impulse.
A reflex.
A moment of insecurity.

I click her name.

The little blue dot flies across the screen.

Across the United States to the eastern seaboard.

But not New Jersey.
Not Spa time.

LIES.

Englewood, Florida.

My stomach drops.
My face melts off.

"How the hell is she in Florida?" I blurt out, interrupting the movie.

My dad and brother turn to me, noticing my shock.
They don't understand what's happening.

"This can't be."

They stare at me in wonderment.
I'm glitching.
Blindsided by my own blatant emotional ignorance.

We all walk out of the theater before the movie even starts.

We hit the street outside the theater.

"How is this even possible? She's in Florida!" I blurt out.

My brother raises his eyebrows.
Knowing.
They aren't stunned.
Maybe they're laughing at how absurd my blindness has become.

And they **do** laugh.

Not out of spite.
Out of relief—that the charade is finally collapsing.

Either way, they know what I haven't wanted to admit:

My iPhone tracker isn't a thousand miles off.

She is.

My dad chuckles again, shaking his head.
"She ain't in New Jersey, son."

I call her.
The phone rings.

They listen.

When she answers, her voice is casual.
Annoyed.

Like I've interrupted her yoga class.

"I'm at the spa," she says.

My heart pounds.

"My phone's in the locker. Why are you calling?"
"You're gonna get me kicked out."

"Kicked out of Florida?" I snap, calling her out.

The pause on the other end extends with apprehension.
She's formulating a lie she didn't foresee having to contrive.

Then her voice—clipped, irritated—fires back:
"It's probably a bad connection. I'm in New Jersey at the spa, and you need to stop calling! I paid a lot of money to be here and get better, and if you don't stop, I can't stay."

Click.

Gaslighting 101.
Make me question my sanity instead of her lies.

But the truth is right smack dab in front of me.

My **gut knows it.**
My **brain knows it.**
My heart doesn't want to catch up.

Her phone is now off.
But her last location—still blinking in my face.

So **I dig.**

I track down a Florida phone number based on his last name. I make calls like a private investigator.

What did I think I was solving?
It's already been solved.

She's **having an affair.**

But I need more info.

I need to connect the two of them together.

I tell myself I'm being clever.
My brother and dad see a drowning man grabbing at the nearest piece of driftwood.

I can't see how **sick I truly am.**

A woman answers one of my calls.

I fumble my words. Choking on my own pulse.

"Hi, I'm trying to get ahold of... " I say, lying through my teeth.
I tell the woman I'm her brother in New Jersey.
"The kids miss her. Her phone seems to be off, and they are desperate to talk with her."

"Oh, they just left!" she chirps. "I'm Devin's aunt. She was here with him. They make such a lovely couple."

Lovely couple?

I spin. The horizon closes in like an old spaghetti Western.

It's high noon, and I've been blasted into a pine box.

I call her again.
The phone rings this time.

This time, she answers.

Silence.

"Hello? Hello..."

Then, another click.

That's all it takes.

One final click of the phone, and the life I once knew goes up in smoke.

She doesn't make contact again for **two days.**
She finishes her party.

My dad places a firm hand on my shoulder. "This is the best thing that's happened to you in a long time. You're finally free from that woman's lies."

My dad probably thought that the relationship was headed for the graveyard at the end of main street with an epitaph that read.

"Here lies the end of nothing great", but I wasn't done yet.

The humiliation has just begun.

RED FLAG MOMENT: Betrayal doesn't destroy you—what you do with it does. Instead of accepting what happened, I let it control me.

The Setup

When she returned from Florida, she didn't come back to apologize—she came armed with a strategy. While my family urged me to toss her belongings into the yard, her family devised their own plan: get me arrested to seize control.

She moved back in for a short time—despite everything. I let her, convinced we could somehow piece together what was left of our family. I need you to consider how weak a man I am at this point. The relapse back to alcohol has me in its grasp. I say this to help you understand its profound effect on my personality. Thankfully, I am not in a fighting mood. I am hurt and defeated. She, on the other hand, was furious to be back. This wasn't reconciliation—it was a calculated takedown attempt.

The Explosion

And after just a few days, it happens.

The kids are in the living room. Everything seems normal.

She stands—walks toward me and erupts.

Like someone screamed **Action** and she switched into character.

Instantly she is screaming in my face, spitting venom with every word.

"I hate you!" Her voice isn't loud—it's possessed.

My children freeze, their eyes wide with terror. This isn't the first storm they've weathered, but something about this one feels different. More deliberate. More dangerous.

She lunges forward, pushing me back against the countertop in the kitchen, nails raking down the side of my face as her face trembles with madness. Pain sears across my cheek as she mouths the words:

"I wish you were dead."

Then she steps back, eyes cold and calculating.

"Hit me," she demands, eyes wild. "Come on—hit me! Do it!"

In that moment, I see it all clearly—the setup, the trap, the endgame. Something inside me stays perfectly still. Calm settles over me like a bulletproof vest.

This isn't working.

She grabs our wedding photo off the shelf, rips open the side door, and hurls it into the yard. Glass shatters across the lawn—a fitting metaphor for what's left of our marriage.

The neighbors hear the commotion. They call the police.

I step outside to assess the damage. She follows, pounding her fists into my chest, forcing me backward against the garage. That's when she slaps me—hard across the face. The crack echoes in the evening air.

"I wish you were dead."

Minutes later, red and blue lights flash in our driveway.

The Reversal

The officers separate us for questioning. Through the front window, I can see my children watching, silent witnesses to another adult failure.

"What happened here?" an officer asks, eyeing the red marks on my face.

"Nothing happened, just an argument," I say quietly.

Meanwhile, she's smiling, telling her own version—but in her lies, she makes a critical mistake. She admits to hitting me.

What she doesn't know is that in California, this admission triggers an immediate arrest. Domestic violence isn't a choice for officers—it's a mandatory booking.

They handcuff her while she protests, confusion replacing her earlier confidence. She is in tears, staring at me as they take her **away**.

"Matt, please help me. Tell them I didn't hit you. Why are you doing this to me?" she pleads.

This wasn't the ending she scripted.

As they place her in the back of the patrol car, I feel no satisfaction. Just exhaustion. And something else—**relief**.

Calm

With her out, the house transforms instantly.

It's like someone turned off a perpetual alarm that had been blaring for years. Silence floods in—not an empty silence, but a peaceful one.

"Let's go to Subway," I tell the kids.

Their faces light up. Simple pleasures without walking on eggshells.

They didn't ask about their mother being away—as if something evil had finally been removed. Like speaking her name might bring it back.

We eat sandwiches at the park as twilight settles around us. No tension. No fear. Just a father and his children existing without bracing for the next explosion.

My son laughs at something, and the sound is so unfamiliar in its freedom that it nearly breaks me. They still remember that evening years later—not because their mother was arrested, but because of how peaceful everything was without her chaos dominating our lives.

The Pressure

Later that night as I tuck them into bed, the calls start.

Her mother. Her sisters. Everyone.

"You need to bail her out." "How could you let this happen?" "What kind of man lets the mother of his children sit in jail?"

The irony is suffocating. They orchestrated the plan to get me arrested—now they're furious their plot backfired.

I call my dad, desperate for wisdom from someone who cares about my well-being.

"Absolutely do not bail her out," he says firmly. "She needs to experience the consequences of her actions."

She spends the night in a cell. Faces a judge the next morning. He sets a hearing date and issues a restraining order—she's not allowed near the house or me.

The Cycle Continues

But by the very next afternoon, she's at the door again.

No police escort to collect belongings. No legal representative. Just her—the restraining order apparently meaningless in her mind.

She literally crawls in on her knees, tears streaming.

"I'm so sorry. I'll never do anything like that again. Please forgive me."

I let her stay.

Not because I believed her. Not because I still loved her.

But because, despite everything, I couldn't bear the thought of the mother of my children carrying a felony charge for the rest of her life.

It was mercy. Or weakness.

What I didn't understand then was that true mercy would have been allowing natural consequences to create real change.

Instead, I was resetting the cycle, delaying the inevitable, and teaching my children a dangerous lesson—that accountability was negotiable.

The pattern wasn't just continuing. It was escalating. And we were all going down with it.

Another chance to step up and be a man worthy of my calling—missed.

The Spiral

*"Too much time spent in your head leaves your hands idle and **your heart weary**."*

We finally separate under the guise that we're going to work on things "for the kids."
But I have to ask myself:
Why did she pack everything we owned one day when I was away and leave?

I get a couch, a bed, a dresser, and an open invitation to the playground of bars right outside my door.

She keeps claiming she is done with the affair, and it was **never sexual**.
Of course it wasn't.
It was only emotional. I wasn't affectionate enough.

Maybe that's why she never cooked a meal in eleven years.

It's all my fault, you see.

She says, "You don't understand—I am the mermaid. Those images he made of me, that's what made me feel alive. He invested time in me."

In my head, the scenes of her "affair trip" play on repeat.
I imagine them holding hands—but only platonically, of course.

An OCD symphony I **can't turn off.**

After that, I become a party animal.
I drink—not the kind of drinking where you have a beer with dinner.
The kind where you have whiskey for breakfast.

The affair becomes the monster inside's best friend.

Deep down, I don't care that she cheated.
I tell myself I'm suffering.
I tell myself I'm in pain.

That I can't believe she had the affair.
That this is the craziest thing that ever happened to me.

I play the victim.

But the truth?
All hail—**King Baby.**

Boo hoo, poor Matt, you got cheated on. You need a drink.

The addict in me treasures it.

The affair isn't a tragedy.
It's a **gift.**

Nobody questions what I've been through.

I was betrayed. I can milk this for YEARS!

The betrayal becomes my **license to drink.**
The affair is my get-out-of-sobriety-jail-free card.

And the ironic part?
I'm already headed to jail the moment that shot of tequila touches my lips.

Every morning, I stand outside the bar on Second Avenue, waiting for it to open like a junkie waiting for his dealer. By noon, I'm three beers deep, and by nightfall, I don't remember where I am.

Panama Joe's becomes my sanctuary, cocaine my communion.

A little bump here, a little bump there.

I lean over a dirty bathroom sink, stare at my hollow eyes in the cracked mirror, and tell myself I'm fine.

She ruined your life, man. How can you keep living after what happened to you?

I'm deconstructing—drink by drink.
Line by **LINE**.

**And the enemy who once reviled me—
Now sits back on his throne, well pleased.**

My father tries to intervene. I remember sitting across from him at a restaurant, beer in hand.

He looks at me as if he doesn't recognize the person sitting there.

"What are you doing? Have you lost your mind?"

I laugh.

"Relax."
"I've got it under control."
"I'm not the same guy I was."
"I'm almost forty. I can handle it now."

Lie.

I'm not a man handling his life.
I'm a walking corpse trying to convince everyone I'm still alive.

That guy—the one from years ago?
At least he had **HOPE**.

I don't have that **anymore**.

The Final Descent

A few months pass, and I give up on Long Beach.
I cancel our lease early.

My father warns me not to leave.
He always warns me.
I should listen.

Instead, I move closer to her.
Closer to the kids.
Closer to **the lie** I'm desperate to believe.

She's spent months complaining I'm *"too far away,"*
that if we're honestly going to *"work on us,"*
I need to close the gap.

So, I do.

And I grow...
Weaker.
And
WEAKER.

Now, instead of stumbling to bars, I'm driving to them.

Bad decisions masking even **deadlier ones.**

Excuses become an hourly transaction in my descent into madness.

I'm no longer drinking to escape—
I'm drowning.

I have dug so deep into darkness that I am manic.

I see no hope for my future. I can only think hours—minutes—seconds ahead.

My only goal now is to **stop the pain.**

I wake up daily at the Residence Inn—one of those sterile, forgettable motels where broken people go to disappear.
To die in slow motion.

But for me? A five-star Google review.

Why?

The lobby bar—steps from my room. Free wine.

Any time of day.

They start hiding it from me in the morning.
The front desk bell expects my ring if it isn't out on time.
Ding. Ding. **DING.**

I complain. "It says right here on your lounge wall. Free wine for all guests."

Alcohol isn't a relief now—it's **oxygen.**

The spiral has almost completely unraveled—**the end is approaching.**

The enemy must have been popping popcorn, eager to watch this catastrophe unfold on the big screen.

Fireworks and Cocaine

It's the Fourth of July!

Five days before the accident.

We take a cooler full of booze down to Huntington Beach to watch the fireworks.
Me and my lovely wife.

She says we're "working on things."
She says we're "rebuilding trust."

When the fireworks fade to black, she turns to me and says:
"You should get some coke."

Of course—I find it.

At that exact moment, I should walk away.
Instead, I stay.

Because I'm still playing the role:
The man trying to save a marriage,
The father doing it for his kids.

But I'm not thinking about my kids.
I'm buying cocaine with them in the car.
Committing a felony with them watching.

The affair is supposedly over, and yet here we are—
Back in my hotel bathroom, drugs in hand, kids asleep outside the door.

Our relationship has become utterly clandestine.
A shameful secret.

She whispers how much she still loves me.
"I hope you're not seeing other women."
She says she's sorry the affair ever happened.
She promises we'll move back in together soon.

What am I thinking?

Let me tell you:
I'm not.

"Just a little more counseling," she says.

Every counselor we see meets with her first.
Every one of them glares at me as if I'm their arch-nemesis.

Why am I still listening to her?
Because damaged people believe the lie that the person destroying them can also heal them.

Am I damaged—or do I just like the abuse?
At least it's attention.

She's the kind of person who can do cocaine and fall asleep.
I'm the kind of person who does it and my eyelids superglue open.

She leaves the next morning.
I haven't slept.

Now I have **coke on hand**—and no supervision.

The gaslighting becomes relentless over the next three days.
She knows I can't handle it.

"I want to make this work. We just need more counseling. I love you."

Looking back, my desperation feels pathetic—but I had to reach the absolute bottom before I could see a way out clearly.

My spikes in drug use turn an already toxic situation into complete **self-destruction.**

The enemy has me so broken, so confused, that I wake each morning like a frightened cadet—waiting for her texts, desperate for orders from my own executioner.

I am no longer blind. My eyes have been removed and put into her purse.

Along with my manhood.

The end is near.

Reflection

Thank God I am on the other side of this now, two thousand three hundred miles away from where she currently lives. It's better that way. No contact has been a blessing. The woman I thought I knew, the relationship I thought I was in—none of it was real. I was living in a carefully constructed illusion. But I was the architect of my own destruction. The King Baby who kept the illusion alive to sustain the monster inside's desires. Without this cycle's continuation, I would have to stop using alcohol and become accountable. I could not do that alone. It was going to take divine intervention.

The irony of it all still stings. There I was, the man who walked away from Naomi Watts at the Chateau Marmont, the guy who turned down opportunities most men would sacrifice limbs for. Hollywood had offered me its particular brand of temptation on silver platters, and I'd walked away from rivers of earthly gold. Not out of some superior morality, but because fidelity mattered to me. I believed in the vows we had taken. I believed those vows meant something.

That's the thing about gaslighting—it's most effective against people who can't imagine doing the same thing themselves. I couldn't fathom living a double life, so I never suspected she was capable of it. I thought my loyalty would be reciprocated simply because it was given. How naive. How catastrophically blind. But it was the perfect lie to believe to feed the demon inside.

Looking back now, the signs were everywhere, blinking like neon lights I somehow refused to see. The contractor's car circling our house late at night, his drunken question about where my wife was months after his job was done—who asks that? The gardener with his mysterious invoices for work that was never done, her insistence that I "just pay it" to make it go away. Each incident was a breadcrumb on a trail leading to the truth, but I was too afraid to follow it.

Los Angeles—"the industry"—preached its false doctrine to me for years, its verses condemning so-called toxic masculinity until I cracked. Men, they insisted, should be safe, tame, and above all, never too aggressive. At one point, an acting coach—a well-respected one, mind you—suggested I wear women's underwear to auditions to ease my nerves. The industry thrives on perversion, sexual confusion, gender ambiguity. It wants you questioning everything about yourself—even if you should identify as a she-wolf, wearing a mask, barking at strangers from the end of a leash.

While I never stepped into a casting suite wearing blue thong underwear to feel more "confident," I did gradually lose my masculine edge. Year by year, my testosterone drained away, siphoned off like blood by a vampire intent on leaving me barely alive—just enough to feed again.

My dad used to say that sometimes the most painful experiences are gifts in disguise. At the time, discovering her affair felt like I was being crushed in a vice inch by inch while she stared at my bulging eyes. But he was right—it was the best thing that ever happened to me. She did me the biggest favor by finally getting caught. Had it continued, I might have spent decades in that fog, questioning my sanity, drowning my confusion in alcohol, never finding my way out.

There's a particular kind of psychological torture that comes with being cheated on while simultaneously being told you're crazy for suspecting anything. It creates a fracture in your reality. Your instincts scream one thing while the person you trust most insists on another. Eventually, you stop trusting yourself entirely. You become a ghost in your own life—present but not fully there, watching but not fully seeing.

Gaslighting is the perfect modern-day example of demonic deception. Satan doesn't only lie to you—he trains you to lie to yourself. He makes you question every truth until his lies become your foundation. He turns your perception inside out until you're living in a world constructed entirely of falsehoods, yet believing it's reality.

Years later, after everything had fallen apart, she said something that still chills me: "I love it when you don't catch me." A casual confession dropped into conversation, as if discussing a preference for chocolate sauce over vanilla ice cream. In that moment, the mask slipped completely, and I saw who she truly was—someone who enjoyed the game more than she ever cared about how it affected others. Even her own children.

I realize now that her infidelity wasn't about me at all. It wasn't because I wasn't affectionate enough or attentive enough. It was about a bottomless need for validation that no single person could ever fulfill. Her seeking validation from everyone was as compulsive as my drinking. We were both addicts, just with different poisons. Both of us desperately filling voids that only God could truly satisfy.

The emasculation I felt wasn't about the betrayal itself. It was about how completely I'd surrendered my autonomy, my instincts, and my self-respect. I had become unrecognizable to myself—a shell of a man who accepted lies because the truth was too painful to face. I accepted blame that wasn't mine because taking responsibility for her actions gave me the illusion of control. If it was my fault, maybe I could fix it. The alternative—that I had no control whatsoever—was too terrifying to contemplate. With all that I had uncovered, I was so terrified of being alone that I chose depravity and self-destruction as my partner.

The iCloud discoveries—the emails, the nude photos sent to multiple men, the bizarre side business of selling worn clothing items to fetishists online—weren't even the worst part. The worst part was realizing that the person I'd lived with for years was a stranger. That every intimate moment, every vulnerable confession, every plan for the future had been shared with someone wearing a mask.

I wasn't innocently sleeping next to a woman who was unfaithful. I was sleeping next to someone who had made deception an art form, who had calibrated her manipulation so perfectly that I questioned my own sanity before I questioned her loyalty. The real horror wasn't being betrayed—it was being betrayed while simultaneously being convinced that the betrayal was all in my head.

In my drunkenness, in my desperate clinging to the bottom of a bottle, I became the perfect target. Addiction doesn't just destroy your body; it dissolves your boundaries, erodes your judgment, and obliterates your self-worth. It makes you willing to accept things the sober version of yourself would never tolerate. I often say that at this time in my life, I was a man with a huge ego and no self-confidence—all swagger on the outside, hollow and afraid within.

The more I drank to numb the suspicion, the more susceptible I became to her manipulation. And the more she manipulated me, the more I needed to drink to quiet the cognitive dissonance screaming inside my head. It was a vicious cycle, each destructive element feeding the other like twin serpents devouring each other's tails.

Looking back now, I see God's intricate design. My children had begun the process of softening my heart, creating the first cracks in my false identity. As devastating as it was, the betrayal became the earthquake that finally shattered it completely. Both were necessary for my salvation. What seemed like abandonment was divine rescue, though I couldn't see it at the time.

As painful as this chapter of my life was, I now recognize it as necessary. The complete demolition of who I thought I was created a clean slate for who I was meant to become. Sometimes, losing everything is how you arrive at the truth.

John 12:24 says, *"Unless a kernel of wheat falls to the ground and dies, it remains only a single seed. But if it dies, it produces many seeds."*

There is profound wisdom in this divine paradox. What appears to be death becomes the birthplace of new life. What feels like failure becomes the foundation for true success. What seems like abandonment becomes the beginning of authentic connection—first with God, then with yourself, and finally with others who see the real you.

I had to die to the illusion in order to truly live in truth. The betrayal felt like death, but it was the necessary death of the false self—the *"me"* that was tolerating dysfunction and addiction and calling it love. In losing everything I thought mattered, I gained the only thing that truly does—a life anchored in reality rather than fantasy, in truth rather than lies.

If you're in a similar place right now—questioning your reality, drowning in gaslighting and manipulation—know this: your instincts are still there, buried beneath the confusion. The voice telling you something's wrong isn't crazy. It's the last honest part of you fighting to be heard. Listen to it. That small voice is your compass in the fog, your lighthouse in the darkness.

Healing from gaslighting isn't only about escaping the relationship—it's about reclaiming your perception of reality. It took me years to trust my instincts again, to believe what I saw with my own eyes rather than what someone else told me I should see. Every time I honored my own truth instead of accepting someone else's version of it, I reclaimed a piece of myself that had been stolen.

Your children, your responsibilities, your genuine self—these aren't burdens that hold you back from some glittering alternative life. They're lifelines extended to you by a merciful God, anchors that can keep you from drifting into deeper deception.

What feels like your greatest loss could be your most profound salvation. What seems like the end might truly be your beginning. It might just save your life, as it eventually saved mine. But first **I had to die.**

The Death of The Ego

I'm a pathetic man. Fully emasculated. She throws out a line of text without any good bait, and I chase it. Another hook in the water, another glint of false hope and I gobble it up.

The hook is **deep in my cheek.**

I am the most loyal follower in her cult of self-love.

The cult's goal is to watch me **disintegrate into oblivion.**

July 9th, 2014. This very morning, I wake up in my usual startled panic.

Shotgun blast over my head.

Move—have to keep moving.

Scramble to find leftover booze from last night.

Down a glass to chase away the morning shakes.

Jump in the car.

Snort a few lines.

Drop the bag in the cup holder.

And blast off toward Los Feliz.

Why?

Because she's been texting me all morning.

> *I'm up by our old house. I miss it. You should come up.*

The Devil purrs in my ear.

Follow her. You need to find her. Fix this. It's all your fault. You were not loving enough.

She is the mother of your kids.

Madness radiates through me. I'm no longer in touch with myself. The demon has taken over. My eyes roll back in my head. The Devil's plan is underway.

Like a starved shark chasing a fake seal. I start the car and begin driving.

I can't tell you what I think I'll find by searching for her in LA. Some closure, maybe. Some answers. When you're this drunk, everything feels like a revelation.

Twenty miles of gridlocked traffic stretch between me and that illusion. I pilot a thousand-pound missile through LA's concrete arteries, cocaine dust forming constellations on my shirt. The steering wheel feels alive in my hands—as if it knows better than I do the final destination.

Her last text before she goes dark.

I'm still at the same spot we used to hike. Where are you?

But when I arrive—she's not there. I can't find her. She vanishes, and the texts stop coming in. She knows I've been drinking. Now I'm twenty miles from home and coming down fast.

The Dresden materializes as I search. Our old haunt. The place where it all started—and the place where, for me, **it all ended.** I sit outside in the car, debating if I should go in. When I'm this high and start to feel it fade, the emotional pain takes over. The override button to calm that raging current isn't just needed at this stage of my addiction—it's mandatory. If I don't get a drink, that raging current becomes convulsions. That's how far along I am.

Inside, the bar's wood grain slithers beneath the lights, shifting, alive.

One glass of wine becomes three, becomes who knows. Time does funny things when you're pickling yourself in regret before noon on a Wednesday. The bartender's face keeps morphing—concern to disgust, then to that special kind of pity reserved for the truly gone. Maybe he throws me out. Maybe I walk out. Memory's funny that way—it protects you from your own stupidity until it doesn't.

I get back in the car.

Every person who ever ended up as a statistic has said those words.

I got back in the car.

The perfect epitaph for the possessed.

Am I a selfish child?

Absolutely.

The Crash

My brother says he was on the phone with me when it happened.

He says he heard the tires screeching, the crunch of metal folding into itself, and my ragged, choking breaths.

I don't remember the conversation.

Maybe there isn't one.

Maybe I'm already gone.

Here's what I do remember:

I'm upside down.

The car flips. My body is weightless, spinning in slow motion.

Soaring over the median of Harbor Blvd—hovering, floating—suspended in limbo.

Through the sunroof, I see the tops of other cars.

Perfect, **unknowing strangers** driving to lunch. People with plans.

People who don't deserve to be trapped under the wreckage of my choices.

For a moment, I'm not flipping.

For a moment, I'm frozen in time.

Then the roof of my car smashes into the tops of the other vehicles.

I feel it, even in the free fall.

The **clank and scrape.**

Enough to make me wonder:

Have I killed someone?

In that moment, flipping through the air without a seatbelt, I know I've crossed a line.

If I've taken a life, do I even deserve to live?

When I finally crash down, the metal twists—a corpse folding in on itself.

Cocaine explodes into the air, shrapnel in the wreckage.

It mixes with the dust, the blood, the glass—painting the inside of the car white.

It settles on my skin, **war paint.**

It clings to my mouth, a final mockery.

My forehead shatters. Blood fills my eyes.

And then...

SILENCE cascades in softly.

No more screeching tires.

No more twisting metal.

For a moment—a single solitary moment—I am calm.

Smoke drifts past my eyes, a faint siren builds in the distance, and fuel drains from the vehicle like the **final heartbeats of a dying thing.**

The Near-Death Experience

I read once that your heart stopping sounds like a bass drum underwater. They're wrong. It doesn't sound like anything. One minute, you're there; the next, the cosmic DJ cuts the music.

I flatline. That's what the chart says. But charts don't tell you what happens in the space between heartbeats—in that infinite pause between *is* and *isn't*.

Here's what they tell you about near-death experiences: You float above your body. You see a tunnel. Maybe Jesus high-fives you on your way to the light. Here's what happens: none of that.

Instead, imagine diving into pure light. Not the kind that dilates your retinas at the eye doctor. More like being inside the sun's living room. Infinite warmth. No edges. No boundaries. A vast, endless something that feels more like home than anywhere I've been in thirty-eight years of breathing.

The weird part? It isn't empty. The light is alive. Conscious. Like being cradled in the mind of God—if God thinks in photons instead of words. No harps. No angels. Just an overwhelming, all-consuming presence that makes everything else feel like a cheap knockoff.

Then comes the question. Not in words—words are too clumsy for wherever I am. More like truth hitting me straight in the soul:

Stay or go?

Simple as that. Heaven's multiple-choice exam to see if I get in. No pressure, just the weight of the rest of my existence confronting me.

My kids' faces flash through my mind. Not the happy memories—the real ones. Being the father they didn't deserve but got stuck with anyway. The thought of them growing up knowing Dad chose the exit ramp over them.

Little faces.

Who **deserve better.**

I don't need to speak. Don't need to move. The choice makes itself—as if my soul has already filled in the answer sheet while my consciousness is still trying to find a pencil.

Reality **SLAMS** me back into my body.

A piston firing.

PAIN DETONATING across every nerve.

The hospital room materializes in fragments—beeping machines, nurses shouting coordinates of my continued existence, the smell of industrial clean desperately masking my pitifulness.

The doctor hovers over me, Death's temp replacement. Funky magnifying glasses make his eyes cartoonishly oversized, like they belong in a Pixar film. He's putting my head back together with staples, casual as IKEA furniture assembly, when he hits me with:

"Maybe you should quit drinking."

Understatement of the century.

Like suggesting someone on fire might want to consider getting wet.

If I weren't fresh from meeting the light of creation, I might laugh. But the cosmic joke isn't funny anymore. Something has changed in that space between heartbeats. The punchline doesn't land the same way.

Even still, **I'm not done with my rebellion.**

The Warning

The doctors, the nurses—they all wear that look.
 The one that says *you screwed up.*

That's probably why they never bother to clean the glass out of my wounds. They know exactly who I am.

A criminal.
A disruptor.
An enemy of their good works.

But my denial is bulletproof. Their judgment doesn't penetrate this tank of an addict.

They wheel me down for the CT scan. Nausea slams into me instantly. My skin crawls, itching from the inside out. Withdrawal sinks its claws deep. The machine whirs to life—a metal coffin designed to show me precisely how broken I've become.

Then, a thought hits me:

I killed someone.

It isn't a question. It isn't uncertainty. It's a fact now. My damaged mind accepts it immediately. I've **murdered someone**—maybe multiple people.

I can't remember the crash itself. Can't picture how it ended. But I vividly see the courtroom, the jury, the verdict, the prison bars.

Life in a cage.
That's my **future now.**

The machine whirs and clicks, sealing me inside my own mind. This is my tomb—a place to wait until they open the doors, cuff me to the gurney, and wheel me away forever.

Who did I kill?

My breath comes in shallow gasps. My pulse hammers inside my skull. Withdrawal isn't just physical anymore—it warps my thoughts.

Hot, then cold.
Shaking, then still.
Every nerve screams for something—**anything**—to make this stop.

The moment I'm out of the CT scan, they handcuff me to the hospital bed. The doctor returns, scans in hand, his face a mask of professional concern.

"You broke your wing-tip vertebra." He points at the crack at the top of my spine as if showing me a map of my own ignorance. "One inch to the left, and you'd be paralyzed from the waist down. For life." He pauses, letting it sink in. "You got lucky."

Lucky. Right.
This sure feels like my lucky day.

They never test me for cocaine. The cops search everything—my clothes, wallet, hospital room—but find nothing except blood and broken glass.

Nobody died.
Somehow, I make bail. They beg me to stay in the hospital. I demand to leave.

"Take these handcuffs off," I tell the officer sternly.

They hand me a waiver: If you die, don't blame us. My signature is likely a death certificate.

My clothes are shredded, blood-soaked, embedded with shards. Tiny fragments rain onto the floor when I pick them up. I opt for the hospital gown instead—a white flag of defeat.

My phone is shattered, useless. The lobby phone becomes my lifeline—one final tether to a world I'm hellbent on leaving behind. Trembling fingers dial a cab.

Five minutes later, I'm slumped in the backseat of a Yellow Cab, holding my neck brace in place as glass shards spill onto the upholstery. Blood cakes my face, crusted evidence of yesterday's chaos. The cabbie's eyes keep darting to me in the rearview mirror—wide, concerned, maybe afraid. He's probably seen plenty of wreckage on these late-night runs, but I'm gunning for first place.

"What happened to you?" he finally asks, voice barely above a whisper.

"Life," I mumble. "Take me to the liquor store."

The store is empty. I shuffle inside, hospital gown flapping open in the back, exposing my bare dignity. The security monitor above the counter reflects exactly what I've become: a creature from a low-budget horror movie, trailing glass and blood barefoot across the linoleum.

I grab the first bottle I see—bottom-shelf whiskey, the kind that strips paint and kills brain cells. The clerk watches me shake broken glass from my wallet to pay, his face blank. In a city this large, it's impressive to be the worst thing he's seen in a long time.

Back in my darkened room at the Residence Inn, I close the curtains tight. Darkness feels comfortable, familiar—like an ending. Sitting on the edge of the bed, agonizing pain floods my body as the hospital drugs fade away. My neck swollen beneath the brace, face ballooned two sizes too big. I stare at the bottle in my trembling hands, twisting off the cap—not from fear, but from anticipation.

People say insanity is doing the same thing repeatedly and expecting different results. But they're wrong. Insanity is knowing exactly what the result will be—seeing the train barreling toward you—and stepping onto the tracks anyway.

I take that first burning sip. Then another. And another.

In the darkness of this room, I don't want to live. I don't want to die. I just want to disappear—and for a while, I almost succeed.

I sob—a broken soundtrack for self-destruction, a pitiful soundtrack for a pitiful man.

You might think gratitude would finally creep in, some awareness of the second chance I've been given. It doesn't. My neck throbs in its brace, every pulse a brutal reminder of how close I've come to leaving this world.

The bottle grows **lighter.**
The room grows **darker.**

Could I go back to that hospital bed and choose differently—to reach for God, instead of this bottle?
Or am I already in hell?

Let's find out.

Reflection

My hands are still trembling. Just moments ago, after recording a podcast about my darkest hour, I fell to my knees in prayer before sitting down to write this. The weight of what happened in that hotel room—the night I nearly traded my eternity for another drink—still anoints me with a clarity deeper than humility alone could ever illuminate.

I collapsed onto that hotel bed, whiskey burning down my throat, neck brace tight against my skin, glass fragments still embedded in my flesh from the accident—I didn't just lose consciousness; I lost hope. If death had come for me that night, I'd have reached out and gone willingly. The man lying in that darkened room wasn't just tired—he was finished. Done fighting. Done trying. Done existing.

But this went beyond despair. I wasn't merely lost—I was inhabited. It wasn't just darkness around me—it was within me. People talk casually about spiritual oppression, but I was fully possessed. My soul was under new management, and I'd handed over the keys one compromise at a time. My spirit hadn't yet been reborn, so it was still dormant. But my soul—my mind, my emotions, my will—was fully hijacked.

Let's talk about what *"the end"* means. Remember the first blueprint step I shared? Writing your own eulogy? I approach this topic not as some theological scholar with theories about the afterlife, but as someone who's actually been there—someone whose heart stopped beating on a hospital table, who was given a choice by the Light itself, and who chose to return. That experience qualifies me to speak about what waits beyond our last breath with a certainty most cannot claim.

Even the concept of *"nothing"* must come from something. I can verify through my own near-fatal folly that after death, there is absolutely not *"nothing."* The term "atheist" literally means *"without God."* Back then, I arrogantly claimed there was no afterlife, no judgment, no Creator waiting. But let me challenge anyone holding this belief: If death leads to nothingness, why was I given a choice by the Light itself when I was clinically dead? Why wasn't it simply darkness, silence, absence?

That Light wasn't empty—it was alive. Conscious. Present. It wasn't just brightness; it was Being. Like resting in the very mind of God, where communication comes not through words but through pure understanding, an overwhelming presence. No harps, no clouds, no angels with wings. Just this all-consuming, all-knowing Presence that made everything else I'd ever known feel like a cheap imitation—a child's crayon drawing compared to a masterpiece.

But here's the terrifying truth—I hadn't accepted the Holy Spirit. I'd rejected every warning, mocked every conviction, numbed every chance at redemption.

Thankfully, I hadn't blasphemed the Spirit. I hadn't cursed the Light. Not yet. I hadn't sealed my fate.

I was on the **road to perdition.** And yet... mercy. He still came for me. The Light I saw wasn't judgment—it was invitation. One final offer. One final choice. *Stay or go?*

Now I understand: I hadn't merely broken my body—I'd come to the razor's edge of shattering my soul beyond repair.

I clearly didn't understand the eternal stakes. There's a reality Scripture calls the Second Death—not physical death, but permanent separation from God, a fate far worse than simply ceasing to exist. The one Revelation warns about: where cowards, liars, and idolaters experience eternal separation in a lake of fire. That was the path I'd been paving with every drink, every line of cocaine, every calculated lie—each one another brick in a road leading straight to hell.

What I couldn't grasp then, but see with painful clarity now, is why I kept returning to that same destructive pit despite desperately wanting freedom. Paul explained this inner war with devastating accuracy:

"For I do not understand my own actions. For I do not do what I want, but I do the very thing I hate... I find it to be a law that when I want to do right, evil lies close at hand." **(Romans 7:15, 21)**

My flesh craved sin even as my soul ached for freedom. I wanted to stop the madness—truly, deeply wanted it—but my flesh demanded something else entirely: **destruction.** Sin doesn't only tempt us; our own nature demands it.

Like being shackled to a corpse, forced to drag it everywhere:

"Wretched man that I am! Who will deliver me from this body of death?" **(Romans 7:24)**

That's exactly how I felt in that hotel room—wretched, trapped, hopelessly lost in a battle I couldn't win alone.

This brings me to what might be the greatest shame of my life. Prior to the accident, after our separation when I had custody of my children, I paid little attention to their needs. I transformed from an involved, loving father into someone who used them as tools to extract information about their mother. All they needed was comfort, stability, a father's love—but I gave them nothing. I was sick, drowning in selfishness. After getting whatever information from them that justified my drinking, I would feed them, place them in front of screens, and retreat to the bathroom to get drunk. They were effectively abandoned during these times, left to raise themselves, their developing minds surrendered to the enemy's digital playground.

I knew what I was doing was wrong. I felt it in the pit of my stomach every time. But I chose evil anyway. I chose myself. I chose escape.

This question used to keep me awake at night:
Why would God give me another chance?
Why extend mercy to someone racing toward destruction?
But now, I don't ask that anymore.

I know the answer. I didn't deserve it. I wasn't seeking Him. I wasn't repenting. I was rejecting, rebelling, self-destructing—and yet... **He reached in.** That Light didn't come as judgment—it came as an **invitation.** One final offer: *Stay or go?*

I had no idea how close I was to eternal separation.

Hebrews 9:27 says, *"It is appointed for man to die once, and after that comes judgment."*

That appointment was on the table. I was a heartbeat away from facing it unprepared.
But in His mercy, God showed me grace I didn't deserve. The answer to my torment was always there, waiting. Not in self-control, not in willpower, not in trying harder, but in surrender:

"There is therefore now no condemnation for those who are in Christ Jesus." **(Romans 8:1)**

My pride nearly cost me eternity. My stubbornness almost led me to **perdition.** But grace interrupted my fall.

Remember the hospital's warning? "If you drink, you have a high probability of death. You've been through a serious accident, and there is potential for blood clotting." Yet there I was, whiskey bottle in hand, stepping directly onto railroad tracks with the train's headlight shining in my face and its horn blaring in my ears.

If I had died that day, it wouldn't have been a tragedy. It would've been **justice.** I hadn't merely rejected God—I'd allowed darkness to live in me. But He didn't let me go. He didn't let me fall into perdition. He offered me one last chance to **fill the empty house** before the seven returned. And by His grace alone, I said yes.

Scripture warns us about this precarious spiritual state in **2 Peter 2:20–21:** *"For if, after they have escaped the defilements of the world through the knowledge of our Lord... they are again entangled... the last state has become worse for them than the first."*

I was worse than a backslider. I was **spiritually bankrupt** and **possessed.** The only reason I'm here now is because God reached in when I couldn't reach out.

Have you ever felt so utterly lost, so completely hopeless, that you couldn't see any way forward? When you want the world to simply disappear, no matter the cost?

If you're in that place right now, hear me clearly: There is always—always—a light at the end of that tunnel. It may be only a pinpoint, barely visible through the darkness surrounding you, but it's there. Start walking toward it, even if you have to crawl. That journey is your only path to life.

I am grateful every single day that I chose to return from that Light—grateful for another chance at salvation, grateful for the opportunity to help others find the path I nearly missed forever. Some send messages of hate, others of love, in response to the truths I now share openly. But after facing death and glimpsing what waits beyond, I speak with absolute certainty—this message is real, and eternity truly is at stake.

Let me ask you directly, friend to friend: Where do you stand regarding that appointment none of us can avoid? Are you truly ready? If your heart stopped beating tonight, what would be waiting for you—the welcoming Light of presence or the darkness of separation?

I have no doubt about my answer now, and I pray with all my heart that you don't either.

My full reckoning—the true beginning of my awakening—was still hours away from that hotel room. But that brush with death planted the seed that would eventually break through the hardened soil of my heart. The journey from that hotel floor to genuine transformation wasn't instant or easy, but it began with one critical realization: I couldn't save myself. I needed something—Someone—greater.

Today, by God's grace, I have a restored relationship with my children. The same ones I abandoned for the bottle now look to me for guidance. The same little eyes that once watched me disappear into bathrooms with vodka now see a father walking in purpose, led by the Spirit that once seemed so distant. This restoration isn't my doing—it's further evidence of God's redemptive power, His ability to rebuild what seemed utterly destroyed.

Heavy stuff, I know. But I'm not sharing this to preach at you—I'm just a broken man who's seen both sides of eternity and desperately wants you to choose the brighter one. Because once you've truly seen the Light, nothing else will ever be enough.

The Morning After

The leaf blower hits first—a distant drone slicing straight through my skull. Then comes the rest: blood-crusted eyelids peeling open, the copper tang of dried blood coating my mouth, the popcorn ceiling of a Residence Inn slowly spinning into focus. Not heaven. Not hell. Just another layer of my private nightmare.

My first instinct: move.
Bad choice.
Lightning bolts shoot down my spine—white-hot electricity frying every nerve—my vision goes **static.** The sheets peel away from me like duct tape from bare skin, glued by blood to my wounds.

Rolling to the bed's edge takes forever, each inch punctuated by the sickening sound of raw skin separating from soaked cotton. Finally, the floor rushes up to meet me. I crash onto my knees, the impact rattling shattered bones and torn muscles.

The nightstand clock blinks mockingly: **8:16 a.m.**

My palm smears wet against the wall as I drag myself toward the bathroom. Later, I'll realize I'm leaving bloody handprints—a trail of evidence leading back to the scene of my crime.

The crime of still being alive.

I flick the switch. The bathroom lights strobe harshly: on-off-on-off. Each flash reveals another piece of my horror show: blood pooling on white tiles, glass shards glittering like diamonds, a neck brace painted crimson.

Then the mirror catches me.

What stares back **isn't human.**
Not anymore.

Its face is a roadmap of trauma—valleys of split skin, mountains of swollen flesh, dried rivers of scars waiting to take shape. A gaping wound across the forehead marks exactly where my skull met the windshield. Empty eyes stare from blackened sockets, seeing everything and nothing.

"Who are you?" I whisper.

The monster mouths the question back, mirroring every word. That's when I realize there's nowhere left to run. No more lies. No more blaming others. The monster isn't in the mirror—it's beneath my skin, wearing my face, whispering in my voice. And it's been there for decades. Am I ready to face it?

I grip the porcelain sink until leaving red crescent moons from where my nails dig in. The truth hurts. But it also awakens. This was the latest stop on a descent I'd engineered myself, one bad choice at a time.

Outside, the leaf blower drones on, indifferent to my misery. Blood drips rhythmically into the sink.
Tick. Tick. **TICK.**

Legal ramifications flood into my battered mind.
I am in the biggest trouble of my life.

A countdown to whatever hell comes next.

Sliding down the wall, my back hits the cold tile floor. And then I do something I haven't done in years:

I pray.

Not the formal prayers from childhood—words recited mechanically. But the desperate kind. The gut-wrenching plea that erupts when you have absolutely nothing left to lose.

"God... if you're real... I can't do this anymore."

No thunder.
No angels.
Just the leaf blower, still humming outside, and my ragged, shallow breaths.

Real change doesn't explode from heaven like lightning.
It's a slow, painful crawl back toward life.

But that moment on the bathroom floor—broken, bleeding, begging—is the first honest prayer I've whispered in decades.

The phone rings, jolting me out of the moment.
The moment shatters.
I haven't heard a landline ring in years. I pull myself up, gripping the wall.

Ring.
Ring.
RING.

I stumble toward the noise, tangled in the cord.
"Hello?" My voice barely audible.

"So, you're alive."
My mother-in-law's voice slices through the static—no greeting, no concern, only icy contempt.

"You're a loser, you hear me? A complete loser. She's never going to stay with you after this."

Each word lands like a slap. The room spins, bile rising in my throat. A familiar bitterness inside me nods along, whispering its cruel agreement: *She's right. Who could love this?*

I try to respond, but silence strangles my voice.

"Did you hear me?" she demands.

"Yeah," I manage.

The call ends abruptly, leaving only dial tone and me holding a corded phone.

I rip the phone from its cradle and hurl it across the room. Big mistake. Pain detonates in my neck, dropping me again to the floor.

When I look up, the nightstand drawer has flown open.

A Bible stares back at me.

You're thinking, *Now he'll pick it up.* Surely, this is the moment.

But I'm sorry to disappoint you.
I'm **still blind.**

CHAPTER 6

The Kids

Sometimes, when God throws you a lifeline, it's not a book or a verse.

Sometimes, it's the eyes of your own children, reflecting exactly who you've become.

I don't know what I expect when my wife calls. Sympathy, maybe. An ounce of support. Instead, she tells me I need to take care of the kids. Moments later, she shows up with them.

Her reasoning is as brutal as it is simple:

"They're your kids. You need to take care of them. It's your day!"

I look at the kids, then back at her.

Clearly, this is not my day.

She gives me a final disgusted look and shoves them inside.

"Good luck, buddy."

The door slams shut.

I can barely take care of myself.

I've become a character from one of my own movies—stitched together, bloodstained, bruised, broken—and now I'm supposed to parent?

I'll never forget their faces: my son—ten years old, trying to be tough, but not ready for this; my daughter—eight, watching everything, absorbing every detail like only daughters can.

Eyes wide. Tears streaming down their cheeks.

They don't just see the wreckage—I can see it in their faces.

They see what I've become.

And for the first time, I see it too.

A father **failing his kids.**

A man who's lost everything—except them.

I spend the night trying to manage the pain without letting it show.

She thinks she's punishing me by forcing them on me, but she's done me a favor.

They warm up quickly, their tiny hands anchoring me in a time of dire need.

For the first time in a year, I stop worrying about what their mom is doing.

It doesn't matter.

Because when I look at them—with sober eyes—I see what I've been too lost to notice in all this disaster.

They need me.

Not as a man drowning in his own misery.

Not as a victim of circumstances.

But **as their father.**

I'm still a long way from the man I need to be.

But for the first time—it's enough to start **crawling toward the light.**

The Breakdown and the Lawyer's Truth

I call my dad—the one man who's never abandoned me.

He flies out a few nights later, and in the middle of the darkness, I lose it.

I don't cry. **I collapse.**

I'm shaking in his arms, sobbing like a child—because that's what I feel like.

A child. A son.

He doesn't say anything at first. He holds me.

And I don't know what's more humbling:

That he has to pull me up from my own wreckage…

Or that he does it without question.

Without judgment.

Just love.

With his insistence, I call a lawyer. My father gives me patience; my lawyer gives me the truth:

"You need recovery. You need it yesterday. If you don't get it, you're going to jail. There's no way you're getting away from this accident unless you act now."

I don't want to hear it. The addict in me wants to crawl back into the darkness, numbing the pain with booze and cocaine. But I can't escape the truth.

"You flipped your car into oncoming traffic," the lawyer repeats. "You're lucky you didn't kill anyone. Lucky doesn't come twice."

Fear gets me into recovery—not wisdom, not health, not some grand realization about my life.

I can't hide.

In reflecting on that moment, I can see that unconditional fatherly love was preparing my heart to further understand God's grace.

Rehab

"Rehab doesn't fix you. It removes the distractions so you can finally see how **broken you are."**

Cornerstone isn't the kind of rehab where you swim with dolphins or pet horses. There are no sunrise yoga classes overlooking the ocean, no mocktails with Charlie Sheen in Malibu. This is Santa Ana, California—where the August sun melts the pavement, and recovery doesn't come with a side of luxury. Cornerstone is concrete, linoleum, and a million regrets. It's a probation-approved, no-frills, tough-love rehab.

And let me tell you—that's **exactly what I need.**

Had they sent me somewhere with pony trekking and therapy games to get me in touch with my feelings, I'd have relapsed on day one. They'd have found me blackout drunk, face-planted on the back end of a confused horse. I probably would've figured out a way to crash the horse into a gas station.

My first meeting is with one of the owners of the recovery center—a guy with the kind of confidence you earn from delivering broken people from the outer edges of madness back to sanity. He sits across from me, calm and steady, and says, "I know where you are right now."

I blink at him. "Where's that?"

"I have been in your seat. You're looking down a dark tunnel. There's no light. I get it. But here's the truth: there is a light. You don't see it yet, but it's there. And we're going to help you find it."

He leans in, eyes locked onto mine, reading every excuse before I can speak. "Right now, you're dealing with a monster. It's out of the cage, and it's raging. But here, we're going to help you face it, shrink it, and lock it back up."

I stare at him, unsure whether to believe him or laugh. *A monster.* It's the perfect word—a metaphor that matches exactly what I'm dealing with. I can't deny his insight.

Sitting here, shaking from withdrawal, skin crawling, thoughts racing, muscles aching, it dawns on me:

Maybe I **am** an addict, staring at a wall wondering how I'm going to survive the next five minutes without a drink.

I end up under the care and supervision of a psychiatrist named Stephanie. She's incredible at her job—a liaison to the court, an advocate to help reduce jail sentencing. The debt I owe people like her is immeasurable. People like Stephanie aren't mere helpers—they're guides, a pathway back to life. There's a phrase you hear a lot: "to hell and back." The only problem I have with that idea is you have to go there first before you can start the return trip.

Now that I'm checked in, it's time to meet my house manager.

The Rules of the House

Rubin doesn't waste time with pleasantries. Fifty-five years old, face carved by hard living, ex-Mexican gangbanger—he's my welcoming committee.

"Sit down," he says, pointing to a kitchen chair that's seen better days. "Here's how this works."

He points to a calendar on the wall, each square filled with names and tasks. Chore rotations.

"Every week, you get something different. Bathroom duty. Kitchen cleanup. Your room with your roommate—that's every Saturday." His finger stabs at my name. "You mess up once, it goes in the book. Mess up enough times, you're out. Simple as that."

The rules come rapid-fire: "Back by 9 p.m. No leaving before 5 a.m. Miss curfew, it gets reported. This isn't some halfway house with flexible guidelines. It's probation-approved, everything is recorded, and sent to the court. One strike and the courts will know."

"Consider this work release," he says, eyes hard. "Except the work is fixing your messed-up life."

Rubin pauses, looking me up and down as if measuring how many pieces he'll have to put back together.

"You ever heard of King Baby Syndrome?" he asks, voice rougher now.

I shake my head. Rubin's eyes narrow slightly, a half-smile creeping onto his face—dark humor hidden behind battle scars. "You're about to."

He leans forward, arms folded on the table, and begins. "A King Baby blames everyone else for their mess. They cling to enablers, think rules don't apply to them. They act as if the world owes them something." He jabs a finger into my chest. "Sound familiar, princess?"

I feel a sting of resentment but swallow it. Truth always stings the first time you hear it.

That's exactly who I was, Rubin continues. "It's who most addicts are—entitled, angry, refusing accountability. Hell, it describes half the people running the world today. It's all about more—more money, more power, more validation."

He leans back in the creaking chair, eyes steady on mine. "But here's the truth, man. Happiness ain't in more. It's in self-sacrifice, love, and the Holy Spirit. Took me fifty years and two prison stints to learn that."

Rubin glances around the tiny kitchen, shabby but spotless. "You know, I once heard a story about a billionaire in therapy. Guy had everything money could buy, but he was miserable. Therapist finally says, 'I got something you'll never have.' Billionaire leans in, curious: 'What's that?' Therapist smiles and tells him, 'Enough.'"

He stands abruptly, knocking back the chair. "You're here to learn what enough means. To find peace in discipline, not chaos. To stop half-showing up your way through life."

Rubin becomes my unwanted alarm clock. At 5 a.m., his boot hits my bed frame: "Get up, princess. Let's check yesterday's work."

He drags me to the dryer, pulls out the lint trap. It's full from my laundry. "You trying to burn down my house? This is why your life's such a mess. How you do one thing is how you do everything."

Cornerstone doesn't expose my lack of discipline—it strips away my identity. That's the point. The person I thought I was? The masks I wore? Stripped down. **Removed.**

I'm a 38-year-old man-baby on the verge of a nervous breakdown every hour of the day. The first few nights, I stand outside on the little patio, smoking cigarettes, staring at the stars, wondering, *How did I get here?* That quiet doesn't last long. They send me a roommate. Someone they think will be perfect for me.

Mark walks into the room—a guy in his fifties who looks like he's gone a few rounds with a meat grinder. He has two black eyes, bruises up and down his arms, and walks like every step is a regret.

We look at each other with a nod of shameful recognition.

"What happened to you?" I ask him.

I got wasted, grabbed a baseball bat, and stumbled over to confront my wife's lover, who happened to be her boss. The guy disarmed me and beat me up in front of her.

If the definition of emasculated had a picture, Mark's beat-up mugshot would be next to it. Not that I have any room to point fingers. Liquid courage is a myth. Mark is living proof.

Mark paused.

"What happened to you?"

"Something similar," I say quietly. "Something very similar."

I put out my cigarette and shake his hand.

The Night Shift

5 to 8 p.m. That's when they **strip us bare.**

Group therapy is a bad movie set: plastic chairs arranged in a circle, nicotine withdrawal making everyone's demons visible. The rules are simple—show up, shut up, and when it's your turn, tell the truth.

Big Black Barry sits across from me—six foot two, two hundred fifty pounds of stubborn. He takes one look at my neck brace and busted face and loses it.

"What the bleep happened to you, bro?"

I stare at him blankly without saying anything. I'm not in a chatty mood.

Rick runs the show. He's our counselor—Colorado-born, with what he calls his "claw hand," a birth defect he's turned into a running joke. But Rick isn't always laughing.

Rick starts us out. "Fifteen years ago I was smoking crack for weeks straight, I ran out and was so strung out I convinced myself the popcorn ceiling was crack. I got out a ladder—scraped it off—loaded it in my pipe, and smoked it. I ended up in the hospital, half-dead from inhaling asbestos and who knows what else."

"That's a bottom," he says, waving his claw hand for emphasis. "Some folks quit after one bad hangover. We call those lucky people 'high-bottom drunks.' But most of us?" He gestures around the room. "We're the ones who had to lose everything first. You'll grow to understand this if you don't already understand that. That's why you have to do three AA meetings a week minimum and get signatures to prove you went on top of the work we do here. Understand?"

Weak nods of agreement from around the room in unison.

Introductions begin.

The girl who goes before me is barely twenty. Last week she rear-ended a family, breaking both of the driver's legs she rear eneded. She was drunk. But that isn't her first dance with disaster. At seventeen, she killed someone while drunk driving. Did two years in juvie.

When it's her turn to introduce herself, she sits up straight, chin tilted in defiance:

"I'm a victim of being accused of being called an alcoholic."

The room goes quiet. Even Barry stops fidgeting. Rick nods slowly, recognizing a hopeless case when he sees one.

Step One of the twelve steps stares down at us from a poster on the wall:

We admitted we were powerless over alcohol—that our lives had become unmanageable.

Admission. Powerlessness. **Unmanageable?**

Thorns in my mouth.

Rick looks at me.

Now, here I am, expected to say I'm an alcoholic.

The girl's words swirl in my mind: *Victim of being accused. Maybe that's what we all think we are. Victims of bad luck, bad choices, bad timing.*
"I'm Matt. I'm an alcoholic. Six days sober."

Rick motions with his claw to elaborate.

"And what brought you here Matt?"

"I've had some relationship issues and I started drinking a lot. Obviously, I broke my neck in an accident."

Barry chimes in.

"Looks like you broke your pride"

Rick snaps.

"You're one to talk—aren't you working on your sixth DUI?"

Light laughter emits.

Rick looks directly at the girl, the one who feels abused and is being forced to admit she has an alcohol problem. His clawed hand taps against his knee. His look says it all: "Denial isn't only a river in Egypt. It's an ocean, and we're all drowning in it."

The stories start flowing. Each one a different flavor of earthly disaster. The minister who lost his congregation to meth and women. The doctor writing himself prescriptions. The undercover cop who lost his job to vodka.

And me? Neck in a brace, fresh from flipping my car six times, still picking glass out of my skin. Still believing I can fix this on my own.

Three hours every night. That's how long they give us to face ourselves in the mirror of each other's stories. Some nights, I want to run. Some nights, I almost do.

But something keeps me in this chair. Maybe it's the court order. Maybe it's fear. Or maybe, somewhere beneath the junk pile, a new voice is breathing through: *Listen. Just listen.*

I look up at Step Two:
Came to believe that a Power greater than ourselves could restore us to sanity.

At the end of the session, everyone stands up and joins hands.
An uncomfortable moment for me.
They start chanting.

"Our Father..."

What is happening right now?

Every night after the group we end with the Lord's prayer.

I play along this first time. Pretending to know the words. Mouthing them without sound. Barry squints—looking at me. Still chuckling.

The Morning Ritual

Mark's rooster alarm tears through darkness. *Cock-a-doodle-do*, good morning, cruel world.

5 a.m.

My hands are already fumbling for cigarettes before my eyes open. Need nicotine. Need something. Anything.

Panic is **hardwired** the moment my eyes open.

I light up before I even clear the sliding glass door. Smoke hits my lungs, calming me. The nicotine steadies me, but the startled awakening is always the same—a **shotgun blast over my head.**

My brain catalogs everything hanging over me: court case, cheating ex, my kids, empty bank account, no car. A few T-shirts, worn pants, sandals. And, of course, the fashion statement of the season—my flesh-toned neck brace.

Dawn in Santa Ana. Santa Ana's streets are already cooking. The sun hasn't even cracked the horizon, but I'm already burning asphalt.

Have to move.

CAN'T STOP.

Every morning, same routine.

The neck brace has rubbed my skin into hamburger meat. My feet are blistered, and my flip-flops are worn paper-thin from miles of concrete. I push on. I am walking nine miles to my first AA meeting in Anaheim. I have no headphones, no music, just me and the sound of the urban jungle.

I walk under the underpasses where homeless guys are rolling up sleeping bags crusted with pee and desperation. Past strip malls and liquor stores open 24/7. Chain-smoking keeps my hands busy. One cigarette lights the next, until my lungs burn and my throat becomes sandpaper. Anything to stop the feeling that is always bubbling inside. If I stop moving it boils over. As I cross over the freeway I stop on top of the bridge. Eight lanes of traffic fifty feet below me. *Should I jump? Get this over with faster? Nah, I've already caused enough accidents for the week.*

Some people probably thought I was homeless— a wild-bearded guy in a neck brace, pacing the streets, leaving a trail of cigarette butts and sweat. But I couldn't stop. Standing still meant thinking. Thinking meant feeling. And **feeling**? That wasn't an option yet.

I don't **eat.**

Don't **shave.**

Don't cut my **hair.**

As I cross the bridge—thoughts of suicide still brimming—**emerald** lightning against concrete gray.

Green parrots. **HUNDREDS** of them.
Screeching overhead like **living stained glass** against a **smog-painted sky.**

They stop me.

Dead in my tracks.
My neck cranes upward—as much as it can—**cigarette forgotten** between my lips.

I had heard stories about them but never seen them.

These weren't native birds. They were **descendants of smuggled captives,**
released decades ago when a **bird smuggling ring was busted.**
Thrown into a world they never asked for.
Not meant to **survive a single California winter.**

Yet here they were.
Not just surviving—**THRIVING.**

Most released pet parrots die within days.
These **tropical refugees**?
They'd been multiplying for **decades.**
Building colonies.
Taking over palm trees.
Turning Southern California into their promised land.

Nobody taught them how to live here.
Nobody showed them where to find food or how to avoid predators.
They figured it out.
Adapted.
Made this concrete jungle their home.

I'd watch them closely,
hundreds of them returning to their roosts,
their calls echoing through streets that weren't designed for their voices.

An entire community of outcasts that shouldn't be here—but were.

I wonder if they remembered their original home.
If they carry the memory of **captivity in their DNA.**
If they know how impossible their survival should have been.

Maybe it was my own mind, searching for meaning.
Or maybe—just maybe—there was something more.

I wasn't listening yet.

But the message was still there.

Speaking to me through contraband parrots against an urban skyline.

I was trying to figure it out.

Something was speaking.

Showing me that sometimes, the ones who shouldn't make it—
are the ones who soar the highest.

First Steps into AA

I'm here to make my first of three AA meetings a week, signed off.

Nine miles in the blazing heat.

A place called **Redeemers**. I quickly make my way to a guy that looks like he may be in charge. I show him my sign off sheet.

"Hey man, can you sign this for me?"

"Sure. Right after the meeting, partner," he shot back directly.

I curse him under my breath and make my way for a seat close by.

I am in a church basement. It reeks of stale coffee and broken promises. Metal chairs scrape against linoleum, echoing off cinder block walls painted institutional beige. I look down at my feet. Dark tan lines.

I'm too good for this. I've made movies. I've grown fan bases to millions. I am better than these people. What do these people know about my life? How could they possibly relate to someone like me?

The sharing begins.

"I'm Sharon, and I'm... I'm an alcoholic."

Everyone. "Hi Sharon!"

For the love of God, do we have to say hi to every single one of these people? Is this introduction thing really necessary?

"Some of you all know me..."

Not me, Sharon, not me. I think to myself.

"Without you all, I would have gone back out last week. For those of you that don't know me, my daughter died a couple of weeks ago," Sharon tears up.

Well, that sucks Sharon. I'll give you that.

"I want you to know that because of the people in this room, I was there for her when she got sick. I was there for her in the end, and I was able to promise her to care for her daughter, my granddaughter, with love and compassion. That was the greatest comfort to her in the final moments..."

Great. Now I feel like a jerk.

"So, thank you."

They clap and pat her shoulders as she sits down, crying.

As they went around the room, sharing their testimonies, their stories had a throughline related to mine—this **demon they all carried.** They called it a spiritual malady—a defect of character. But I didn't want to see that back then.

Me? Defective? Please. Maybe if I was playing a "defective" role.

Then came the hand-holding post-meeting.

The Lord's Prayer.

Here too.

AGAIN.

Are they serious?
More Christians?

I grit my teeth.

The last time I thought about religion was at Griffith Observatory, staring at an expanding universe hearing scientists talk about the **Big Bang.** *When you die,* **it's nothing. It's black.** *No judgment. No second chances.*

But if that were true, why did I see that light after the crash?

I look around the room. These people believe in **virgin births and resurrections.** *Turn my life over to a higher power? Me? Right.*

The guy reduced to pounding pavement in sandals because he can't submit to anything bigger than himself—he doesn't need **humility**. Not a stitch.

It's painfully clear—I am my own biggest problem. But I'm not ready to admit that. **Not yet.**

Not even close.

Walking away from that first meeting, court card signed to prove I'd been there, I was already plotting how to game the system. Get signatures without showing up. Forge them if I have to. Three meetings a week? We'd see about that.

That's how I started. Not with surrender. Not with acceptance. The same old hustle in different shoes.

But hustles have **expiration dates.**

The Conference Room

Cornerstone didn't do half-measures.

You **faced it.**

No running. No excuses.

That's how I ended up in that air-conditioned coffin of a conference room, staring at my soon-to-be ex while Rick got ready to drop the hammer. She arrived dressed for an Oscar acceptance. Hair? Perfect.
Makeup? As flawless **as she could manage.**
Her expression? Contrition—custom-tailored, designer brand.

But the eyes?

Still **EMPTY.**

Rick didn't waste time.

"Are you still having the affair?" he asked, voice flat.

Her face **cracked**—a little.

"I'm so sorry," she murmured, her voice trembling enough to seem real.

Her hands shake on cue.

"I touched a hot stove," she says. "I learned my lesson."

What is this—kindergarten? I think to myself.
Like she's been caught sneaking extra dessert, not blowing up a marriage.

Rick sits back; his claw hand taps the table like a lie detector.

He's seen this movie before. Probably has the **script memorized.**

She wasn't done.

"I'll quit drinking," she added. "Whatever it takes. I love him. We can fix this."

The same **lines.**
The same **delivery.**
Different **stage.**

Rick lets her finish. Then he leans in.

"Thirty days. No contact."

"What?" I said.

This was a **sucker punch.**

"No contact at all?"

Rick didn't flinch.

"No calls. No texts. No emails. Nothing."

I look at her.

She **nods.**

"That's best for us babe. We need to heal before we can come back together."

Too eager. **Way too eager.**

Looking back at Rick, *"I can do that. I promise,"* She said.

She walks out, heels clicking against the linoleum until **the sound fades.**

Rick turns to me.

"I want to believe her. But do you?"

Something in my gut **twists.**

That warning bell.
That **sick feeling** I'd ignored a hundred times before.

The same feeling I had when she said she was going to New Jersey.

But **I still wasn't ready to listen.**

"No Rick, I don't."

Divine Moonlight

Tonight, I'm lying in my tiny rehab bed, journal in hand. Mark snores loudly in the bed next to me like an elephant seal giving birth. I try to block it out, focusing on the moonlight streaming through the window. The moon is full, impossibly beautiful, its serene glow drowning out Mark's sleep apnea. I stare at the moon and begin to see the face of a beautiful woman. I don't know her. But the features are unmistakable.

As I stare at it, a peace settles over me.

Just as my eyes become heavy and my lids inch together, my phone buzzes: a notification from Airbnb.

I frown.

What's this about?

My account login has changed. Confused, I scramble to log back in, eventually regaining access through Facebook. When I finally do, my hunch is confirmed.

The message in the account glows like a crime scene photo. My wife's face smiling in the chat icon:

> Hi Marco, I am so happy this is working out. My new boyfriend from Canada will be staying for a month while he gets to know my two small children from my previous marriage.

Previous marriage—as if I'm already history. As if we hadn't sat across from Rick hours ago, her promising change, promising sobriety, promising whatever lies she thought would work.

Huntington Beach.

The address sears into my retinas.

My hands start shaking.

How can someone lie like this? What is the point?

At least it isn't on my credit card—a small blessing.

I haven't been prosecuted for the accident yet, so I can still rent a car.

You can probably guess where this is going. The rational part of me knows it's a terrible idea, but obsession has already taken over. I need to see this with my own eyes. I drive to the address and wait outside like a cliché from a bad detective novel. Eventually, her car pulls up—and there he is. He looks like he's been plucked from the reject pile at a casting call for "loser boyfriend."

She is wearing a tiny skirt.

But the relationship was **only emotional.**

They go inside.

They are probably just having a long talk about their feelings.

I wait.
I should stop here—but **I can't.**
The monster is steering now.

Boiling.

When they finally come out, I follow them to a waffle shop in Torrance.

The Waffle Shop Confrontation

I park a few spaces away from the front windows of the waffle shop. My ears buzz as I peer through the window. There they are—giggling, acting like newlyweds, holding hands. Comfortable, ordinary—as if they haven't just blown my kids' lives apart.

I know walking inside is a terrible idea, but the rational voice—the one saying, *Don't do it; walk away*—is drowned out by the screaming mockery in my head.

I step out of the car, cross the parking lot, and push through the door.

The bell jingles above me, obnoxiously cheerful, as if this is another normal morning.

I watch them—sipping coffee like this is a normal breakfast date. My stomach knots at the sickening sight.

I march straight to their table. *"What the hell is this?"*

They look up. Not scared. Not guilty. Slightly disappointed, like I've ruined their day.

I stare at my ex, stunned by her apathy, then at him—the guy she's brought to meet my kids.

He **leers at me.**

My mind breaks even further—I'm pretty sure a few staples holding my forehead together pop loose.

Without thinking, I sweep their coffee off the table. Mugs explode against tile floor. Hot liquid streaks across the floor. Time freezes. Forks stop halfway to mouths. Toast turns to ash in stunned throats.

Every head turns, staring at me—the deranged man at the center of the chaos. I've officially become Michael Douglas in *Falling Down*.

Unhinged.

"Let's talk outside," I say to her, my voice shaking but low. I'm not about to stage a full show for the Sunday morning crowd.

She sighs, exasperated—like I'm leftover laundry she forgot to dry—and slowly stands, following me out the door.

The California sun blazed overhead as we face off in the parking lot. The heat bakes my neck brace, and my skin glistens—slick with sweat, but I don't care. I turn to her,

"What is this?" I spit.

"It's not what you think," she says flatly, not bothering to sell it.

I laugh bitterly. "Not what I think? You brought him to meet our kids." Then he boldly appears, walking out of the restaurant with an oblivious shuffle. My shirt—my freaking shirt—hangs on him like a costume two sizes too big.

"You gave him my clothes!"

She shrugs. "I thought you were done with those shirts."

I stare at her, stunned. "Done with those shirts?"

He doesn't look at me. **He looks at her.**

"The pancakes are getting cold," he says, his voice high and whiny. "Could we eat them, then you guys can talk?"

This can't be my life.

My fists curl at my sides. My adrenaline spikes. If there was ever a moment to unleash every ounce of rage it is now. One move—that's all it would take. Short shuffle forward. Quick grab. Then a satisfying bone crunch.

But then: **STILLNESS.**

Stillness blasts into my body. The same choice—death or life. Violence or peace. The monster inside me roared, clawing for release. But something else spoke louder. A calm swept over me—a presence, steady and unseen, resting a hand on my shoulder.

I stare at the two of them: her, still blank and bored, and him, fidgeting in **my shirt**, oblivious to the monster standing inches away. I feel it—coiling tighter, clawing at my insides, begging to be let loose. But the voice is louder:

No. Walk away.

It wasn't me. At that moment, God infused me with remnants of whatever shred of humanity I had left, but the message was clear: If this is what they want, **let them have it.**

I take a long beat. My breathing slows, and my fists unclench.

I take one last painful long look at each of them.

I make them squirm.

And as I look at them, I see two children standing in front of me.

I hear a voice.

You have no control over this. If they want each other. Let them have it.

I turn around and leave, and as I walk out of that parking lot, the scraping of my flip-flops against the pavement is **louder than their silence.**

I never look back.

Letting It Out

As soon as I hit the driver's seat and slam the door, the calm shatters.

Go eat your pancakes. Enjoy your new wardrobe.

The silence is too much, and loathing explodes out of me. The windshield becomes my sounding board; the steering wheel my punching bag.

"How did it come to this? **My** shirt? You gave him **my** shirt?"

My voice ricochets off the glass, shaking as my grip tightens on the wheel, knuckles turning bone white.

"Is this what my life is now? Is this the bottom?"

Every thought I've buried for months—years—claws its way to the surface.

They're a joke—both of them. But me? I'm the punchline. I'm the one who let it get this far. **I LET THIS HAPPEN!**

My eyes flick to the rearview mirror, and that's when I see it clearly—the monster.

Sweat on my forehead. Red flush across my face. Wild, desperate eyes glaring back. This isn't new. I've seen you before. He was in the driver's seat after that tequila shot that erased eleven years of sobriety. He was there the day I flew over the median, fueled by coke, booze, and lies. He's always there, feeding off my anger, my pain, my worst impulses.

His voice whispers clearly now:
You should've beaten him up. He stole your shirt. Stole your wife. She ruined your life, Matt. Destroyed you. Your pathetic walking away.

"STOP."

I recognize you now. I know this pattern—it repeats, again and again. And if I don't end it now, I'll be meeting my maker soon.

My breathing slows, and the silence returns, tense but honest.

The monster didn't suddenly materialize—I invited him. I allowed him in, piece by piece, excuse after excuse.

But this time?

I'm not letting him win.

By the time I pull into the rental car parking lot, I'm done. Done with her. Done with this toxic cycle. Done funding their Waffle House dates with my credit card.

It ends here.

My past isn't memories—it's an active force trying to kill me and my future.

It lives in the people I know.
The places I go.
The things I do.
The habits that own me.

I return the car and make my way back to the safety of my recovery home bed.

I cut off my credit card, the texts flood in relentlessly:

> **Visa is declined**
> **Visa is declined**
> **Visa is declined**
> **Visa is declined**

They continue into the night.

> *I get it—OK—you don't care about me because you can't—because you don't love yourself in the right ways. Please stop torturing me with your sick games. I deserve better than this!!!*
>
> *It's always a game for you. You have to win, or be right. Even with 'no contact,' you're still just you!*

I shut off my phone, silence the gaslighting, and close my eyes.

As sleep claims me, one final thought settles in:

I have to purge everything pulling me under, cut loose every anchor keeping me weak, small, and trapped in cycles that threaten my future. That's how I break free. That's how I finally win.

Now it's your turn.

Are you ready to purge the anchors holding you back?

Are you ready to fight for the life you were meant to live?

> *"Pain is a great teacher—but only **if you're willing to listen.**"*

BLUEPRINT STEP 3: BUILD A WARRIOR'S VISION

(Purge Everything That Keeps You Weak)

"Your growth will offend the ones who stay stagnant. Let them go."

WAR STRATEGY:

Your environment isn't neutral. It's a battlefield.
Every relationship you tolerate either **fortifies your calling** or **feeds your destruction.** Every text thread, every voice in your ear, every open door—it's either **Kingdom or compromise. Mediocrity is contagious. Distraction is spiritual seduction.**
And loyalty to the wrong people is rebellion in disguise.

ACTION ORDERS:

1. Execute a People Audit

Not everyone deserves access to you. Identify those who hold you back:

- **The Dead Weight**—they aren't evil. They're just *comfortable*. Comfortable in dysfunction.
- **The Chains**—these people are emotionally dependent on your weakness. Your healing threatens their identity. Your growth means they lose control.
- **The Traitors**—the ones who *pretend* to support you.
  But behind your back? They mock your mission.
  They're "concerned" when you change—but only because they've lost power over you.

Write down every person who fits these categories. Cut them off. Block them. Move on. **No exceptions.**

> *"I called these people friends, but we were co-conspirators in our own destruction. I wasn't better than them—I was done dying slowly."*

2. Cleanse Your Environment

Every place you go either strengthens you or weakens you.

- That bar where you used to drink—**it's an altar to your past self.**
- That dating app you lost yourself in—**it's a minefield.**
- That office that drains your soul—**it's a prison you must escape.**

Identify three places that trigger old patterns. Stop going there. **Find battle-ready environments that maximize your growth.** Your surroundings shape your thoughts. **Shape them deliberately.**

3. Eliminate Toxic Habits

Your routines aren't neutral. They're either sharpening your blade or dulling it.

- Morning social media scroll—**feeding distraction.**
- Netflix binge that kills your night—**stealing your future.**
- Procrastination that prevents execution—**self-sabotage in disguise.**

Identify your top three destructive habits. Replace them with **warrior protocols:**

- Study Scripture instead of scrolling
- Journal instead of mindless entertainment
- Train your body instead of indulging weakness

Execute **without hesitation.** Your habits become your life.

4. Destroy Your Comfort Zone

Comfort is the **enemy of progress.** Every compromise for comfort is surrender to mediocrity.

- That easy job that pays "just enough"—**golden cage.**
- That relationship that's "good enough"—**draining your purpose.**
- That life that's "not that bad"—**slow death of your potential.**

Your comfort zone is your **coffin. Stay in it? You die in it.** List areas where you've settled. **Make comfort your enemy.** All in or nothing.

WAR CRY:

Victory comes to those who **execute without mercy.** Cut the people. Change the places. **Kill the habits.** Destroy the comforts. Your environment is a battlefield—treat it like one. Weakness thrives in comfort. Strength is forged in resistance. Lukewarm doesn't work. The world doesn't need another comfortable man. It needs **warriors** who refuse to settle.

You don't level up while surrounded by people afraid of heights. You don't transform while chained to the past. You don't become a lion by living for comfort. The soul wants easy. The Spirit trains for war. **Purge what keeps you soft. Purge everything that keeps you weak. Now.**

BLUEPRINT RECAP:

BEFORE: *(Trapped in the Comfort of Chaos)*

"I couldn't handle being alone. The silence was deafening. My own thoughts were too loud, too harsh, too real. So I surrounded myself with noise—people who didn't challenge me, places that kept me numb, things that distracted me from myself. I called these people "friends," but they were weak accomplices in mutual destruction. We weren't building each other up—we were holding each other down. We didn't celebrate victories—we celebrated escapes. We didn't talk about tomorrow—because we were too busy hiding from today."

Pro Tip: The next time your "friends" want to party, **suggest doing something healthy instead.** Watch how fast they **ghost you.** Then you'll understand **what your friendships were truly based on**—not connection, but mutual destruction.

AFTER: *(Finding Strength in Solitude)*

"The key indicator that Step 3 was working in my life was simple: I could handle loneliness without running to a chemical escape. I became good with me. I started recognizing that the vices controlling me had propelled me toward negativity, often landing me around people who either used me or were in equally as bad shape as I was. I began to surround myself with people who had a life. They didn't party excessively. They enjoyed a steady, calm existence. They didn't need to inebriate themselves to have fun. I found myself communicating on a different level. When I could take the risk of allowing myself to believe I was worthy of adapting my personality to enjoy the freedom that comes with success—that's when I knew I was there."

Remember, you are the sum of the people you surround yourself with. For a while, that sum might only be you—be the model of what you want to attract. Toxic relationships aren't a weight—they're handcuffs. The loneliness you fear isn't punishment; it's your proving ground.

VICTORY INDICATORS:

You Know You're Succeeding When:

- Your social circle is noticeably different from six months ago
- You've changed environments that were dragging you down
- You're uncomfortable more often because you're growing
- People from your old life criticize your changes
- You experience resistance but push through anyway
- You recognize toxic patterns faster and avoid them
- You've established clear boundaries that you maintain

RED FLAGS:

- Your phone still has the same contacts
- You still hang out in the same places
- You keep making exceptions for people who hold you back
- You justify maintaining connections to your old life
- You fear isolation more than you desire growth

REALITY CHECK:

This step will hurt. When you cut people off, some will attack you. When you avoid old places, withdrawal will set in. When you kill old habits, your brain will rebel. You might even feel worse before you feel better. Accept this resistance. Isolation might feel unbearable at first—your instinct will be to run back to what's familiar, even if it's destructive. The void will test you. Some warriors need a complete environmental reset—new city, new job, new everything. Others can rebuild where they are. Either way, the discomfort isn't failure—it's confirmation you're dismantling what kept you trapped. The withdrawal symptoms prove you're breaking an addiction to mediocrity.

WAR ORDER (FINAL COMMAND):

Identify **ONE** thing in your life you know is making you weak. The person. The place. The habit. The comfort. Cut it out for 30 days. **Complete elimination.** No compromise. No exceptions. No halfway measures. **DESTROY it.**

"No soldier gets entangled in civilian pursuits..." **(2 Timothy 2:4)**

Translation: If you're trying to win a war, stop playing house with your enemies.

"Most men have a price. That's why they lose. They trade their integrity for comfort. Their strength for validation. Their soul for attention. The ones who win? They refuse to cave to the system."

CHAPTER 7

The Pink Cloud

Barry's Laugh

*"Cutting out weakness is the start. But real strength is built day by day, moment by moment, in the trenches—**one sober breath at a time.**"*

You think change happens fast? Think again. 5:46 p.m. Two months into recovery, sobriety was reshaping my world—slowly, painfully, inevitably. But old battles don't vanish overnight. Some days, they knock on your door in new disguises.

Barry's voice shook the room. He didn't enter a room; he took it over. His laugh could shake the walls, and when he spoke, his voice rumbled with hurricane force.

I told the group about the pancake house before the session started, about finding my wife's new boyfriend wearing my shirt. Barry's laugh nearly brought down the building.

"Hold on," he wheezed, his shoulders heaving like tectonic plates. "He was wearing your shirt? Your actual shirt?" Tears streamed down his face as he doubled over, barely able to breathe. "That is the most bleeped-up thing I've ever heard!"

That was Barry—finding humor in the darkness, even when his own life was far from light.

Tom, our new counselor, walked in and shot Barry a look that said "shut up" without saying it.

We graduated to new counselors as we moved through the program. I was two months in, and Tom, our new counselor, had seen it all. He could look at you and detect a lie in a single hair follicle on your head. He scared the living daylights out of us. Nothing was going to squeak by Tom.

He scanned the room with intensity, reminding me of the Headless Horseman from *Sleepy Hollow*—if the horseman had reclaimed his head, it would've looked exactly like Tom's. With his long gray hair and wild beard, he seemed ready for the hunt as he opened the meeting.

He began by introducing himself.

"I'm Tom and I've been sober thirty-three years. You've made it sixty days. Congratulations. About this time you start to feel like you are floating. Your body is detoxed and clean, you're sleeping better, and you're starting to see the roses. You're floating on a pink cloud. It doesn't last. Real life is still waiting for you out there. You think you've won the battle because you quit the booze or the junk, but the truth is you're just learning to crawl. You ain't even walking yet. So, each one of you is going to lay it on the table in these meetings. What is said here stays here. I'm no different than you. I've had my fair share of problems. I lived under a bridge in Newport Beach for two years before I got sober. I drank and used heroin for so long I lost the use of my right arm. I was so far gone I robbed a liquor store in a blackout. That's what they told me. I don't remember a thing. When the judge sent me away for nine years, it was like ordering lunch. I didn't care. Now, let's introduce ourselves."

When it was my turn to share, I rambled on about the pancake house, the monster I'd felt rising inside me, and the strange calm that stopped me from violence.

Tom took a long pause, stroked his beard, and finally said, "You keep saying something stopped you," leaning back in his chair. "Maybe it was God. But maybe it was also you, for the first time, realizing you can't let her—or anyone else—control you anymore. Sounds like she's been the nail in your coffin long enough. Maybe it's time to stop handing her the hammer."

He paused, then dropped a truth I've carried with me ever since: "Sometimes, the people closest to you are the worst influences. Even if they are blood. Blood doesn't always mean good advice. Sometimes, you've got to cut people out, no matter who they are."

Tom was right. This wasn't about her anymore.

I thought to myself, *I can't keep giving weight to anything my wife says. It's over.*

A girl who had recently joined our group chimed in.

She was twenty-three, fresh-faced, eyes still bright with the kind of hope life hadn't beaten out of her yet.

The most attractive woman in a predominantly male group.

She would smile at me in sessions.

Laugh at my jokes. And respond to my vivid stories.

"You're lucky. Your wife's not worth it. It's not like you can't find a better girlfriend easily. You shouldn't give her the time of day anymore," she said, winking at me.

Barry nudged me.

Her wink stoked that validation in me.

Was she flirting?

Stop. *This is the start of the same cycle.*

The Girl Who Couldn't Let Go

When she offered me a ride that night, I saw myself in her—that same desperate need to believe in fairytales.

Her corolla hummed through the dark streets while laying out the real story about her boyfriend, the same dealer whose "business" had landed her rehab.

Cops found a **huge** stash of ecstasy in his apartment.

A drug dealer.

She was living with him when the raid happened.

She was given an amazing deal: thirty days in rehab or ten years in prison.

She would not go to prison if she stayed **away from him** and out of trouble.

If she breaks the rules, she does the full suspended sentence.

Simple math. Simple choice. But **addiction doesn't do simple.**

"He's different now," she said, her voice thin with desperation. "He's changing."

Silence filled the car.

Something shifted. The old me would have been lustfully checking her out, playing along, telling her what she wanted to hear. But tonight? Genuine concern overtook me.

"If you keep seeing him," I said, "you're going to end up in prison."

She laughed—that young person's laugh that says life hasn't taught them the hardest lessons yet.

"You don't understand. He's turning over a new leaf," she said.

And I knew.

She needed **the hard lesson.**

"Listen," I tried one more time, "Would love make you risk ten years of your life?"

She laughed, totally **ignoring** what I said.

I knew I couldn't reach her.

Nothing I could say at that moment would change her mind.

When she dropped me off, I thanked her quietly and walked inside.

Mark was already grinning. *"She drove you home? What happened? She's so hot."*

I barely looked at him. "Nothing happened, Mark," I muttered. "She's a lost kid."

Mark was disappointed. He wanted a story I didn't have to give.

I flopped on the bed victorious and defeated at the same time.

*If God is real, why all this **pain**.*

The sky faded to black.

I started making an inventory right there in the dark. I knew I was powerless. I knew I had to turn my life and will over to God. Could I do that? I guess I could try.

Two weeks later, she left rehab.

He was out on bail.

Still dealing drugs.

Another raid.

And just like that.

She went to prison—ten years.

Changes

I've been in recovery for ninety days. Ninety days clean. Ninety days sober. I've gone to the AA meetings, every single one of them, no excuses. I'm walking to one now, late October air cool against my skin. I glance down at my shoes—real shoes this time, not flip flops. A sign I'm slowly becoming human again.

As I walk, the familiar rhythm returns. Thoughts swirl in my head—the doubts, the fear, but also—what I've learned, what I'm still learning. Each step forward is another commitment kept. Another battle won. I repeat the words of the Serenity Prayer to myself as I walk:

"God, grant me the serenity to accept the things I cannot change, the courage to change the things I can, and the **wisdom to know the difference."**

The words take on meaning. **Bold. Unshakable.**

Years ago, I would've laughed at myself walking along the street mentioning God.

Acceptance? I wrestled with everything I couldn't control.

Courage? I never had the courage to even try to tell the difference.

Wisdom? I figure out that this is a prayer to be gifted with the **wisdom to differentiate.**

But today, something's different. Today, the words are sinking in. Practical. Necessary.

I swing my backpack up onto my shoulder as it slips. The neck brace falls off and hits the ground.

I stare at it.

And instead of picking it up, I walk away.

I don't stop. I don't look back.

Let it go.

It's behind me now. It belonged to another life—another movie coming to an end.

I continue walking, and more realizations come at me.

In group last night, someone dropped this treasure:

"Your serenity is inversely proportional to your expectations."

Translation?

The more you dream up impossible scenarios the more disappointing your life will be.

I'm halfway to the meeting when my phone buzzes in my pocket. I stop beneath an underpass, transients asleep in their encampments. The phone's pale glow splashes over my screen.

> Wife: Your son is out of control again. You need to step up and be a father. He needs consequences. He can't talk to me like this. Fix it! **Now.**

My jaw clenches. Instant anger starts bubbling beneath the surface—familiar, old, automatic. She does this often. Starts trouble with him to draw me in. My thumb hovers over the screen, ready to launch back a speedy reply, ready to dive headfirst into another pointless battle.

That hand on my shoulder stops me.

A voice. Quiet but clear.

You can't control her behavior.

Those five words connect. I can't respond. Break the cycle.

Awakening.

I type four words into my small victories journal instead. The letters stare back at me on the glowing screen:

Can't control her behavior.

The pressure drops from my body.

I pocket my phone without responding.

Look around at life moving.

Why am I investing my time in her sickness?

Peace replaces frustration, quiet but undeniable.

I take another step forward and keep walking.

Not today.

Small surrenders bring peace.

Small victories add up.

Watching myself try to play God—then choosing to step down from a throne I was never meant to sit on.

It wasn't about giving up. It was about growing up.

It was about learning which battles were mine to fight—and which ones were ego charging into wars I was never meant to win.

Every time I wrote down a small victory—a pressure released from a valve I didn't even know existed until that moment.

And I got better.

Better at knowing what I could control. Better at accepting what I couldn't.

Serenity isn't some mystical state achieved through enlightenment.

It's practical. Mathematical, even.

Control leads to expectations.
Expectations lead to **disappointment.**
Disappointment **destroys serenity.**

Lower expectations. Be practical. Be reasonable.

Your serenity remains intact.

It's simple.

Not easy.

But simple.

The Minister's Performance

Family group therapy night was, at times, our most entertaining night. Barry and I were always solo. No family showed up. The minister was the star performer—all perfect teeth and blue eyes that could sell salvation door-to-door. But beneath his polished exterior, meth and affairs had turned his ministry into *Dante's Inferno*.

He landed here after getting caught fooling around with most of the women in the church choir—in his office.

From the side, Barry and I played critics. Comedy was our armor against truth.

Then **his wife walked in.**

She was beautiful in that way that made you question his sanity. But her eyes—they carried a familiar pain. I'd seen it before, staring back from my own mirror on nights when my wife was in "New Jersey."

As their turn to share rolled around she blurted out,

"I want the truth! " Clutching her designer purse.

"For once!"

The minister's face scrolled through his chameleon catalog. Years of altar calls had taught him exactly how to look sorry. The minister, the picture of solemn regret, nodded. "I'll tell the truth," he said, his tone dripping with practiced remorse.

Barry leaned in close. "Yeah, right," he muttered.

His wife didn't waste time. "That day when I went to your brother's house in the morning—I knocked, and a woman answered—wearing nothing but a bra and underwear. You told me you were staying to take care of your brother's dog while he was out of town!"

The group froze. Even Tom tilted his head down to look over his glasses in deep wonderment.

"What was going on?" she demanded, her voice trembling.

The minister didn't flinch. "She's my brother's friend," he said smoothly. "She needed a place to stay."

Barry was already choking on suppressed laughter. She shot back, "And why did she slam the door in my face?"

"She was embarrassed," he said.

Her voice rose. "Why were you half-dressed? Why did you ignore me, get in your car, and drive over the lawn to get away from me?"

There was a long pause.

"I panicked," he finally admitted. "I didn't want to fight."

"She wasn't even wearing pants!" she shouted.

The minister tried to recover. "She's having renovations done at her place. She had nowhere else to go, so my brother let her stay."

Barry's laughter boomed like judgment. "Renovations?" he wheezed. "Come on, man!"

I laughed too. Until **I saw her face.**

The tears cutting through her makeup weren't funny. The way she clutched that purse like it was holding her together—that wasn't comedy. Her pain filled the room, thick as smoke, **choking out the laughter.**

"I've stood by you through everything," she whimpered. Her voice carried years of swallowed truth. "The affairs. The drugs. The lies."

The minister reached for her. She pulled back as if his touch hurt. Her mascara running."Nothing happened," he said desperately, his voice hollow.

The room fell silent. Barry leaned over to me, "This guy's unbelievable."

Tom quickly blurted out, "Let's take a ten-minute break."

Her face haunted me. The desperate hope in her eyes. The way she wanted—needed—to believe him. I knew that hope.

Had worn it like a crown of thorns during my own marriage.

I saw myself in both of them. In her endless capacity to believe lies. In his masterful ability to tell them. In the dance they did around the truth, both knowing the steps by heart.

Hope can be its own kind of addiction.

Barry saw a show that day. I saw a mirror.

And in that mirror, God was carving something new: The beginning of empathy. The first cracks of real humility. The painful gift of seeing yourself in others' wreckage.

Sometimes, laughter dies so **wisdom can be born.**

Rehab has its own rhythm. Between groups, between meltdowns, between revelations—there are smoke breaks. These are the real therapy sessions, where truth slips out between exhales, where guards drop alongside ash.

Barry and I stood in the designated smoking area, California sun beating down on us as we shielded our cigarettes from the Santa Ana winds. From here, we could see traffic rush by—close enough to hear, too far to make out car models. It was constant in this city.

Barry exhaled slowly, eyes distant. "Some of these women in here are ready to hook up, bro. Like their addictions are starving, and they're just looking for a fix."

I nodded. "Yeah, looks like the minister's wife will be single soon enough."

He shook his head, smirking. "Right? He's gotta be out of his damn mind. She's fine, that's all I got to say. But I can't be with white chicks, bro."

I took another drag, tasting bitterness. "What? That makes no sense."

Barry stared at me, suddenly serious. "Last time I dated a white girl after high school, she cheated on me. You feel me?"

I let his words settle. "Yeah, but that's kinda... prejudiced."

Barry flicked ash onto the pavement, gaze softening. "Dude, I caught this chick with another man and broke a stereo over his head. She called the cops, and I had to hide in a bush—in the neighborhood—for a whole day while they looked for me."

The smoke hung between us, carrying our truths. I shook my head.

"When we went to court, she cried in front of the judge, said I was crazy—violent. I did nine months for that."

I chimed in, "My wife—"

Barry cut me off. "Stop saying my wife, bro. She ain't your wife. She's getting roofed by some Canadian with horns."

We laughed.

"It's his mermaid now," I said. Barry's laughter was so loud that everyone in front of the building looked over.

"But seriously," I continued, "she called me one night when I was new here. Told me the kids were sick. It was after hours. I snuck out, went to the apartment. When I knocked, nobody answered. She slid back the curtain, took a picture of me. Dude, Tom called me the next day and told me she called him seventeen times to say I snuck out and was harassing her."

Barry's mouth dropped open. "See, that's what I'm sayin'. These women will get you killed. Did he bust you?"

"No. He told me never to listen to her again. Said she's psycho. That was it."

They call us back into the group. Barry and I put out our cigarettes, shaking our heads.

"Women," Barry muttered, "gonna be the death of me."

The Hallway Meltdown

It wasn't long after family night that Barry and I were walking into rehab when the minister gave his final sermon. We'd barely stepped through the door when he collapsed onto the floor, clutching his head and screaming like a televangelist possessed by a demon.

"I'm having an aneurysm!" His voice boomed through the hall, ricocheting off the linoleum—more desperate plea than medical emergency.

Everyone froze.

Staff scrambled, radios crackling, but nobody moved to help.

We'd seen this act before. It was drug test day, and the minister wasn't about to pee in a cup. Addicts are bad magicians when it comes to escape.

Fake a **brain bleed.**

Dodge **accountability.**

To his credit, he kind of **sold it.**

Paramedics arrived, wheeling in a stretcher and loading him like a tragic hero. But the audience wasn't buying it. Not this time. We all stood there, silent, watching him perform his swan song for people who'd seen the script a hundred times.

The church had sent him here—clean up or lose your pulpit—but we knew he'd already been fired. Rehab wasn't redemption for him; it was the epilogue to a career already burned to ash.

He kept showing up after that, going through the motions without conviction. Then, one day, he didn't.

No **goodbyes.**

No **curtain call.**

Just an empty chair where **denial** used to sit.

Barry laughed about it later, calling it the best performance he'd seen since he got here. But I couldn't laugh. Watching him cling to his lies while being wheeled out, I saw myself. The lies might change shape, but their weight always drags you down.

The Weight

The envelope waited on my bed that night after group. A snake coiled in white paper. Nine years. Enhanced charges.

Great bodily injury.

My charges had been upgraded to first class. Free champagne and extra leg room. I was looking at **more jail time.**

The room closes in on me.

The air leaves my lungs.

The **deepest silence** engulfs me.

My legs buckle under the weight of my own ruin. My knees hit the floor. Desperate for mercy I do not deserve. I bow my forehead, my neck feels the pain, the coarse fibers of the carpet stare up at me. Tears mixed with sweat, drip into the silence. My voice comes raw, broken:

"I get it. I'm not in control. You have control. If You want to take me right here, I won't fight it. I deserve it. Whatever You want, it's Yours. I submit. I am powerless and I turn my will over to you God."

There are no bargains. No conditions.

No escape plan.

This is a prayer—**finally humbled.**

The man who thought he could control everything, manipulate everyone, and run his life into the ground without consequence **DIED** right there on that floor.

What rose in his place was fragile, unfinished, and new.

I felt a weight lift—not gone, but shared. As if someone had taken hold of the **cross I'd been dragging.**

The system wasn't done with me. But for the first time, I stopped running. Stopped fighting.

My spiritual life started there, face-down on that floor. God had finally **broken me.**

So He could build **something better.**

I laid down on the bed. My thoughts slowed, and a calm came over me. I drifted off to sleep.

The Morning After

The next morning, my eyes open slowly.

No shotgun blast of panic? No jolting awake to Mark's ridiculous rooster alarm blaring like a prison siren three feet from my ears. Just quiet.

I blink once. Twice.

Still quiet.

Sunlight seeps through the blinds, warm and gentle—unfamiliar. For nearly four months, every single morning felt like waking up in crosshairs. An already wounded animal searching for a place to hide. My mind racing. Heart pounding. Panic rising before my feet even hit the floor.

Not today.

I sit up carefully, my fingers touching my neck. Still real. Still sore, but I don't think of its negative connotation. Inside feels different—lighter, steadier. My heartbeat isn't a jackhammer. My thoughts aren't a tornado. Instead, an unexpected peace pulses gently beneath the surface of my thoughts.

What is this?

Sliding my legs out off bed, bare feet touch the cool floor, grounding me. I breathe deeply—fully—for the first time in months. It's not that the charges are dismissed or the consequences are erased. The threats are still very real. Worse actually, but today, something stronger fills me: **surrender.**

Reflection

Looking back now after ten years of genuine sobriety, I see that night on the bedroom of my rehab floor wasn't about avoiding prison—it was about the death of pride. What good would physical freedom have been to a man still imprisoned by his soul's insatiable thirst? I had to be utterly broken—not bent, but shattered—before I could finally beg God for mercy and submit myself completely to Him, to truly listen.

That night, as I knelt on the stained carpet, crushed by the reality of enhanced charges, something extraordinary happened—the constant noise within me subsided. For perhaps the first time in my adult life, silence enveloped. This silence wasn't only external; it was a profound inner stillness I had spent decades fleeing. You see, my perpetual motion was tethered to the corrupt, soulish life I desperately clung to. In that constant, furious movement—the parties, the drinking, the endless distractions—stillness could never take root. My soul would not—could not—permit it. My attention remained utterly consumed by the immediate impulse to restore my soul to pleasure, to numb the pain, to escape reality. But that time had passed.

The very stillness I had spent a lifetime avoiding is precisely where God connects most powerfully with us. There was no climbing back up the slide I had descended. I had reached the bottom, trapped in a pit of mud so deep I couldn't pull myself out. Like a man lost in the desert, staggering forward day after day until finally collapsing face-first into the sand and whispering, "It's over. I surrender." Only then—only when all my thirsting ceased—could I finally listen.

When I knelt, I did more than merely incline my ear to listen—I spoke to God from a place of genuine, reverent humility for the first time in my life. This moment transcended my desperation to avoid jail. It marked my first authentic grasp of what it truly means to surrender to a power infinitely greater than myself. I wasn't bargaining or presenting terms—I was waiting, emptied of self, desperately needing to hear from Him.

Twenty years after lying broken on that cold jailhouse floor in Seattle, true submission had finally arrived.

"My son, attend unto my wisdom, and bow thine ear to my understanding:" **(Proverbs 5:1, KJV).**

To *"bow the ear"*—this ancient phrase captures what modern language struggles to express: the deliberate act of humbling oneself before truth.

"Bow down thine ear, and hear the words of the wise, and apply thine heart unto my knowledge." **(Proverbs 22:17, KJV).**

This message resonates now with piercing clarity: Stop ignoring Me. Receive the truth from those I've entrusted to speak it. Let My truth reshape your thoughts, redirect your decisions, and recalibrate your character.

Here's what they don't tell you in rehab—what they can't tell you because it would empty their centers: turning your will over to some vague, comfortable "higher power" is profoundly insufficient. Recovery centers often sell serenity without providing the key. "Pick whatever works for you," they say with well-meaning smiles. "Door knob, universe, collective consciousness, whatever feels right." But when you're drowning in the wreckage of your own making, comfort isn't what you need—you need truth, even when it cuts.

Truth functions as both destroyer and builder. It first demolishes the false self you've meticulously constructed—that identity built on shifting sand. Only once that facade crumbles completely can truth become the rock-solid foundation upon which something enduring can finally be built. This explains why half-measures and vague spirituality inevitably fail. They're like applying fresh paint to a house that's rotting from the inside out—temporarily beautiful, ultimately worthless. The bottom is not the end if you seek truth. It's the beginning—the necessary foundation.

The psychiatrist at Cornerstone once told me something that I only now fully comprehend: "It's almost a shame you quit drinking for eleven years. White-knuckling sobriety for over a decade? That's infinitely harder than hitting rock bottom. The guys who come in completely destroyed—bodies wrecked, marriages shattered, careers obliterated—don't have eleven years of buried anxiety eating them alive like acid." She was right. My earlier sobriety never brought genuine freedom—it was merely a pressure cooker of restraint. I wasn't healing; I was simply starving the monster within, making it hungrier, angrier, and more calculating with each passing day. Religion without authentic spiritual connection operates exactly this way: starvation disguised as discipline. It hands you rules without revelation, lessons without transformation. You're reading Scripture blind—seeing the words without hearing the truth vibrating within them.

But when you finally surrender everything, when you bend your knee in true humility rather than begrudging compliance, something miraculous occurs—the Bible begins reading you. Verses you've skimmed a hundred times suddenly seek you out with laser precision, revealing what you've carefully hidden, confronting truths you've spent decades avoiding.

Walking out those rehab doors, I understood with startling clarity that the war hadn't ended—it had merely changed battlefields. Getting physically sober is essentially mechanical: remove the substance, monitor the vitals, wait for the body to detox. But staying sober? That's psychological and spiritual warfare of the highest order.

This is precisely where most people break. Not because they want to relapse, but because they never learned how to live comfortably inside their own skin without some spiritual escape hatch. The monster doesn't die when you put down the bottle. It adapts. It studies your weaknesses with predatory patience. It waits for the perfect moment.

The enemy understands that the unguarded mind is his preferred playground. This is why Scripture urgently commands us to *"take every thought captive"* **(2 Corinthians 10:5)**. When we fail to fill our minds with truth, lies rush in to fill the vacuum with terrifying efficiency. And those lies invariably lead to the same destination—bondage ingeniously disguised as freedom.

Our culture screams false liberation at every turn: *"Live your truth!"*; *"Don't let anyone judge you!"*; *"You do you!"* Empty platitudes that sound liberating but lead nowhere. Because when you're bound to sin, your only real choice is which chains hurt less. Alcohol or drugs. Toxic relationships or crushing isolation. Shopping addiction or gambling debts. Pick your poison—you're still poisoned, still enslaved, still dying.

Real deliverance—the kind that breaks chains instead of merely painting them gold—only comes through Christ. This is the ultimate paradox that our self-determining age cannot comprehend: surrender to be truly free. Be bound to Him to be released from everything else that binds you.

Solomon understood this profound truth when he wrote, *"The fear of the Lord is the beginning of wisdom"* **(Proverbs 9:10).** Notice he calls it the beginning—not the end. Acknowledging God's authority over your life isn't the destination; it's merely the starting line of an extraordinary journey. It's where true transformation began for me. That night on the floor, I wasn't confessing to save my skin from legal consequences. I was finally understanding that physical sobriety represents the beginning. Without emotional sobriety—the ability to fully feel without needing escape, to sit honestly in discomfort without running, and to build a life so meaningful you no longer want to numb it—we remain ticking time bombs, merely awaiting detonation.

But emotional sobriety never arrives alone; it demands a spiritual awakening that reshapes everything. These two realities—emotional and spiritual restoration—are inseparable, much like regeneration, new birth, justification, sanctification, and glorification in Christian theology. While each can be identified and described distinctly, none ever happens in isolation. They are threads intricately woven together, forming the seamless fabric of God's sovereign and complete work of redemption within a broken human heart.

God hadn't merely broken me that night; He had revealed the true battlefield where the real war would be fought: not against the bottle, but against an enemy that was after my heart itself. The bottle was just one weapon in his vast arsenal—one of many he would strategically deploy throughout the coming years.

Back then, I had no conception of how challenging inclining my ear to hear and then speak God's word would ultimately be. It required time, persistence, failure, and renewal. But you are about to read how God kept encouraging me, pursuing me, even when I struggled to pursue Him.

The true miracle in my story isn't that I stayed sober. Countless people achieve physical sobriety through sheer willpower, fear of consequences, or enlightened self-interest. The genuine miracle was that God used my absolute brokenness to initiate a complete renovation—not just of my external habits, but of my heart's deepest chambers. He wasn't remotely interested in making me a better version of the old me. He wanted something far more radical—to make me an entirely new creation.

As Paul wrote with profound insight, *"Therefore, if anyone is in Christ, he is a new creation. The old has passed away; behold, the new has come"* **(2 Corinthians 5:17).** This verse captures the essential difference between true spiritual transformation and mere behavior modification. One changes what you do; the other fundamentally changes who you are at the most elemental level.

The old me wouldn't recognize the man writing these words now. Not because I've achieved some state of spiritual perfection—far from it. But because the desires that once dominated my every waking thought, driving me relentlessly toward self-destruction, have been replaced by something immeasurably stronger. Not suppressed through willpower. Not managed through techniques. Replaced at the root.

This is the astounding promise of the Gospel that most people tragically miss. God doesn't forgive your sin as an isolated transaction; He changes your heart's deepest desires from within. He doesn't merely give you rules to follow through gritted teeth; He gives you a new nature that genuinely wants what He wants. The old heart that craved destruction gives way to a new heart that hungers for righteousness, for wholeness, for Him.

As the Psalmist wrote with profound insight, *"Delight yourself in the Lord, and he will give you the desires of your heart"* **(Psalm 37:4).** Most people misread this as God simply giving you what you already want—a spiritual vending machine for your existing appetites. But the deeper, more beautiful truth is that He gives you entirely new desires—desires aligned with His character, desires that satisfy the soul rather than enslaving it further.

That's the journey you're about to witness in these coming pages. Not simply a man staying sober—though that's part of it—but a man being made new from the inside out through divine craftsmanship. A painful process. A beautiful process. A necessary process. The only process that leads to genuine, lasting freedom.

Sharon

Before I was released from rehab, there was one more conversation I needed to have. I never stopped attending the Redeemers AA meetings in that old church basement. Over five months, I'd gradually collected phone numbers, built relationships, and communicated regularly with people in the group. I started participating actively—arriving early to set up chairs and staying late to put them away.

After one particular meeting, everyone got their court cards signed and scattered—everyone except Sharon and me. Sharon was the first person I'd ever heard speak at an AA meeting.

"Hey, Sharon... it's Sharon, right?" I asked.

"Yeah, that's me," she smiled warmly. "Your share today was so powerful. Wild story."

"I have to tell you something," I said reluctantly.

She paused, giving me space. "Okay."

"You were the first person I ever heard speak in an AA meeting. You talked about losing your daughter. Back then, I was so jaded, it hardly made me blink. But I never stopped thinking about it. Every day, for five months now, it's been on my mind." My voice softened. "I wanted to say—thank you."

She met my eyes, quiet for a moment. "You know, you can be cruising along, and then one day, everything changes. Nothing in this world is certain. But I'll tell you this—you saying this right now means you've changed. God is working on you."

I nodded, something catching in my throat. The old me would have dismissed her mention of God, would have found some way to deflect the sincerity of the moment. But standing there in that basement, surrounded by empty chairs we'd soon stack away, I felt something shifting inside me—like a door long rusted shut had been gently pushed open. Not kicked down. Just open enough to let some light shine through.

"I think you might be right," I said finally.

We didn't hug. We didn't need to. Something more important had passed between us—an acknowledgment that pain, when witnessed and honored, can transform both the teller and the listener. I walked out of that church basement a different man than the one who had first shuffled in five months earlier. Not fixed. Not perfect. But finally, **finally listening.**

The First Test

Five months of living in rehab are finally behind me.
Now I'm here, standing in a **Seal Beach apartment I still pay for,** facing my first real test.

My "wife" disappears into the bedroom, her voice trailing behind her like **bad perfume.**
I've been out of Cornerstone exactly **one hour.**
All I want is to see my kids.

She returns. **Topless.**

"You need a place to stay, right? We've stayed in the same room for years. Just sleep here," she says, like we're discussing **the weather.**
Like the last year of destruction was a minor inconvenience.
Like this is normal.

I avert my eyes, but the familiar pull is there.

Not **attraction.**
Toxic **Patterns.**
Five months of sobriety. Five months of rebuilding.
And here's the old life, standing in front of me, **knowing I've been caged up for months.**
Preying on **my carnal weakness.**

This is how **the Devil operates.**

He doesn't show up with fangs and fire.
He waits. Patient. Watching.
And when you're vulnerable?
He offers comfort—**poison disguised as comfort.**

"I'm good," I say.
The words **aren't for her. They're for me.**
"When the kids wake up, tell them I stopped by. I want to see them later."

Her face **floods with shock.** Her wheels start **spinning.**
She realizes that **a new man is standing before her.**
One she **can't control.**

This simple exchange **sets the wheels of revenge in motion.**
I knew this wasn't the end.
The enemy **doesn't take rejection lightly.**
He **reloads**.

I would end up sleeping in that bedroom.
Without her in it.

A short time later, I'd **take over this apartment** when she became dissatisfied with it and moved out.

A recurring theme in my kids' lives. The woman was never satisfied. Constantly wanting the new.

But that was later.

For now, I walked out the door, lungs exhaling the weight of **not giving in.**

Discipline wasn't simply about resistance. It was about **identity.**

I've got to do something to get this energy out. I have to fight this demon.
And the first place I go?

The Iron Church

*"You don't need motivation to succeed. You need a work ethic that **doesn't quit when life gets hard.**"*

I sign up to train in a dungeon-like facility off Pine Avenue in downtown Long Beach.

Gold's Gym. A cathedral of **sweat and steel.**

Descending into the belly of the beast, I hear it:

Clank. Clank. **CLANK.**

Ex-cons and bodybuilders working in metallic harmony—a melting pot of physical prowess. Real men doing **hard work.**

God doesn't call men to sit idly.

Sitting on the edge of a worn counter, I watch them train. A surge of energy rushes me. I remember saying these exact words to myself:

I'm tired of being weak. Tired of letting the old voices win.

Men need to lift heavy things. Men must be physically strong.

It's deeper than muscle. I need to set goals, fight for them, and win. A man must follow through. If I can't follow through on my goals, my life will remain a series of small train wrecks.

If I achieve what I set out to do—without giving up?

Everything changes.

Right now, I'm scrawny. Weak.

But I know—if I give this gym one year, day after relentless day, I'll forge a new path. More respected as a man, more attractive to women, respected by peers.

You can do this.

No, scratch that—I will do this.

I will become **JACKED.**

That day, salvation comes in the form of heavy iron.

Doctor's orders? *"You shouldn't lift heavy weights."*

Translation: You probably shouldn't even be alive—but here we are.

I go all in. Defy medical advice.
No pills. No follow-up doctor appointments.

Just pure will.

Being alone with your thoughts as an addict is a rabbit hole Alice never escapes.

That's why I hit those plates twice a day.

The first month, I lift alone. Others watch, silently measuring my determination.

By month two, Franco—a beast built of equal parts Danny Trejo and Fabio—finally speaks up.

Franco is fifty-eight, five foot ten, and two hundred sixty pounds of pure muscle. He's sober too.

Franco sees the fire in me, offering pointers now and then. Over the next month, he reveals his story: raised by a heroin-addicted father who abused him relentlessly, he battled addiction himself, nearly dying several times before getting sober.

Before his father died in the '90s, he'd sold nearly everything the family owned, investing in land around Long Beach Airport. Months later, when JetBlue unexpectedly opened operations there, the land skyrocketed in value.

Franco became extremely wealthy overnight—two hundred thousand dollars a month in hangar fees.

He didn't waste the opportunity. With his newfound financial freedom, he hired one of the world's top Mr. Olympia trainers, paying him for an entire year. He absorbed every secret, endured every brutal workout, and internalized every ounce of hard-earned wisdom.

Now Franco passes it to me. He becomes my bodybuilding mentor.

"You want strength?" he asks bluntly. "Forget the fancy workouts. Compound lifts. Heavy weight. Hard work."

Under Franco's guidance, it takes eight relentless months to go from pressing sixty-pound dumbbells to hammering one-twenties.

Hours. **Every day.**

Those weights crush my thighs before I even lie back to press. This isn't only about building muscle—it's about building resilience.

It's pure will.

A hunger for more pain. **Medicine for the mind.**

There's power in redirecting pain into purpose.

Same time.
Same place.
Every day.
Hard work.

The iron. It hardens my hands, leaving calluses—physical proof that discipline and effort change you. My body transforms. **My mind follows.**

One night, sprawled exhausted on my couch in Seal Beach, muscles screaming, windows open to the Pacific breeze, a truth hits me square in my sore chest—

This was never just about muscle.

This was about forging armor.

Weakness won't win. Neither will hesitation. The enemy reloads—so do I.

Every rep. Every set. Every drop of sweat. It's training.

For war.

Not just against the enemy, but against myself.

The old me.
The one who stayed complacent.
The one who feared the void.
The one who listened to doubt.

They are the enemy's victims.

I'm not going to be one of his victims.

I wasn't waiting for motivation.

I was building discipline.

If you wait until life is easy to start, **you never will.**

Back then, I realized I needed a **WAR-PLAN**. And that's exactly what I built. The war plan you're about to read. Follow it, and you can transform your life radically in a short period of time.

Are you ready to build your war plan?

BLUEPRINT STEP 4: FORGE A WAR PLAN

(Discipline Over Motivation)

"Motivation is a mirage that disappears when you need it most. Discipline is the well that never runs dry."

WAR STRATEGY:

If you wait to feel ready, you'll never move. If you wait for motivation, you'll die waiting. The enemy of transformation isn't resistance—it's reaction. Impulse is his front-line soldier. The warrior's advantage isn't strength—it's strategy. Without a battle plan, distractions will destroy you. Without discipline, chaos will reclaim you. Your feelings lie. Your inspiration fades. Only systems and structures survive the fog of war. A warrior doesn't show up hoping for a win—he prepares, trains, and executes regardless of how he feels.

ACTION ORDERS:

1. Establish Your "Non-Negotiable Three"

These are your daily weapons. No excuse. No skipping. No negotiation.

- **Spiritual**—prayer, Scripture reading, fasting—anything that builds faith.
- **Mental**—journaling, self-examination, eliminating mental toxins.
- **Physical**—training, cold showers, fasting—discipline that strengthens your body.

These aren't "good habits." They're **weapons**. Artillery. Armor. Write down your three **non-negotiable** daily disciplines. Commit to them. **Zero compromise.**

2. Schedule Your Battles

Every morning, **set your battle plan.** If you don't define your priorities, the world will define them for you.

- List your **top 3 priorities** for tomorrow **before you sleep.**
- Assign specific time blocks for execution.
- Eliminate distractions during those blocks.
- Execute with ruthless focus.
- Review and adjust daily.

Wake up with a mission, not confusion. Structure kills chaos.

3. Attack Discomfort Daily

The enemy wants you soft, weak, and controlled by comfort. You must actively attack what's uncomfortable.

- **Do one hard thing daily.**
- **Do one thing you don't feel like doing.**
- **Do the work, even uninspired.**
- **Rise early**—own the morning; it sets the tone.
- **Kill distractions**—delete apps, block sites, create barriers to weakness.

Discipline is the bridge between destruction and freedom. Pick one specific discomfort to attack tomorrow. Then do it without hesitation.

4. Build Spiritual Warfare Discipline

- **Start with God**—prayer and Scripture **before the world gets you.**
- **End with God**—reflection and repentance **before sleep.**
- **Fast and sacrifice**—strengthen your soul **against weakness.**
- **Fight with Scripture**—*"The Lord is my strength and my shield; my heart trusts in Him, and He helps me."* **(Psalm 28:7).**

Spiritual discipline isn't optional—it's survival. The warrior who kneels before God is the only one truly ready to fight.

WAR CRY:

VICTORY COMES TO THOSE WHO EXECUTE WITHOUT MERCY

Cut the excuses. Follow the plan. Win the day. Motivation is the enemy's illusion to keep you waiting. Discipline is God's gift to keep you advancing when feelings fail. The best warriors don't fight because they feel like it—they fight because they're committed. David didn't wait until he felt strong—he ran toward Goliath when everyone else cowered. Gideon didn't wait until he believed in himself—he obeyed while still afraid. Paul didn't wait until life got easier—he wrote letters that shaped the world from inside a prison cell.

They didn't move because they **felt ready.** They moved because they had a **mission**. A **PURPOSE**.

BLUEPRINT RECAP:

BEFORE: *(Trapped by Ego & Excuses)*

"I thought other people were built different. I told myself they had better genetics, better circumstances, better opportunities. I looked at men who trained hard, who built success, and thought: They have something I don't. I made excuses instead of changes. I waited for motivation instead of building discipline. I let comfort sedate me while warriors trained.

In rehab, I finally understood: I was blessed to even be alive. I had wasted time. Wasted strength. But I was still here. I saw men who didn't make it. I saw a young warrior-in-the-making who had every reason to succeed—but something was missing. Gratitude. Humility. Perspective. Two weeks later, he was dead. Sobriety wasn't enough. Strength wasn't enough. Without humility, the demon won."

Pro Tip: If you think discipline is about proving you're strong, you've already lost. Test yourself: Wake up at 5 a.m. for a week straight. Cut out all sugar for 30 days. Train when tired, not just when you are motivated. Watch how quickly your ego tries to justify quitting. That's when you know the real battle has begun.

AFTER: *(Training with Humility, Not Ego)*

"Before, I saw discipline as suffering. I thought sacrifice was loss. But humility changed my perspective. I realized self-sacrifice wasn't weakness—it was the price of something greater. The best warriors don't fight for themselves. They fight for something beyond themselves. Humility turns self-sacrifice into a weapon.

I learned the strongest men weren't superior to me—they had simply **endured more**. They learned that comfort is a lie. I stopped making excuses and started making progress. I stopped being too proud to struggle and started training like a man who had to fight for his life.

Now? I don't train to look strong—I train because some men don't get the chance to wake up today. I don't execute my war plan to prove something. I execute because my second chance is a gift. Humility isn't weakness. It's awareness. When you understand how fragile life is, you stop wasting time."

VICTORY INDICATORS:

You Know You're Succeeding When:

- You complete non-negotiable daily disciplines even when you don't feel like it
- Your calendar reflects your priorities, not just obligations
- You no longer need motivation to do what matters
- You've established systems that make discipline easier
- You can point to specific discomfort you've embraced daily
- Your mornings have structure instead of chaos
- You finish what you start

RED FLAGS:

- You still rely on motivation to take action
- You make excuses for skipping your disciplines
- Your schedule changes based on how you feel
- You can't name the last uncomfortable thing you did
- Your day happens to you instead of being directed by you
- You procrastinate on important tasks while staying busy with minor ones

REALITY CHECK:

Discipline will fail you—not because it doesn't work, but because you're human. You'll oversleep. You'll skip workouts. You'll give in to distractions. You'll have days when your plan collapses before noon. These failures aren't the end—they're data points for improvement. The difference between a disciplined warrior and everyone else isn't perfection—it's recovery speed. How quickly do you get back on track after derailing? The enemy will use your failures to convince you that you can't change. He's lying. True discipline isn't about never falling—it's about getting up faster each time. When discipline falters—which it will—don't waste energy on guilt. Reset immediately and execute the next time correctly.

WAR ORDER (FINAL COMMAND):

For the next 7 days, wake up at 5:00 AM and complete your Non-Negotiable Three before 8:00 AM. **No excuses.** No snooze button. No negotiations. If you fail, start over. Small victories. Stack them. Build momentum.

*"Every excuse you make? The enemy **LOVES** it. Every time you hit snooze, every time you reach for the bottle, every time you stay quiet when you should roar—he laughs. What are you going to do about it?"*

CHAPTER 8

The Judgment

Discipline prepares you for battle. But some battles aren't fought in routines—they're fought staring into your own reflection, the night before your fate is decided.

Ocean views and sea breezes **do not cure a lonely heart.**

The night before my sentencing, I stand in the bathroom of my tiny, outdated apartment, staring in the mirror. I see someone different. The bruises—gone. The neck brace—gone. The scar on my forehead is still red and puffy, a crimson testament to my brokenness. My face leaner, sharper. My muscles beginning to take form beneath skin that has known too much poison. The wildness in my eyes—replaced with something steadier, something that holds my gaze instead of darting away from it.

For the first time in years, I see someone I respect—someone imperfect who is finally trying.

But at night, when darkness presses against the windows and silence amplifies every thought, the voices start again.

One drink won't hurt.

You're already screwed—why suffer?

You're going to jail tomorrow. Why not go out on your terms? One last party.

Addiction doesn't die. It morphs. It creeps under doors, finds new shapes, new disguises, new compulsions to fill the void. It recognizes the scent of fear, the tremble of uncertainty. It knows when you're nearing a breakthrough, and that's precisely when it strikes—when victory is within your grasp but doubt still lingers in the shadows.

Nine years hanging over my head. That's three thousand two hundred eighty-five nights in a cell. That's birthdays missed. That's my kids growing up without me. That's my mom and dad visiting me through bulletproof glass. That's me waking up daily with a number instead of a name.

Tomorrow morning, I'd face the judge. The guillotine was in place—waiting for my arrival. I'd done everything asked of me since leaving Cornerstone. But now, staring at myself in that mirror, my mind spirals into the abyss, and I have to stop myself.

Face the void: *What is true in this moment?*

That I'm powerless? That's true—I have no control over tomorrow's outcome.

That I'm afraid? Also true. What man wouldn't be?

But what else do I believe?

I believe in taking responsibility.

I believe in being a man of my word.

I'd spent the last few hours reading about judges giving harsher sentences before lunch, lighter ones on Friday mornings. Internet research fails to ease my tension. Instead, I hit my knees.

"God, I'm at your mercy. Whatever punishment you give, I'll accept."

My prayer is simple. No bargaining. No promises. **Just surrender.**

Resolve replaces fear. If I get prison time, I'll use it—write, work out, prepare for what comes next. If I get freedom, I'll honor it. Recovery is working, turning this fear into fuel. Real men face their consequences. That's who I am becoming.

I am able to sleep.

The Morning of Judgment

Morning comes like an executioner's footsteps—methodical, inevitable, final.

I dress with deliberate care—each movement a meditation. The suit and tie feel like armor, though I know they won't deflect what's coming. I'm not the same guy that flipped a car six times. But will the judge see that?

I catch myself spiraling again.

Redirect the fear.

The courthouse swallows me whole. The walls press in, the air stuffy—heavy with the weight of consequences. I hear the shuffle of handcuffs clicking as they bring in the detained prisoners, the distant sound of someone crying, the quiet, ticking tension of bad decisions about to meet their final reckonings.

I'm not the only one facing judgment today. But I might be the only one with a plan to turn my sentence into purpose.

My attorney sits to my left. Stephanie to my right. They'll speak for me to start, tell the judge how I've changed. But, this moment is between me and God—the true judge.

Other cases go first. I watch the judge's face, trying to read his mood, wondering if he's had lunch, if he's having a good Friday.

STOP.

Control what you can control. Accept what you can't.

"Matthew Farnsworth."

My name echoes through the courtroom—two words carrying the weight of my entire past, present, and future. I stand, shoulders back, chin up, not from pride—from acceptance. Whatever comes next—I've earned the consequences.

Stephanie speaks first. *"Your Honor, in my years of working with recovery, I've rarely seen someone dedicate themselves to recovery like Matt..."*

The words she speaks blur into the intensity of the moment. Over a year of waiting for this atonement order is coming to an end. *Control what I can control—this moment is His, not mine.*

I hear my attorney lay out the legal arguments. Hear the prosecutor push back.

I clear my mind again.

FOCUSED.

I've done the work.

The judge's gaze finds mine. *"Mr. Farnsworth... they sure have a lot to say about this mess."*

Each second an eternity of suspended breath and pounding heart.

"What say you, Mr. Farnsworth?" the judge asks.

I bow my head before looking back up.

This is it. Be honest. You are not a victim of being accused of anything. You are the perpetrator.

From a place of acceptance, words form in my mind and rise from a soul steeped in accountability. The crime I committed demands nothing less than complete honesty.

I say verbatim:

"What I say doesn't change what happened, your honor. My actions since that day speak louder than my words. I can only offer these two witnesses to testify about my behavior since July 9th, 2014—the day my terrible choices caused disaster for everyone involved. What they say is true and whatever punishment you see fit to give me, I am ready to accept. I desire to be accountable for my actions."

The judge leans back. Letting the silence settle. The blade hovers over my neck.

You can feel the whole courtroom stop moving. The air itself seems to wait.

My pulse pounds inside my skull.

He glances down at the paperwork, then back at me.

One word from him, and my life takes a different path.

He squints his eyes and points at me before saying these words:

"I'm going to suspend all jail time and give you time served for your five months in rehab. Your license is revoked for a full year. No driving."

His words rush past me, too fast for my mind to comprehend. For an instant, everything goes silent—the courtroom, my heartbeat, even the breath caught in my throat. Stephanie gently nudges me, pulling me back into reality. Only then does relief flood in, raw and overwhelming.

"Yes, thank you, your honor."

"But hear me loud and clear: One mistake—one—and you'll serve the full sentence."

I nod, not trusting my voice. What? Unexpected mercy. Me? This isn't only freedom. This is God's grace materialized in a courtroom where grace is rarely seen.

The relief doesn't hit all at once. It comes in waves, each one carrying a new realization: Twenty-four months of probation. No license for a year. No drinking, no second chances. My freedom has a razor-thin edge.

But now I have something that I didn't have five months ago:

A foundation.

A way to turn consequences into counteraction from outside a prison cell.

Walking out of that courthouse, I watch Stephanie and my attorney walk away. They had been angels in my corner, divine messengers disguised in legal attire.

I stop and look up at the vast sky—cloudless, endless, like the mercy I've just received.

I am not sure yet what you are looking for from me, but thank you. I'll follow my punishment through whatever they ask me to do. No matter how difficult it may be. I will not waver.

This grace weaves a fabric of belief into my heart. That something bigger than myself had mercy on me that day. That God is approving of my recent choices. The punishment has been dealt. Now it is my job to fulfill the terms without faltering.

The question hangs in the air, both challenge and promise:

Am I up to the task?

The man in the mirror—the one with steady eyes and a puffy scar—believes I am.

And for the first time in years, **I trust him.** But right now I'm holding a court order:

> *Report within thirty six hours to be fitted for electronic ankle monitoring for sixty days. The cost will be assessed at the time of the fitting. If you fail to comply with this order you will be found in contempt of court and be brought before the court for re-sentencing.*

House Arrest

"Even when life tries to bury you, remember: **seeds grow in the dirt.**"

Freedom has many faces. Mine wore a blinking red light.

House arrest wasn't solitary confinement. It was a leash. A chain. A sentence without a cell.

A curfew. No drinking—the monitor can detect even a trace of alcohol, and I am never to remove the device.

Every night, that pulsing crimson eye on my ankle reminded me I wasn't free. The device itself was heavier than it looked—two pounds of hard plastic and electronics that grew slick with sweat during workouts, chafed my skin raw on long bike rides, and beeped randomly in the quiet hours, waking me. A constant companion documenting my submission to the system.

And I accepted it—because I knew **I deserved it.**

The ankle monitor tracked my every movement. Every step logged, recorded. Sometimes, I'd stare at it, that blinking red light like a parasite, feeding on what was left of my freedom.

Claustrophobia would wrap around me like a noose.

I wanted to rip it off.

But cutting it off meant one thing: jail.

You can do this. Sixty more days.

I'd ride my bike or longboard from my apartment to the bus stop along the Pacific Coast Highway in front of *"In-N-Out"* burger. The same burger joint where I'd once pulled up in my Infinity, windows down, music blaring. Now I was inside looking out, watching people live normal lives while mine had boundaries programmed into a GPS parameter.

Every silent moment on the bus served me another slice of humble pie. Nobody cared who I used to be. Nobody cared about my IMDb credits—not that they would've recognized me anyway. This forced step-down in my status pushed me into conversations that never would've happened otherwise—conversations with people I'd overlooked behind the tinted windows of my former life.

This day on the bus was like any other.

Until a gentleman sat down across from me.

He glanced at my beard. "I used to have a beard like that."

"Why'd you shave it?" I asked.

"It reminded me of my daughter. She used to pull on it."

I paused. Did I want to know more? My stomach tightened, sensing what might come next.

Before I could ask, he continued. "She was killed by a drunk driver last Halloween. Hit crossing the street. Her and my mother."

His eyes were dry—like he'd cried every tear possible, now existing in the hollow space grief carves out. My mouth went dry. The monitor suddenly weighed a thousand pounds around my ankle, absorbing the mass of his words.

How close had I come to being that driver? How narrow was the space separating me from destroying lives? I swallowed hard, feeling a crushing wave of shame wash over me. One different choice—one fraction of a second—and I could've been the one responsible for extinguishing a child's life for leaving a father with nothing but memories and a missing beard.

In recovery, we call these moments **"God Shots"**—when God reaches down and shakes you awake. This was a brutal, unforgettable reminder of what I'd nearly done to someone else's life.

Accountability.

I decided to honor that ban on driving. No shortcuts. No *"just this once."* When you're staring down the barrel of a suspended nine-year prison sentence, you don't test the system. You walk the line.

At times, it felt like punishment.

It's supposed to.

I'd bike forty to fifty miles a day—commuting to the gym, the grocery store, and everywhere in between. My thighs burned each evening, lungs scorched, back aching. But the physical pain felt justified—like penance, like earning every inch of freedom.

Probation check-ins meant my PO watching me urinate into a plastic cup. The mirror tilted down, his gaze ensuring I hit the fill line. To this day, I still send him flowers on our first drug test anniversary, a small token of thanks for keeping me accountable, even if it came with a side of humiliation.

They required employment. I took my test to become a personal trainer, passed the certification and satisfied them.

Then came surprise inspections. Nothing jolts you awake faster than probation officers banging at your door at 5 a.m.—flipping drawers, pulling couch cushions, searching your space like you're running a cartel. Except there were no drugs. No secrets. Just me, my Viking beard, and workout plans.

A drug bust with nothing to bust.

Was it tough? Absolutely. Every inspection, every humiliating drug test, every grueling mile burned into me one undeniable truth—I was finally doing something right. The monitor wasn't a punishment; it was a path. My life became a living oxymoron: discovering true freedom within confinement. Accountability, honesty, and humility rose from the ashes. This wasn't the end of my story—it was the first honest chapter I'd written in a lifetime.

Breadcrumbs Back to Purpose

When I didn't jump on the bus, I rode my bike.

Those miles became meditations. Every ride was a victory—proof that I was honoring my commitments, even when no one was watching. The rhythm of pedaling, the constant forward motion—it became a metaphor for the man I was trying to become. Steady. Persistent. Present.

My daily ride to Gold's Gym takes me through Naples, past Mothers Beach, toward a Med Spa tucked beneath the Naples Bridge. Today, I pause at the bridge. Boats glide quietly past, the water calm, gray skies promising sunshine later. Below me, families set up umbrellas, laughter drifting upward. Below the bridge, there is a Med Spa. Each morning, I notice it—but don't know why. Perhaps because it feels like a symbol of renewal, of restoration—a subtle reminder of the healing I crave. Something about it calls to me, subtle but insistent, whispering beneath the noise of traffic.

I lean my bike against the railing. Watch a father teach his young daughter to build a sandcastle. Watch her laugh when the waves destroy it. Watch them start again. The cycle of destruction and rebuilding playing out in miniature before me—a lesson I'm only beginning to understand.

That scar on my forehead—still puffy, still pink—glares back at me in every reflection, an angry constellation marking the map of my mistakes. The accident I caused. The lives I nearly ended. Fixing it would feel like repairing a broken part of me.

Why not now? I think.

But I don't have the money. Not yet.

I need more clients.

I ride through Belmont Shore.

The very place I used to inebriate myself. Where I once stumbled between bars, in a drunken trance seeking an answer to my pain in **poison.**

Now I see it with sober eyes.

The stores are all opening up.

Smell of stale beer—still present.

It's beautiful but if you look close enough, you see the truth. Paradise with a hangover. A postcard image with vomit in the margins.

There are stairs to my right that ascend to the top of the bluff. I dismount and begin sprinting up and down; my legs start burning. Motivational music blasts through my headphones, but my voice shouts louder.

I'm releasing the monster from the past.

You're not the same man you used to be.

*This is your **comeback.***

*This is your **comeback.***

The ankle monitor, covered in sweat, reminds me that I must have **humility.**

You let yourself be deceived. It's nobody's fault but yours. Own it, bro. You'll never let it happen again.

One more set.

One more round.

One more push to keep the **monster in its cage.**

I pour myself into work instead. Sharing every lift, every meal, every small win on Instagram like therapy. Every interaction, every like, every comment—I start grasping for crumbs of validation. Searching for proof that I still exist, that I still matter, that I can rebuild something from the wreckage.

I'm sober, yes. But emotionally healed? **Far from it.**

The monster became quieter those days, but it didn't vanish. Instead, it waited patiently, shapeshifting, wearing new masks. Validation, attention, empty connections—another drug. Another distraction. The desperate search for something outside myself to fix what was broken inside.

The truth I hadn't fully grasped yet: You can't heal a wound by covering it. You can only heal it by cleaning it—and cleaning it stings deeper than the original injury.

I thought: *God has me exactly where I need to be—alone enough to face myself. Restricted enough to learn discipline. Humbled enough to grow.*

The sunset casts long shadows as I ride home. The beachgoers have packed up their day. The air thins—degrees drop and briskness sets in. I take a deep breath. The tide is coming in, erasing footprints, smoothing the sand for tomorrow's visitors. Nature's reset button.

Each evening, before I sleep, I write down one victory from the day. It's often small—staying calm when my kids spill cereal, biking an extra mile, resisting the urge to feel sorry for myself. Small steps, but they're moving me forward.

I endure learning patience. Discipline. Structure.

And in the my punishment, I learn delayed gratification—something my addicted brain never understood before—I find an unexpected gift:

Hope.

Not the flashy, instantaneously vapid kind sold in commercials.

But something sturdier. Something that builds slowly, day by day, choice by choice.

The kind of hope that only comes from the true source.

The kind that doesn't promise an easy path, but promises that the path leads somewhere worth going.

As my wheels turn against the pavement, something else turns within me—slowly, almost imperceptibly, but turning nonetheless. Something new is being built, even as the waves of my past continue to crash against uncharted shores. But no matter how far forward I move, the tides of my past always threaten to pull me under again.

Facing My Past

My wife never stopped tormenting me.

From the moment I left recovery, **she was plaguing me.**

The texts came in waves.

A normal text message before picking up the kids.

> *You are such a brainwasher and scumbag. Just go away please. I just want you to go away and leave my children and their love that I have given them alone. You are a bad person, Matt. Just leave my kids out of your disturbing and disgusting display of negativity. You were lucky to have ever had the love and loyalty I gave you for as long as I did.*

My responses became business only.

> *What time are you dropping them off?*

> *What time are you picking them up?*

This spurred even more erratic behaviour.

One day it was:

> *You deadbeat. You drunk loser. You're not a father. What kind of man doesn't support his wife and kids?*

The next:

> *We are a family—and we will always be a family. You know me, Matt. I've always loved you. It's time for us to fix this. The kids need their father.*

The manipulation was relentless.

I had to stop the insanity she was bringing into my life.

She was repeating the same cycle.

The only option.

Break it.

I finally had enough.

I went no contact.

Blocked her number.

Even if it meant not seeing my kids.

No Contact Didn't Stop Her

I made it a month before she started showing up at my door.

Some nights, she wanted to talk.
Other days, she wanted to fight.

"I saw your Instagram. Are you with those women you're training?"

"You should train me."

The accusations and rekindling attempts never stopped.

The pattern continued.

She **discarded me first.**

But I was not **allowed** to discard her.

How dare I block her?
How dare I move on?
How dare I date without **her approval?**

Half the time, she was trying to claw her way back into my life.

The other half? She was attacking me.

Then came CPS. Child Protective Services.

She made **false claims about abuse.**

Tried to weaponize the system against me.

When she finally filed for divorce, I was relieved.

She said:

"I filed so you would talk to me. I want our family back."

I agreed to the divorce immediately.

I thought it would be straightforward.

It wasn't.

She kept coming to the apartment.

Started slipping notes under my door.

Waiting for me in the parking lot.

One night, she threw herself at my feet.

Clinging to my ankles, sobbing.

"Please, please don't break our family up!"

I ripped my legs away.

Breaking her grip.

I looked down at her and calmly said, "Get ahold of yourself."

Back then, I didn't have The Blueprint laid out the way it is now.

But I knew one thing. The voices that allowed me to listen to her rhetoric wanted to **destroy me.**

And **I wasn't about to let them.**

The Divorce Circus

The divorce wasn't a courtroom drama.
It was a bloodbath in slow motion.

Two years. Nine hearings. Endless depositions.

The lawyer fees stacked up like ransom notes.

Lies thrown like daggers. Accusations stacking like bricks. The walls closing in.

This wasn't about fairness. It was about war.

She'd walked into court like she was stepping onto a **movie set**—she's sit across from me, whispering to her attorney like she was scripting a soap opera.

Like this was **her moment.**
Like she had spent weeks rehearsing the role of a **wronged woman** instead of a **destroyer in disguise.**

And me?
I sat there. **Silent.**
Letting the weight of **every accusation** press down on me.
Every demand.
Every lie.

She would call me, screaming into the phone before court—
*"You're gonna pay, buddy. **PAY!**"*

If hell has waiting rooms, they probably feel like family court.

She didn't want money.
She wanted **everything.**

She tried to **rewrite California law** to include my **father's financial support** for our kids as part of child support.
The entitlement knew no bounds.

She wasn't after **justice.**
She delusionally believed she could change California law.

The Paper Cuts

Deposition after deposition, I learned something new:
This wasn't a fight.
This wasn't a legal battle.
This was a **slow death by paper cuts.**

So, I stopped seeing the court as a battlefield.

I fired my attorney.
I took it on myself.

Because **I could see the truth—**
The only people who were winning were the ones getting paid to sit there and **pretend** to do something.

Even her lawyer saw it.
One day, he pulled me aside and **apologized** to me.

"I'm sorry for all this crazy stuff, man," he muttered, avoiding my eyes. "But I want to retire, and her family is funding this basket case."

The future **Blueprint at work.**
Nothing was going to change the outcome.

I reframed it all.

This was not a war.
Not an attack.

It was a **training ground.**

Every five-hour deposition?

Patience training.

Every **ridiculous claim?**
Mental endurance.

Every hour spent listening to fabricated accusations designed to **break me?**
An exercise in **breaking toxic patterns.**

The Final Gavel

By the time the **gavel finally dropped,** I felt **nothing**.

Not relief.
Not anger.
Not victory.

Finally... **closure**.

She got **nothing**.

She had divorced me at my lowest.

50/50 custody of the kids.

No alimony. No child support.

No **Hollywood ending** for her courtroom performance.

The **final scene?**
A woman **blasting out of the courtroom**, eyes filled with abomination, realizing she had lost.

And me?
I walked away.

But here's what they don't tell you about exes.

They don't need to **see you** to **haunt you.**

Social media?
It's a **stalker's best friend.**

She still found ways to **creep into my life**, even through **blocked numbers,** even from **behind a screen.**

Little **digital attacks.**
A comment here.
A **fake account** there.

A reminder that **recovery doesn't mean the challenges stop.**

It means **you're STRONGER when they come.**

CHAPTER 9

Online Dating

The Void's New Shape

Winning battles in courtrooms doesn't end wars. Especially when the battlefield is your own mind, and your enemy takes on new forms.

I'm alone now. **Often.**

Wake up.

Coffee.

Workout.

Eat.

Train clients.

Eat.

Sleep.

Repeat.

I got antsy.

Addictions don't die—they shapeshift, like cancer, finding a new organ to eat. That same gnawing void that once mainlined cocaine and tequila? The monster crept back in. It found a new drug: **validation.**

Here's the truth: those half-hearted prayers I'd tossed skyward to save my broken self were not nearly enough. I was dancing on a razor's edge, believing sobriety alone meant I was safe, blind to the Devil laughing in the shadows as I shuffled back toward the edge of the abyss.

The flesh wants what it wants, and mine desperately wanted to fill that loneliness void.

Enter the Roman Colosseum of modern romance: dating apps. Swipe right for heaven, swipe right for hell—usually straight to hell. The attention happened fast. Women liked the sober guy, the one building muscle, reconstructing his life from the ground up. Validation is a **powerful** drug.

And the comedown? Absolute brutality.

The instant messages stopped; the moment the screen went dark, silence crashed back in—**withdrawal,** all over again.

Swipe. Swipe. **Swipe.**

Back in my day, in the 1900s, connection required courage—you had to look someone in the eye, risk actual rejection, remember their name, and write down their phone number. Now? It's a digital meat market, and I became a popular butcher.

With my license restored, mobility became my new fix. Like a sixteen-year-old tasting freedom, except I wasn't some wide-eyed kid. I was a recovering middle-aged addict deliberately laying out silverware at the banquet table of my own destruction—**again.**

Want the express lane back to rock bottom? Chase the very poison that almost killed you. Addiction resurrects itself, uglier and hungrier.

Rehab counselors called this beast "cross-addiction." Your brain always finds new ways to get its fix. Cocaine morphs into sex; alcohol morphs into validation. One master replaced by another, but always serving the same demon.

I saw every red flag clearly, yet still walked straight into the fire. Sobriety hadn't cured me—it had exposed the brokenness I'd spent a lifetime running from.

This wasn't some revelation descending from heaven—The Blueprint was forged from the fires of my own stupidity, one painful mistake at a time.

What was I chasing after? Not love. Not even companionship. It was noise loud enough to drown out my own brokenness.

Am I sober?

Yep.

Am I emotionally healthy?

No.

I'd swapped bottles for dating apps and empty, lustful exchanges. **It made me feel ashamed, but that shame wasn't enough to stop me.**

My actions had consequences. Sober or not. A new realization I had to "realize."

And the women I attracted were mirrors, reflecting my jagged edges and cracked foundation. Broken calls out to broken—and **broken always answers.**

There was the twenty-five-year-old who tried to move in after a month and sliced her own arm open with a kitchen knife when I finally asked her to leave. I'd never seen self-harm in real life—no Hollywood prop blood here. Darker. **Angrier.** The guilt consumed me because that's what addicts do. We wrap ourselves in guilt like a comfort blanket—then watch it catch fire.

The Blueprint was being forged through my own mistakes:

- Face the void: What am I chasing?
- Inventory reality: Was this healing or destroying me?
- Audit your circle: Were these connections lifting me or dragging me under?

I ignored it all.

And ignorance is fuel for the enemy.

He doesn't care if you're sober—only that you're vulnerable. And loneliness made me the perfect target.

THE ENEMY DOESN'T SLEEP.
He doesn't rest.
He doesn't care if you're healing, progressing, or building your war plan.

He waits.
He waits until you're tired.
He waits until you're alone.
He waits until you're scrolling.

He waits until you're convinced, **I've got this under control.**

Then—
You swipe.
You match.
You message.

You tell yourself, *This is different.*
You whisper, *This is harmless.*
You reassure yourself, *I deserve this*.

The flesh never stops craving.
The past never stops whispering.
The enemy doesn't care what the drug is—
He wants you hooked—on **something.**

I decided to stay away from her. Two months of peace shattered in seconds. I'm walking across the street on Main Street in Seal Beach when she pulls up. In the middle of the crosswalk, she honks, drawing my attention. She'd been stalking me—God only knows for how long. Nearly runs me down, flips me off, screams something savage, and speeds away.

Then the texts start, a tidal wave of hatred:

You're a scumbag. I hope you die.

Then her mom jumps in, leaving voicemails calling me fat, short, and a deadbeat loser. Meanwhile, my ex-wife was stalking my social media, messaging every new woman I dated, screaming that these women were trash, and feeding off the chaos.

My genius solution? Double down on insanity. Date someone else—because gasoline always puts out fires, right?

The girl from the gym I start dating makes the self-harm psycho look like Mary Poppins. She might as well have been a bottle labeled ***Step One: Relapse Here.***

There was something about her that drew me in. Not unlike my ex-wife. Every red flag slapped me in the face, but addicts don't stop to read signs. Her energy was off—*dark, twisted, unnatural.* One night, I snapped a casual photo of her. Nothing special. But when I looked at it later, something stopped me cold. Her fingers weren't normal—they looked like **claws**. Long. Sharp. Distorted. Not a camera glitch. Not a lighting issue. *Actual claws.* It was the first time something dark came through digitally—and it felt like a warning.

I showed Franco at the gym. His face went pale.

"Bro," he said, "that's not normal."

I tried laughing it off. "Maybe it's weird lighting."

He wasn't smiling.

"Matt, that is not weird lighting. She's possessed. I know it sounds crazy, but it's real. It happens."

Franco wasn't a conspiracy guy. Definitely not a church guy. But he recognized something dark, something real.

"I had a similar experience," he admitted quietly." That's why I quit using. You need Christ, man. She'll get you killed."

It was the first time anyone said it outright—not just that she was dangerous, but that something else was working through her. He gave me a prayer to say at night.

Psalm 27:1-3 (ESV)

"The Lord is my light and my salvation; whom shall I fear?
The Lord is the stronghold of my life; of whom shall I be afraid?
When evildoers assail me to eat up my flesh, my adversaries and foes,
it is they who stumble and fall.
Though an army encamp against me, my heart shall not fear;
though war arise against me, yet I will be confident."

I ended the relationship. I told her that I needed space. The drunken messages at all hours of the night started coming in. I had to block her.

Then came the final straw.

Two months later, at 3 a.m., I'm stark naked—no AC, don't judge—when I hear someone breaking into my place. I dial 911, grab a blanket, and shut the bedroom door. A few minutes pass.

Footsteps approaching.

When I step into the hall, a cop stands there, gun drawn, shouting, "Raise your hands!" I comply, blanket dropping.

Nothing screams *"life on track"* like debating property rights with a Glock aimed at your chest while your undercarriage catches a draft.

The cop exhaled sharply: *"I nearly shot you!"* Outside, the same woman Franco said would get me killed is telling the cops she lived with me.

She goes to jail, calling me from behind bars: *"How can you do this to me, Matthew? I'm a total catch!"*

Rock bottom has a basement. That basement has a basement, furnished wall-to-wall with your worst decisions.

These were the brutal post rehab lessons that helped build The Blueprint. Rehab advice alone wasn't enough—I needed spiritual weapons to battle an enemy equipped with **devastating artillery.**

The enemy doesn't care about progress or plans. He waits until you're tired, alone, **vulnerable.**

Every disaster sharpened my vision, each scar mapped a clearer path. God was using my ignorance to shape the lessons that would one day save others. First, I had to survive long enough to learn.

> **RED FLAG MOMENT:** If you don't recognize the shift, you'll trade one form of self-destruction for another. Getting rid of the bottle doesn't mean you're free. The void will tempt you to find something new to fill it with—unless you fill it first.

Back to Building The Blueprint

The wake of the break-in settles, but I can't sleep.

I stare at the ceiling fan spinning endlessly.

It's hot. Sticky. **Uncomfortable.**

What am I doing with my life? I nearly died again—without a single drink. Sobriety alone clearly isn't enough. Evil is real; it's out there waiting. This feels like my first night at Cornerstone, minus the legal consequences. And for what? Cheap sex? Validation? I don't even care about these women. They're using me, and I'm using them.

I have to stop.

I'm a liar—a fraud.

I stare into the void again and finally see it clearly—I'm still finding new ways to destroy myself. The void never vanished. It switched masks, like putting lipstick on a piranha.

Tom's words from Cornerstone take over:

When I got sober, I thought I'd never find love. I spent months alone, to make sure I was good without anyone. And then it happened. I met the love of my life. And it'll happen for you too—when you least expect it.

Tom—the guy who spent nine years behind bars for something he couldn't even remember, a blackout crime—his words still guiding me, years after rehab.

It becomes clear to me that I have to get back to my roots of change.

Face the void: I'm terrified of being alone. Inventory reality: These relationships are addictions in disguise. Audit my circle: Every swipe right is **another step backward.**

Women have always been my gateway drug—the first domino before the collapse: emotional attachment, drinking, self-destruction. The pattern is always the same. The first hit's free; then you're chasing the high straight to your own funeral, without salvation in sight.

I throw myself into training clients.

I am done with women. For a while, anyway.

Delete. Delete.

DELETE.

Reflection

I'm sitting at my desk now writing this, years removed from that night revealing claws in that digital photo, my hands steady on the keyboard though my spirit still trembles at the memory. With time and spiritual maturity, I understand something I couldn't possibly comprehend then: What transpired wasn't merely a dangerous relationship or another self-destructive choice in a long catalog of poor decisions. It was spiritual warfare made momentarily, terrifyingly visible.

That photograph captured a rare instant when the veil between worlds—between what we can see and what truly exists—grew thin enough for me to glimpse what had been working against me all along. The enemy rarely shows himself so plainly. He operates in shadows, preferring subtlety and deception, the patient poisoning of your perception until the line between truth and lies blurs beyond recognition. But occasionally, when he grows confident in his grip on a soul, he becomes careless. Arrogant. He reveals himself, believing his victory so certain that concealment no longer matters. You may even grow to prefer it.

Looking back with spiritual eyes now opened, I understand with chilling clarity what Jesus meant in **Luke 11:24-26,** *"When an unclean spirit leaves someone, it wanders through waterless places seeking rest. Finding none, it returns to the place it left. If it finds that house swept clean but empty—it brings seven spirits more wicked than itself."*

My hard-fought sobriety had indeed swept my house clean. I'd removed the alcohol, purged the drugs, and abandoned the self-destructive behaviors that had nearly killed me. But—and here was my fatal miscalculation—I hadn't filled that newly emptied space with Christ. I was still running from loneliness with desperate energy, still avoiding the cavernous space inside my soul that screamed for meaning, purpose, and connection. The demon's strategic decision to return to the place it left suggests that it recognized me—a previously inhabited person—as a potential stronghold once again. My weakness. Women. It knew me so well. The house had been *"swept and put in order,"* temporarily improved, but critically, it remained empty. This symbolizes someone who has experienced momentary moral improvement or partial deliverance but has not been filled with the Holy Spirit—the only genuine protection against darkness.

Mere self-improvement, I learned the hard way, is catastrophically insufficient. My efforts at external righteousness, divorced from true transformation through Christ, left me more vulnerable to deception and bondage than before. This perfectly aligns with Peter's warning in **(2 Peter 2:20)**, where those who escape corruption through moral reformation only to fall back into it find themselves in a state worse than their original condition. This is why you hear the term addiction is a progressive disease. It only gets worse.

While Scripture clearly affirms the reality of demonic possession, it also indicates that unclean spirits can exert influence across a spectrum of degrees. A person who has not truly received Christ—who is spiritually empty, even if they appear outwardly reformed—might not necessarily be fully possessed, but they become increasingly exposed to deeper forms of deception and influence when not actively rooted in Christ and filled with The Spirit.

When the unclean spirit returns, it brings *"seven other spirits more evil than itself"* **(Luke 11:26)**. How frightening is that reality? This deliberate escalation carries profound significance:

The Symbolism of Seven: In biblical numerology, seven represents completeness or fullness. The presence of seven additional spirits signifies not just partial influence but complete domination by evil—a total invasion.

Degrees of Wickedness in the Spiritual Realm: Jesus explicitly states that these spirits are *"more wicked"* than the first, revealing a sobering truth: there exists a hierarchy of malevolence within demonic realms, with some entities possessing greater capacity for destruction than others.

This passage illuminates the uncomfortable reality that spiritual forces actively and strategically seek influence over people. This isn't paranoia or superstition—it's the clear teaching of Scripture. Vigilance and consistent spiritual discipline—immersion in prayer, Scripture, and authentic fellowship—aren't optional extras but crucial defenses against these forces **(Ephesians 6:10-18)**.

True spiritual regeneration stands in stark contrast to mere moralism. Many people, myself included, can temporarily clean up their external lives yet remain spiritually vacant if they do not embrace Christ completely. Only through genuine faith and living union with Jesus can one be truly secure from the powers of darkness **(Colossians 1:13)**. A cleaned house requires a new occupant—the Holy Spirit—or it remains vulnerable to reoccupation.

This woman I'd become entangled with wasn't inherently evil herself—she was a vessel. A conduit. Something darker was working through her, exactly as Franco had recognized instantly upon seeing the photo. Franco possessed a spiritual sensitivity forged in the fires of his own battles with addiction. His suffering had given him eyes to recognize darkness when it manifested. Some truths you can only discern after you've personally faced their terrible reality.

The claws visible in that photograph weren't a technical glitch or peculiar lighting effect as my rational mind desperately wanted to believe. They represented a momentary glimpse into spiritual reality—that brief, terrifying instant when the physical world and the dark realm aligned with perfect transparency. A flash of the enemy's true nature bleeding through the carefully maintained human mask.

The break-in wasn't merely a disturbed woman's obsession or the actions of someone mentally unwell. It represented the culmination of a calculated spiritual attack designed to destroy me completely. The enemy didn't just want my sobriety—he wanted my life extinguished, my testimony silenced, my redemption story eliminated before it could be written and shared with others who might find hope through it.

Why am I certain of this interpretation now? Because the timing was too perfect, the escalation too rapid, the danger too precisely calibrated. The enemy typically strikes hardest when you're making genuine spiritual progress, when you're vulnerable yet moving toward God. When you're swept clean but not yet filled completely with the Holy Spirit—that transitional space between old and new creation represents a threat, and he doubles down on you. This also happens when you are initially baptized. **Possession ends the moment Jesus takes residence.** Once you are sealed by the Holy Spirit, the enemy loses his claim to inhabit.

Ephesians 1:13 says, *"Having believed, you were marked in Him with a seal—the promised Holy Spirit."*

The enemy may still knock. He may still whisper. But he no longer owns the house.

I see now with painful clarity that we don't merely battle flesh and blood—other humans with their own wounds and agendas. We battle principalities and powers, rulers of darkness operating in high places beyond our physical sight. The enemy is real, and he hunts with strategies most of us can't recognize until we've been caught in his jaws at least once, if we are lucky enough to survive, bearing the scars of the encounter. Make no mistake—the enemy's ultimate goal is **death.**

That night fundamentally changed me. It wasn't Franco's warning or the terrifying break-in that altered my trajectory. It was the bone-deep realization that I was fighting something infinitely bigger than myself, and I could never win this battle alone. I needed weapons I didn't yet possess. I needed protection beyond my own resources. I needed God—not as a concept or a comfort, but as a living, active presence filling every empty space within me.

Perhaps you're reading this and thinking I've completely lost my mind. That's entirely fair. Before that night, I would have thought the exact same thing about someone sharing such a story. But I ask you to consider this: What if the most dangerous, most effective lie the enemy has ever told is that he doesn't exist at all? What if our modern dismissal of spiritual warfare isn't enlightenment but blindness—making us easy targets?

The enemy is undeniably real. But so is God and he is infinitely more powerful. So is redemption. So is the transformative power to fill that empty house with something the darkness cannot touch, cannot overcome, cannot withstand.

I share this story not to scare you needlessly, but to prepare you for battles you may not yet recognize. The enemy doesn't announce himself with dramatic music or obvious warning signs. Throughout this book, I've explained that he comes disguised in forms so familiar we welcome them without question. Often, he appears as the very human desire you most desperately seek to fulfill—validation when you feel worthless, companionship when you're lonely, escape when your reality feels unbearable. He studies your unique weaknesses with calculating patience, identifies your particular blind spots, catalogs your specific addictions.

And he waits—sometimes years—for the perfect moment to make an offer that appears not only safe but necessary for your happiness.

But here's the truth I now know with absolute, unshakable certainty: *"Greater is He that is in you than he that is in the world"* **(1 John 4:4).** This isn't merely a comforting verse; it's a declaration of spiritual reality.

The enemy is powerful, but he is not all-powerful. He's clever, but he is not all-knowing. He can attack with frightening precision, but he cannot ultimately claim what rightfully belongs to God. His authority is limited, his defeat already assured, his time running out.

I wasn't remotely ready for that battle then. I lacked the weapons, the knowledge, the faith, the spiritual maturity to recognize what was happening, let alone effectively counter it. But God protected me anyway, using Franco—another broken believer who had battled his own darkness—to sound the alarm I desperately needed to hear. He sent the warning through an unlikely messenger, proving once again that He can and will use anyone, anything, to reach those He loves.

The photograph with the claws has been deliberately deleted, permanently erased from digital existence. I have no need or desire to see it again. Some glimpses behind the veil separating our physical reality from spiritual truth are enough to last a lifetime. Today, my house isn't just swept clean—it's filled with something stronger than myself, something eternal rather than temporal. **Let me say this plainly: If you belong to Christ, you cannot be possessed by darkness.** You can be tempted. You can be attacked. You can even be tormented. But you cannot be taken. The enemy can't break into a house that's already occupied by the King.

Yet I harbor no illusions that the battle has ended; spiritual warfare doesn't cease this side of heaven. Every day requires vigilance, surrender, and a conscious choice to let the Holy Spirit fill what the darkness once occupied with such destructive efficiency.

The enemy still prowls, still seeks, still waits for moments of weakness or pride. But now I recognize his tactics, sense his approach, understand his limitations. And most importantly, I know with certainty who holds ultimate victory. It isn't me. It was never meant to be me. It is and always will be Christ alone, working through vessels willing to be both broken and filled.

Consider this carefully: What occupies your spiritual house right now? Is it empty, swept clean by mere self-improvement, or truly filled with the presence of God?

The Divine Setup

Months go by. I keep my head down and focus on work. That scar on my forehead—still puffy, still pink—gnaws at me. I want to fix it. Not out of vanity. Not really.

In 2018, four years sober, I finally walked into the Med Spa I'd ridden my bike past a hundred times. The place smells like eucalyptus and essential oils and everything I'm not. I'm just here for a fix—a simple scar revision. But God is playing chess while I'm still learning checkers.

That's the thing about divine love: It arrives disguised as coincidence. As ordinary moments that **rewrite your entire story.**

Amber didn't pay attention to me that day. Her friend sure did. Later, Amber admits her friend had dragged her from her workstation to glance at me waiting in the lobby.

"That guy?" Amber said, unimpressed. "He looks like a Viking. Nice man bun—not my type."

My beard is massive, my hair even longer—I barely resemble the man I once was.

But her friend, curious, tracks me down on social media anyway and shows Amber my profile. Amber scrolls to a photo of me clean-shaven, and something shifts.

"Okay," Amber says. "That's attractive."

Preparation for Something Greater

Amber has her own reasons for avoiding men, online dating, and empty validation. Like me, she's ready to file online dating permanently under "Not Worth the Trouble." After her own hellish experiences, she's done. Finished. Closed for business.

Yet Amber has an idea: "Why don't we train with him? He's probably affordable since he's a new trainer."

It's pure logic—two women simply looking to get fit. Neither of us knows this practical choice would crack open our entire universe. God works like that: using ordinary, practical moments to pull us into something extraordinary.

Meanwhile, Amber's friend's interest in me grows. Life is about to get complicated, because here's the thing about God's plan—the road to what's right sometimes winds through roads that are wrong.

Free will isn't a loophole; it's the whole point. Without it, how could we ever truly be free? Looking back, I realize God isn't watching me. He is preparing me.

Every bike ride, every early-morning inspection, every lonely night—it was spiritual boot camp. I'm learning:

- **Peace in solitude,** instead of chasing chaos in company.
- **Boundaries,** to keep toxic people at bay.
- **Dignity** in rebuilding from nothing, riding a bike after driving cars I couldn't afford.
- **Calm under pressure,** when probation officers show up at 5 a.m.
- **Strength** to cut off people threatening my new life, without looking back.

These lessons aren't just for me. God isn't wasting my pain—He's teaching me to help someone else heal.

The divorce battle? It taught me how to handle a narcissist without losing myself. *(That would matter later.)*

The financial struggle? It showed me how to rebuild from nothing. *(That would matter later.)*

The quiet days? They forced me to sit with pain, trust God's timing, and become someone whole—alone. *(That would matter most of all.)*

Meeting Amber

Amber reaches out on Instagram. Two young kids, stunningly beautiful, and appears single (not that I'm looking). She asks about my rates for training her and her friend.

Something makes me hesitate. Is God pulling back on my reins?

When she sends a follow-up message—a simple "?"—I finally reply, offering a massively discounted rate. Later, I learned it was exactly what they could afford from their tips.

Corner Bakery. Next morning. It's the first time I see her face-to-face.

Let me tell you something about love at first sight—it's not a Hollywood movie moment. It's confusing. I left not knowing what had happened to me. My heart, hardened to love, cracked open a little. I didn't want it. So I tried to pretend it didn't happen.

I can't stop thinking about:

The way her feet move under the table. The curve of her neck when she laughs. How she curls her lip moments before laughing.

Everything about Amber radiates something I'm not used to... Authenticity.

Stop!

Keep it professional. Have to. Must not go there.

My discipline sessions taught me this lesson: **Boundaries matter.**

But God is writing a different story because Amber isn't chaos in cheap heels—she's grace in running shoes. For the first time, I want something deeper than a quick fix.

I ignore it. Convince myself she isn't my type. Too conservative compared to the women I usually prefer. Besides, I have sworn off women altogether.

Her friend—the one showing more interest—doesn't stir anything in me. I firmly tell myself I'm not interested in either of them.

Nope. Done with women.

Period.

The Training Begins

We strike a deal. The hard work is underway.

Amber is **hyper-focused, disciplined, and coachable.**

She listens, asks thoughtful questions, and pushes herself harder than most of the clients I train.

Her friend? Less so. She's distracted—more interested in me stretching her than conditioning.

Amber, though? She doesn't complain. Doesn't fish for attention. She simply shows up without makeup, hair in a bun, and does the work.

That catches my attention.

The first week is **strictly business.**

Form corrections. Adjusting their squat depth. Teaching them how to build strength without getting injured. **The normal routine.**

Amber and I communicate about workout times and how **both of them** are feeling after the workouts.

> *Amber: I dropped a pen at work and stared at it on the ground. I looked at my friend and said it's just going to have to live there. I'm that sore. Your workouts are brutal. But I need that.*

I keep it professional, the same as I would with any other client.

> *Matt: Make sure to stretch and roll your legs out with a foam roller. You need to be vigilant about taking care of yourself when you are first getting back into shape. I do not want you getting injured.*

Sure, I can look at Amber and acknowledge **her beauty.** I play it cool.

There is nothing inappropriate. Nothing beyond professional. But every now and then—for a second—our eyes connect, and I laugh under my breath. Maybe at the absurdity of it. Maybe because some part of me already knows **this is different.**

For weeks, we train. No lines crossed.

No **flirting.**

Just focused work.

The Shift

After several sessions, Amber and I decided to meet again, strictly to discuss **future training plans.**

At least, that's what we told ourselves.

That's the lie we both needed to believe. What started as a work meeting evolved into **something else.**

The dinner we ended up having was **spur-of-the-moment**, but let's call it what it was: **a date.** And not just any date.

July 9th, 2018.

The anniversary of my accident. My sobriety date.

Four years clean to the day.

Want to see how God moves?

He doesn't just **open doors**—He orchestrates coincidences that would make Hollywood blush.

Amber picked a restaurant directly across the street from my old recovery center—the exact spot where everything changed. Carl Jung called these moments *synchronicities*—meaningful coincidences with no apparent cause.

Before dinner, I sit in my car staring at Cornerstone's front doors. Those fluorescent lights still buzz inside, casting that sickly institutional glow I remember too well. That place stripped me down to nothing so I could start over. I don't know what tonight will bring, but I know one thing: without Cornerstone, I wouldn't be here. Grace has a strange way of circling back.

I've said the Lord's Prayer hundreds of times, but tonight it hits differently. God seems to be directing me: *Real connection starts with real honesty. No filters. No performance. Truth—raw and bleeding.*

I drive across the street to meet Amber at Shabu Shabu, a contemporary Japanese restaurant alive with the hum of conversations and the savory aroma of simmering hot pots. She confidently orders beef with veggies, clearly familiar with what she wants. There's an awkwardness between us—both pretending this is strictly professional. But beneath the polite fiction, we feel something else pressing against our **walls built of fear.**

I clear my throat, glancing out the window. "Funny story—I came from across the street. See that building there? That's Cornerstone. Spent five months of my life in that place. Well, not living there exactly—I was in a sober home around the corner. Actually, I lived a couple blocks from here."

Her eyes soften, curiosity peeking through. "Really? How long ago was that?"

"Exactly four years today," I say quietly. "July 9th, 2014. Today's my sobriety date."

Amber's eyes widen, startled. "Wait. Today's your anniversary, and I picked a restaurant across the street from your rehab?"

I chuckle, nodding. "I drove by before coming here, stared at the entrance, remembering what a mess I was... weird coincidence, right?"

She studies my face carefully. "What was it like—being there?"

I lean in slightly, not because it's a secret, but because it feels sacred. "I got into a horrible accident, flipped my car six times. Charged with felony DUI, great bodily injury—the works. Had a near-death experience. Rehab wasn't optional; it was life or death. And I took it seriously. I never did jail time—I was fortunate. When they took my license, I didn't touch a steering wheel, didn't break a single rule. Showed up to every meeting, every probation appointment. Changed me completely."

Amber listens intently. "That had to be rough."

"Absolutely brutal," I admit. "But necessary. Our house manager, Rubin—a hardcore dude, old-school reformed gangbanger—called me out every single day. Told me to quit showing up halfway to my own life. No more hiding, no more performing. Just honesty." I pause, grinning. "I also learned the art of properly cleaning a bathroom toilet."

She laughs lightly, eyes thoughtful. "Funny how honesty's the hardest thing, isn't it?"

I nod slowly, feeling the weight of her words. "Yeah. Isn't that the truth. What's your story?"

Amber hesitates briefly, then lays it out plainly. "Separated, but still married. My ex won't pay for the divorce, and I can't afford it. It's his way of controlling me. He can't let go. He's manipulative, volatile—dangerous. I've spent years clawing back my independence one painful inch at a time."

"I know that fight," I say quietly, recognizing myself in her words.

She glances toward Cornerstone again, shaking her head slightly. "You know, that place almost became part of my story too. My ex was offered a spot there. Turned it down, said it was 'too ghetto.' Went to some luxury rehab in Arizona instead to pet horses."

I laugh, shaking my head. "Guess I went to the 'ghetto' rehab then."

She grins, eyes warm toward me. "Yeah, but it worked for you. That fascinates me."

"Why?"

Her gaze deepens, intense yet gentle. "Because you're proof that change is possible—you just have to man up and do the work. Real work."

Another cosmic connection. God's signature scrawled boldly across our stories.

My heart quickens at her words, sincerity cutting through the last threads of awkwardness between us. "Thanks for telling me that."

The conversation gradually shifts into lighter territory, our laughter becoming natural, the space between us relaxed. When dinner ends, we step outside into the warm July night, humor shielding the connection we've just forged.

"Just to clarify," Amber teases gently, "this was not a date."

I chuckle softly, playing along. "Absolutely. Strictly professional."

We exchange a brief, slightly awkward hug—one that says everything and nothing at all—and part ways, each of us walking back into our separate worlds.

By the end of the night, I feel something unexpected: seen. Not the recovering addict. Just... me. We'd both shared parts of ourselves we normally kept buried. Battle scars exposed to fresh air.

Driving home, her words replay vividly in my head. Her openness isn't something I'm used to. I don't fully understand what tonight means yet, but for the first time, I don't need to.

I glance out my window, and at that very moment—as if punctuating the night's magic—green parrots streak across the evening sky, swooping gracefully into a massive tree in good ol' Santa Ana.

My mind flashes to a memory...

Quicksilver

I'm twenty-one years old, on a flight back home, feeling heartbroken. Plotting the perfect way to win someone back, rehearsing heartbreak monologues and poetic apologies as if I was auditioning for a part. An elderly woman watched me from the next seat, my desperation **radiating.**

I told her my sob story.

She leaned over, her silver hair catching the light, and dropped a truth bomb I wouldn't understand for decades:

"Love," she said, *"is like quicksilver in the palm of your hand. If you try to squeeze it, if you try to control it, you'll find it slips through your fingers and scatters everywhere. But if you let it rest there, if you let it be what it is, it stays."*

Back then, I was too young and too wrapped up in my own pain to get it. But now, thinking about Amber, it hit different.

Quicksilver—mercury—is liquid metal. Maintains its form while remaining completely fluid. If you try to control it—**it slips away.**

Life works the same way. The more you force outcomes, the more everything scatters. The tighter your grip, the more you lose what you're trying to hold onto. **Control is an illusion.**

That stranger on the plane wasn't giving me relationship advice. She was teaching me a universal principle: Some things in life can only be held with an open hand. And now, I was starting to understand it.

Back at home, I didn't overanalyze the night. I let it be what it was. Real connection doesn't need to be forced.

I laid my head against my pillow and closed my eyes.

Then, my phone buzzed. A message from Amber.

Her tone was completely different—playful, teasing—nothing like the testimony energy from earlier. I couldn't stop grinning. Sometimes, when you stop chasing, the things meant for you find their way into your life. That dinner felt strictly professional. Amber hadn't given any sign she was interested beyond our training arrangement.

This is the exact conversation. I still have it saved today.

> **Amber:**
> *Your story moved me.*
>
> **Matt:**
> *Thought I kept it too real.*
>
> **Amber:**
> *No way. Honesty is sexy.*
>
> **Matt:**
> *Good to know I didn't overshare.*
>
> **Amber:**
> *You did. And I liked it.*
>
> **Matt:**
> *I am your trainer, remember.*
>
> **Amber:**
> *Yes, sir. Am I out of line?*
>
> **Matt:**
> *Are you crossing the line?*
>
> **Amber:**
> *Am I in trouble?*

She flipped the switch—professional to playful, formal to flirtatious. The switch I didn't want to touch had been fully turned on.

When you want to find love, **don't look for it**. When you stop looking, love finds you. Amber and I kept flirting on Instagram, and I was instantly into her. It wasn't only her beauty—it was her sense of humor. Everything about her drew me in. By divine coincidence, the next day was her day off. Neither of us had our kids that week.

I asked if she wanted to come over and go to the beach. No pressure.

No expectations.

> **Matt:**
> *Would you like to come over tomorrow? Lay out on the beach?*
>
> **Amber:**
> *Yes.*

She said yes.
A simple

> "Yes," then "Goodnight."

Her response lingered in my inbox. I stared at it for a beat.

Yes.

I hadn't felt this way before.

This was new.

Everything Changes

The moment Amber steps into my apartment, **the air changes—like the moment before a thunderstorm.**

This isn't rudimentary chemistry. This isn't the plastic, manufactured connection I've **learned to fake.**

This is real. Raw. **DANGEROUS.**

We lock eyes.

Words die in my throat. Everything I've learned about control, about playing it cool, about protecting myself, it all evaporates when she looks at me. At this moment, every fear, every doubt we've both harbored about love is no longer. It isn't planned; it isn't calculated. It just is.

"I can't take it anymore," the words burst out, a **dam finally breaking.** I pull her close. And when our lips meet, it isn't simply a kiss—**the world disappears.**

Time blurs. We stay in after our beach trip, caught up in a whirlwind of connection. By the time she leaves that evening, I feel an unfamiliar sense of bliss—an emotion I'd never truly known before.

Settling into my usual solitude, I turn on the TV, but it's impossible to focus. My mind keeps circling back to her—her laugh, her smile, the way she looks at me. She's supposed to be at a friend's boating party, but not long after she leaves, I get a text:

>Can I come back?

I can't respond fast enough.

>***YES!***

CHAPTER 10

The Real Gold

A Weekend That Changed Everything

The most important moments don't announce themselves. You don't see them coming. You don't plan them. They just happen—and suddenly everything is different.

An hour later, she's back, and it's as though she never left. That night, we talk, laugh, and exist together, the way two people do when the rest of the world fades away.

The next morning isn't awkward.
We stroll to get coffee, wandering sunlit streets, conversation easy, pressure-free. The day unfolds effortlessly, spilling into an unforgettable weekend.

I don't want it to end, so I buy tickets to The Orange County Fair. It hits all your senses at once—cotton-candy sweetness blending with greasy funnel cakes, flashing lights bleeding into the twilight, carnival barkers' voices competing with joyful screams overhead. We play rigged carnival games like carefree kids, me trying to win her some ridiculous stuffed animal, both of us knowing it's absurd but loving it anyway. We squeeze into a photo booth designed for teenagers, not adults with histories. Four flashes capture what words can't:

Flash—her laugh, uninhibited, flawless smile—my eyes, softer than they've been in years, fixed on the camera. *Flash*—a kiss, nothing performed, nothing restrained. *Flash*—our goofy faces conspire together. The strip prints, still warm.

I watch her tuck it into her purse with **reverent care.**

"Would you mind if I had a glass of wine?" she asks, voice careful, eyes searching mine for discomfort.

"Not at all," I answer truthfully. Four years sober has taught me this: other people's choices aren't my downfall. My demons don't live in liquor glasses anymore.

What I don't yet know—what the universe mercifully conceals for now—is that alcohol was the scaffolding of her previous marriage. The liquid foundation—that once removed, revealed no love beneath. There's a graveyard of revelations waiting for us, bones we'll unearth together, piece by piece.

The next weeks blur into beautiful inevitability. Our lives interlock with mathematical precision. Even our custody schedules align in ways that defy probability—divine architecture creating uninterrupted stretches where we can exist without outside claims on our time. God doesn't speak to me directly, not yet, but His fingerprints mark these perfect alignments too precisely to call them coincidence.

I vividly remember the anxiety the first time Amber met my kids. I've seen relationships shatter on these rocks, fragile moments where new beginnings falter. But Amber walks in with quiet confidence, natural grace easing the tension. My daughter immediately opens up, chatting comfortably. My son remains cordial but distant—his Xbox calling louder than conversation.

Meeting her children flips the script. Her four-year-old daughter adopts me instantly, squealing at my terrible jokes. But her nine-year-old—that girl could weaponize a glare. Her eyes dissect me with surgical precision, finding me recoiling before I speak a single word. I recognize the look: *You're replacing my father.* I don't correct her misconception, don't compete, and don't push. I simply exist—consistent, until the day her glares soften to grudging tolerance, then dubious acceptance.

We'd both sworn off love, like recovering addicts swearing off their drug of choice. "I'm never getting married again," I'd declared when we first met, words heavy with past failures.
"Me neither, no chance," she'd shot back without **hesitation.**

But the way we looked at each other told a different story.

The words "Never getting married again" were our way of fighting the insatiable connection between us.

I remember thinking:

Her smile is the most magnificent sight I have ever laid my weary eyes upon. I know that if she was the last thing I see before I leave this world, I would die the happiest man that ever stumbled across a second chance.

Still, I can't tell her this. I'd sound certifiable. When you have never truly been in love, you simply can't form the words to do the emotion justice because words are not enough. Words are crisp and clear. This was spiritual and boundless—a language spoken not with sounds but with the silent recognition between two souls.

Another principle from recovery: When something's real, you don't need validation or permission to know it's true.

For the first time, I keep quiet about a relationship. No announcements, no social media updates, no polling friends and family like a desperate politician. Silence becomes another test—one I'm finally ready to pass. I knew that I was in love with her, but given my history with women, I was still cautious.

Here's another piece of The Blueprint: Other people's opinions are borrowed trouble. Even your parents or closest friends don't live inside your skin. They can't hear the whispers of your heart. If you're surveying people about your relationship, you're probably trying to convince yourself of something you know isn't working.

With Amber, everything moves at a different frequency. One evening, about a month in, she bursts out of the bathroom—a tornado of energy. Makeup brush in hand, one eye a masterpiece, the other beautifully bare.

"If you're seeing any other women or talking to anyone else," she blurts, *"I don't think I could handle it."*

I laugh—not at her vulnerability, but at the chaotic honesty of the moment, her standing there, half-glammed, half-natural, all truth.

"No," I say, matching her smile. *"I'm not seeing anyone else. In fact, I plan on making you mine."*

She smiles, relieved. The truth feels clean in my mouth. The dating apps have vanished from our phones like digital exorcisms. Endless Instagram scrolling and the hollow validations I once chased evaporated the moment she walked into my life. The void I'd spent years filling with chaos has quietly filled itself.

Building Something New

They say, "The Devil is in the details." In recovery, we learn that big changes start with small actions—making your bed, showing up on time, and doing what you say you'll do. Love works the same way.

One night, about six weeks into our relationship, I notice Amber's clothes scattered in the corner—not a mess, but it doesn't sit well with me. The sight tugs at something deep in my chest.

She enters the room, leaning down to pull a sweatshirt from her bag. Something about that image—her beauty amid temporary living—awakens a protective instinct in me.

"Hey," I say softly, "you can't keep living out of a bag on the floor."

She smiles sweetly, brushing it off. "It's no big deal. I'm just happy to be here with you."

She climbs into bed beside me, tugging playfully at my beard, checking its reality, making sure I'm real.

"This is the first time I've felt safe in years," she whispers, her voice carrying the weight of every past relationship that made her feel anything but safe.

"That's good," I say softly, holding her hand.

Her eyes soften, vulnerability surfacing. "Nobody ever opened doors for me, held my hand, or took charge. Dating was always halfsies—no real men, just boys looking for fun."

"Is that why you asked if I was seeing other women?"

She nods seriously. "Yeah. Those apps were a nightmare—hookup culture. It's gross. I had awful experiences."

I laugh lightly. "Trust me, I know. I almost died because of someone I met on a dating app."

Amber shifts, meeting my gaze directly. "But we agreed—we weren't supposed to get serious."

"I know," I chuckle gently. "But if we did, how would it work? Neither of us wants marriage again. We have insane exes and four kids between us."

She smiles playfully, cautiously hopeful. "Maybe we could live close and date exclusively."

"That might work," I say. "But no marriage."

Amber dramatically throws her hands up. "Please, no! I'm not even divorced yet—I never want to go through that again."

We laugh together, tension easing as our eyes drift back to her clothes piled on the floor.

That sight still tugs at something deep in my chest. The next day, I buy her a dresser. I spend hours assembling it, cursing at Swedish instructions, carefully ensuring each drawer slides smoothly.

When Amber arrives and sees it, joy lights up her face, making every smashed thumb worth it. She runs her fingers across the wooden surface, opening each drawer reverently. A dresser—six drawers, nothing fancy—but in that moment, it's everything. It symbolizes permanence in a life accustomed to temporary.

"For me?" she whispers softly, almost disbelieving.

"For you," I reply gently. "So you can stop living out of a bag."

Small things matter. Love lives in these little details. Quiet promises without words, the way I tell her every day:

You belong here. This isn't temporary. I see you.

That dresser wasn't just furniture—it was my first real commitment in years, not with words but with action. For Amber, those drawers weren't just for clothes—they were spaces carved out specifically for her, in a world that had been trying to erase her.

That's how we build our foundation, not with gifts or dramatic declarations, but with small acts of care. Each one a brick in something bigger than ourselves. **The small things matter.**

Falling

*"Love isn't about what you can take—it's about what you're willing to give, **no matter the cost.**"*

As that second month curves quietly into the third, something shifts beneath the surface of our lives. It's subtle, like sunrise unfolding in slow motion—you can't pinpoint exactly when night becomes day, but suddenly everything is bathed in new light. I used to tease Amber about the ninety-day rule: if a relationship survives ninety days, it might just stand a chance.

The walls we've carefully constructed—barriers built from lessons learned painfully, brick by brick—start to crumble. We're falling in love, though neither of us dares admit it—not yet, not even to ourselves.

But the truth has its own gravitational pull, drawing us closer. It's that tension, a silent current beneath our everyday conversations, an unspoken reality waiting to break free. Each interaction, each glance, fills us a little more, until it overflows. When you've sworn off love and marriage, when you've made declarations about never falling for this trap again, admitting you're in love feels as if you are committing **high treason** against yourself.

One night, Amber lies against my chest, her head finding that perfect spot where heartbeats align. The room is dark except for moonlight filtering through the blinds, the kind of quiet that makes every breath noticeable.

She breaks the silence softly, almost shyly.
"I like you," she whispers. "Like... a lot."

Laughter bubbles up from somewhere deep—pure joy wrapped in absurdity. We're grown adults, yet somehow, in this moment, we're teenagers navigating first love, aware of the danger yet irresistibly drawn toward it.

"I like you too," I reply, smiling into the darkness. "Like... a lot."

It becomes our inside joke, our gentle dance around the truth we're both afraid to acknowledge openly. Straight out of Dumb and Dumber, though Amber insists she didn't say it like Jim Carrey. (She wants you to know that.) Sometimes, the deepest truths wear comedic masks.

The Turning Point

That same night, sleep **refuses to come.**

The ceiling becomes a canvas replaying every moment leading up to this one—each laugh, each quiet evening, each glance holding secrets neither of us were ready to share until now. Amber shifts next to me—not the restless shifting of sleep, but something deeper. Her breathing is uneven. She's holding something back.

Say it.
That's what the air between us commands. The silence bristling with energy.
When truth needs to be spoken, it creates its own moment. You can fight it, try to control it, try to plan the perfect time—or you can surrender to it.

She sits up first. I follow.

Like we're being pulled by the same invisible thread.

She looks at me, eyes searching, testing the ground before stepping onto it.

She draws a slow breath, bravery gathering in her eyes. Her voice, when it finally emerges, is barely audible—but honest:

"I think I'm falling in love with you."

And without hesitation, without doubt, without fear I say—

"I'm already in love with you."

And there it is—the truth, clear as spring water, solid as stone. All our carefully constructed walls, all our adamant promises to ourselves about never risking this again, melt quietly away like morning frost in sunlight.

No fireworks. No soundtrack. No Instagram filter could capture the raw, simple honesty of this moment. Just two broken people, speaking truth into existence—like **God breathing life into dust.**

The Halloween Incident

I didn't realize how quickly that love would be tested. Sometimes, the most dangerous predators don't look like monsters. They look like mortgage brokers living with their moms. Wearing carefully crafted social masks.

At first, I didn't see it. But the signs were there. The way Amber's whole body would tense when her phone lit up with his name. The way her voice would shift—submissive, apologetic—a fraction of herself. Her eyes darting to the nearest exit, her fingers trembling as she fumbled to lower the TV volume. **Pure prey response.**

This wasn't the behavior of someone dealing with an ex. This was the behavior of someone who'd learned to fear for their life. His attempts to intimidate Amber weren't only controlling—they were dangerous. This wasn't basic toxic masculinity; this was calculated emotional abuse.

At first, I thought maybe there was something still there between them. I'd seen enough toxic relationships to recognize the patterns. But this wasn't love or even longing. This was pure terror—wrapped in a thousand-dollar monthly payment he used like a collar around her neck. Four months into our relationship, I'd had enough of him.

Usually, when her ex was due to drop off the girls, Amber got nervous. **Unsettled.** I'd make myself scarce—part of the unspoken dance we'd all been doing. But that day, sitting in the Circle at Orange, kids in costumes buzzing past, my coffee going cold, I had a moment of clarity:

I had spent years lifting, training, learning discipline. Not only physically—but mentally, spiritually. The man sitting here, drinking his coffee, wasn't the same man from three years ago.

I was living out something primal, something God hardwired into man's soul. Later, I'd come across John Eldredge's *Wild at Heart* and realize—this was it. Every man has three core desires: a battle to fight, an adventure to live, and a **beauty to rescue**.

And when he doesn't find them? He finds **addiction** instead.

A man without purpose doesn't merely wander—he self-destructs. A man without a mission doesn't merely get lost—he numbs himself to the pain. A man without something to fight for will find something to **escape into**.

For years, I had no battle. No adventure. No beauty to fight for.

Even though I wasn't fully connected with God yet, He had already been working. My simple prayers had been enough to give me the grace to learn. To grow.

Without purpose, addiction takes its place. Without resilience, weakness creeps in. Without something to fight for, men **destroy themselves.**

The pattern in my life had changed. And in that change, I found resolution. Confidence. And the woman worth fighting for.

What the heck am I doing? Why am I leaving my girlfriend's house for a man she is no longer with?

The desperation of hitting rock bottom pulled me into recovery—not wisdom, not health, and certainly not some grand epiphany about my life. Sometimes, God allows you to feel the weight of your own choices—not to paralyze you in fear, but to wake you up. And when you finally turn to Him, you realize fear is never meant to lead—faith is. But here's the truth they don't share in those early recovery meetings: true protection often means planting your feet and refusing to move, not with clenched fists or heated threats, but with the quiet, unwavering power of your presence. It's about becoming the immovable object in someone else's battle.

I drove back to Amber's place.

Her eyes went wide when I walked through the door.

"What are you doing?" she asked, startled.

"I'm not leaving," I said, my voice steady. "You're my girlfriend. I'm here."

The smile she gave me—I'll never forget it. A flash of confidence. The look of a woman realizing, for the first time, she doesn't have to **fight alone.**

Then he showed up.

And like clockwork, he **tried to come inside.** Stomp around. Assert his dominance. But Amber cut him off at the knees with three simple words:

"I have company."

And that was it.

He retreated, tail between his legs, huffing as he slammed his car door ferociously and drove away. Later that night, he sent this infamous text:

> *Tell your company to call me tomorrow on my lunch break and give me their number so I know it is them calling. Tell them to text me before they call.*

We laughed about it for **weeks**, mimicking his wannabe-tough-guy voice: *"Tell your company to call me!"*

But beneath the laughter, something darker lingered. A **cornered narcissist** is like a wounded animal—**unpredictable, desperate, and dangerous.** Every text, every demand was another attempt to maintain control as his grip slipped away.

And he wasn't **letting go.**

But now? **She had me.**

I found **my beauty to rescue.**

And for the first time, **she let herself be rescued.**

Our trust deepened.

Then, that night, **she told me everything.**

I knew Amber's past held **heartache and pain.**

But I wasn't prepared for how much it mirrored my own.

She sat across from me, voice steady, but I heard the weight behind every word.

She wasn't just telling a story—she was unraveling years of survival.

And as I listened, I realized:

This wasn't just trauma.

This was war.

This is the story she shared with me...

Toxic Control: The Carbon Monoxide Effect

> **RED FLAG MOMENT:** Toxic control is like **carbon monoxide**—odorless, invisible, and deadly. By the time you realize you're suffocating, **the damage is already done.** If you have to **shrink yourself** to survive, **you're already in danger.**

For Amber, the suffocation came **slowly**—years and two children deep.

The pattern emerged:

- He'd **fail**—at taxes, at bills, at **being a husband, a father, a man**—and she'd pick up the slack.
- Both alcoholics. He got hooked on **opiates**. They ended up **broke, living with his parents.**
- He'd spend his days in a **drug-induced haze**, while she worked, took care of the kids, and carried the weight of it all.

It wasn't **love**. It was survival.

She started losing time.

She'd wake up exhausted, not remembering if she'd even slept.

She'd drive the car just to get away.

She started forgetting little things—the date, what she'd eaten, why she was standing in a room.

Then the bigger things—like who she was anymore.

She knew she needed help. But help never came. And that's when she stopped caring if it did.

Until one night, survival became something **else.**

Amber snapped.

Amber's voice dropped. **The room narrowed.**

"The breaking point wasn't a slow descent. It was a cliff jump."

"It was sudden, violent, inescapable."

"One moment, I was functioning. Or at least pretending to."

"The next?"

"I collapsed in on myself. I went catatonic."

Like a dying star, crushed under the gravity of everything she had carried for too long.

Her body **rebelled.**
Her hands **trembled.**
Her vision **blurred.**
Her mind fractured like glass hit by a hammer—sharp edges, splintering reality, no way to put the pieces back together.

"I couldn't handle it anymore."

"His family. His voice. His control."

"The madness of it all."

"I was drowning in a sea of manipulation, and there was no land in sight."

And then—

The hospital walls swallowed her whole.

5150 hold.
Amber's voice tightened.

"They admitted to the psyche for a weekend. Somewhere in that sterile prison, a question clawed at my brain."

"Maybe I really am crazy."

"Maybe he was right."

"Maybe I deserve this."

Even when he wasn't there, his **voice slithered through her mind, tightening the noose.**

Inside that place, she made **a choice she is ashamed of.**
Not out of love.
Not out of logic.
Out of **desperation.**

She met someone.

Someone just as broken as she was. Someone just as dangerous as her husband. Someone who wasn't an escape—even if she thought it was.

It was **a different kind of trap.**

Because when you're bleeding, you don't notice if the hands reaching for you are clean—or covered in their own blood.

The **affair** wasn't about **love**—it was about **escape**.

Her voice shook for the first time.

"And when I got home and told him what I'd done..."

"I was ready for a fight. I thought this would finally end it."

"I thought he wouldn't want me anymore."

It changed things—but not in the way she'd imagined.

She **wasn't** ready for was **the gun**.

A loaded **9mm** to the chest.

Their **youngest child** in her arms.

Dragged to a **motel room** in the middle of the night, in the middle of seedy area, he made the message clear, she said: "He had the gun pressed against my chest. Our youngest daughter was in my arms."

"He told me—If you leave, you die."

"I don't remember breathing. I don't remember thinking. I remember being cold. The room, his voice, my skin. **Ice cold**."

"I want you to think about what you've done," he said. "If you call 911, you die. If you call anyone, you die. If you leave, you die! He ripped the baby out of my arms, then the door slammed shut, and I was alone."

Her cell **phone gone**—any way to call for help **stripped** from her.

This isn't some **Lifetime movie**—this is **how abused women die.**

The attorney we would later hire to help us deal with him, a former DA who'd handled violent crimes, told us: "Cases that start with a gun and a hotel room end with a body bag. You are very fortunate."

Amber was **not** supposed to make it out alive.

Amber's Quick Thinking

Trapped in that hotel room, she **knew** her life depended on her wits.

She tried to remember numbers. She didn't know who to call.
He made it clear that if she called 911 she was dead.

When he kicked the door back in hours later, survival instincts kicked in.

She **convinced him** she needed help.

"I told him I had a follow-up appointment at the hospital that morning and he needed to take me. I was so afraid it wouldn't work. He just stared at me."

She didn't beg. That wouldn't work. Begging would make him feel powerful. Instead, she broke—enough for him to believe it.

"I need help," she calmly said. "You're right. I need to fix myself. I can't believe I did this. Maybe they can help me at my appointment." His grip loosened. His posture shifted. Good. He wanted her broken. That's how she got him to take her to the clinic. That's how she got out.

At the clinic, Amber **mouthed the words** "Help me" to the woman admitting her.

He was **acting erratic** enough—**pacing behind her**—that the staff took the hint. They got her to safety, and when police arrived, they **found his gun.**

Smart enough to avoid a fully loaded weapons charge, he'd **unloaded it** before they showed up.

He was arrested on the spot. She had her **way out. Or did she?**

Child protective services got involved. Insisting she file a temporary restraining order. Guns and babies tend to do that. They tell her: *If you don't file, your kids will be taken away.*

The System's Failure

Here's where the **system fails women**:

His **attorney** for the gun charge sat her down and explained the dire situation she was in. More manipulation. He knew he had to convince her not to press charges. "You press charges, he can't work. No work means no support. No support means you're on your own. Is that what you want?"

Systems don't fail by accident. **They fail by design.**

These vultures prey on their victims when they are at their weakest.

The **same structure** that's supposed to **protect** becomes another **prison.**

Amber let him walk. Not out of **weakness,** but out of a toxic bond formed over years of abuse and a broken spirit.

She looked at me honestly and said:

"I was so emotionally broken I believed I couldn't survive with him. He told me over and over again that I wasn't smart enough to make money and that without him I'd be nothing."

No Safe Haven

Amber had nowhere to go.

No protection.

So she went to the **one place that should have been safe.**

Her father's house.

Except he wasn't a father.

Not in the way that mattered.

He knew what her husband had done to her.

Her father fed her alcohol and patronized her.

He didn't protect her. He didn't fight for her. He didn't make her feel like she had a home.

He was a man who had once pushed her to marry the man who had **kidnapped her.**

And when her ex started stalking her, calling at all hours, **terrorizing** everyone around her, her father did nothing.

Then came the **2 a.m. break-in.**

Amber woke to the sound of footsteps inside the house.

Her heart pounded.

For a split second, she thought she was dreaming.

Then the door creaked.

And there he was.

The same man who had **held a gun to her chest.**

The same man who had dragged her to a hotel room and promised her **death if she left.**

Her father caught him in the act.

Amber hid in the room.

What did he do? He went and got his daughter and said,

"You should go outside and talk with him. Try and work things out."

With a restraining order in place. Like Amber was a child who needed to be scolded—not a woman who had been kidnapped at gunpoint by a **psychopath.**

Like this was nothing more than a misunderstanding.

He should have thrown him out. Should have called the police. Should have dragged him into the street and handled business.

Instead?

He urged **his daughter** to make peace.

To **hear him out.**

Amber was utterly **ALONE.**

The Apartment That Wasn't a Home

A few weeks later, her husband came back to visit.

Her welcome was wearing thin at her father's house.

He was calm. Polite. The mask of reason pulled tight over his face.

"I honestly want to help. I've been terrible. The way I reacted."

"I'll never do that again."

"I'll get you your own place. I don't plan on staying there."

"You and the girls need stability."

She wanted to believe him. She needed to believe him.

So—she moved in.

A **tiny apartment in Orange.**

The very one I used to walk past every day in **recovery.**

He promised **he wouldn't stay.**

"I'll be at my parents' house," he said. "I'll help pay for it, but it's for you and the kids."

But liars don't change.

The second she moved in—and the temporary restraining order was lifted—so did he.

She clenched her jaw, eyes dark with memories. He wasn't going to hold up his end of the bargain. Healing wasn't an option. **He wanted her destruction.**

Psychological Torture

He didn't **hit** her.

It was **worse.**

It was the slow, methodical dismantling of her self-worth.

Day and night, he broke her down.

"Was he bigger than me?"

"Was he better?"

"Did you think about him when you were with me?"

"You're disgusting."

"No wonder nobody wants you."

"Your own father didn't even protect you."

She tried to ignore it.

But he never stopped. Never let up.

"They put me on five psychiatric medications. Five."

"It drove me mad. I didn't care about anything anymore. I couldn't feel anything. I was completely numb. I convinced myself my kids would be better off without me."

"And then, I decided to end it all."

"I wrote letters. I convinced myself there was no other way out. No way to escape him."

"The medication made it worse. The thoughts wouldn't stop."

"How could I crash the car in way that would end it?"

"How deep would I have to cut my wrists?"

"I landed on wanting something that would make me slip into a coma. Nothing messy."

"At least then, I'd go to sleep before I knew what was happening."

She **tried to pretend she was strong.**

But every woman who has **been through psychological abuse knows:**

It doesn't happen all at once.

It's slow.

It's a thousand little cuts— by the time you notice the bleeding, it's too late.

And then?

The voices become your own thoughts.

She looked in the mirror and **saw nothing.**

Not a mother.

Not a survivor.

Just a broken woman with no way out.

"I didn't want to die."

"I didn't want to exist like that anymore."

"I wrote goodbye letters."

And so?

She **made a plan.**

To **end it.**

To **disappear.**

The Darkest Night

Amber was dying. She wasn't metaphorically dying. She wasn't **"lost in depression"** or **"feeling hopeless."**
She was literally, biologically, on the verge of leaving this world. The hospital machines beeped in sterile rhythm, tracking the fading pulse of a woman who had nothing left.

The **overdose** had done its job.

Three days in a coma.
Her parents were told, "Say goodbye."

As her mom sat by her bed, the air thick with the weight of finality, Amber's ex—the man who had destroyed her, the father of her children, the person who claimed to **"love"** her—never showed up.

Not once.

Not to check on her.
Not to see if she lived or died.

She should've died. That's what the doctors said.
But **God had other plans.**

On the third day, **she woke up.**

Waking Up Angry

Her first emotion wasn't gratitude.
It wasn't relief.
It wasn't even fear.

It was **rage**.

Pure, unfiltered RAGE.

"Are you kidding me? I have to do this again?"

She didn't have a golden light moment.

She didn't want another chance. She wanted **out**.
Out of the 3 a.m. door kick-ins.
Out from under the vodka-stained breath in her face.
Out of the endless cycle of terror.

But God doesn't hand you miracles.
He doesn't wait for you to be ready.

If you are fortunate—He steps in when you're completely wrecked.
When you're absolutely broken.
When you're at the end of yourself.

And that's exactly where **she** was.
Where **I** was.
Where we both needed to be.

Broken. But alive.

Choosing to Live

*"The climb out of the darkness is painful, **but every step makes you stronger.**"*

Three days in a coma. Two more in a hospital bed. Within a week, she was back in that tiny apartment, listening to his footsteps in the hallway, waiting for the next 3 a.m. door explosion.

For weeks, she drifted in and out of survival mode, moving like a shadow through her own life.

The police had shown up again—another screaming match, another door left hanging off its hinges. Another night of explaining her actions and covering up the emotional wreckage. But no matter how many times the cops came, they always left with him still there, lurking like a crocodile she couldn't shake.

And she was left wondering.

Why am I still here?
Why did I have to keep fighting?
Why did life keep dragging me back into this same cycle?

Then, one night, she walked past her kids' bedroom.

She paused at their door, the soft rhythm of their breathing filling the room. They were asleep. Peaceful. Innocent. **Unaware.** Their tiny faces relaxed, untouched by the chaos that waited outside that door. Innocence so pure it made her chest ache.

And in that moment, something broke—and something stronger took its place.

Tearing up, she said,

"I stood in the hallway, watching them sleep. Their soft breathing. Their tiny hands curled into the blankets."

"I thought, somebody has to pull this together."

"Somebody had to fight for these kids."

"And I knew—it sure as heck wasn't going to be him."

The man who woke up walked straight to the freezer, pulled out a bottle of vodka, and took a shot before 7 a.m.

The man who would wake her up at 3 a.m., spiraling, demanding her attention, needing her to validate his brokenness. The man that cut her power at night to terrorize her and the kids.

The man who wasn't in this tiny, broken apartment for his kids—he was here because he had nowhere else to go. Because he wanted to make her pay for discarding him.

She looked at her children.

And that night, she made a choice.

To **live.**
To **fight.**
To pull herself out of this nightmare.

Escape

But that choice wasn't a magic switch.

She cut back on drinking. She started setting boundaries—flimsy at first, but growing stronger with each day. She stopped explaining herself, stopped justifying her existence to a man who couldn't see her worth if it was etched in stone.

Her voice dropped,

"He got even worse when I stopped paying attention to his insanity. I had to sleep in the car a lot."

And when he finally spiraled far enough to get a DUI he landed in rehab, Amber didn't celebrate.

She made a plan.

A plan to never go back. It was over.

But here's the thing about abusers—they don't leave because you've made up your mind. Even when they're out of the house, they still hover, a phantom weight on your chest. And even then, she tried to help him. Another classic move of the abused trying to fix their abuser, clinging to the hope that maybe, just maybe, he'd come back from rehab well enough to be a father, work, and help support his kids.

But he wasn't going to Cornerstone—the place where I'd scraped the bottom of my soul, where I'd faced my demons head-on.

No, that was **beneath him.**
He went to a place that massages your ego and avoids real work.

While I was sweating through withdrawals in a cold rehab house with Rubin, choking down the bitter taste of my own failures, he was sipping herbal tea between mindfulness sessions. I was staring down the abyss, clawing my way out one painful truth at a time. He was riding horses through the desert, pretending the sand under his boots could cover up the wreckage he left behind.

We both went to rehab—but only one of us faced the truth. I am grateful I finally chose humility.

I am grateful that he didn't pull it together because he gave me the greatest earthly partner a man could ask for.

When he finally got out, Amber waited to hear something—anything—that would suggest he'd changed. But his first words out of rehab?

"I can drink again someday."

He had become *"spiritually enlightened"* while he was there.

And that's when she knew.

There was no fixing him.

No **saving him.**

His family would not allow him to live with them, so she had to take him back in. He took the bed, but he didn't own her anymore. Every night on that couch—or worse, in her car again—was another silent promise to herself: *This ends soon.*

And then, one day, **it did.**

She played the long game. The lease had been in his name, but after a year of him barely paying attention—and countless police visits—the landlord was done. Even he wanted them separated. Amber saw the opening and took it.

She convinced the landlord to put the lease in her name. Waited until the ink was dry. Then, one day while he was out, she changed the locks. She said:

"Once the lease was finally in my name—while he was out—I changed the locks."

"I packed his belongings. Left them on the porch. Sent his mom a text."

It's over. Please have your son pick up his things off the porch.

There was nothing he could do. He moved back in with his parents. Again. A place he still lives today.

She wrapped up her wild story with an exhausted laugh. *"Honestly, it was like having three of the worst-behaved children ever move out,"* trying to make light of the years of hell she had endured.

I sat there listening, realizing that for the first time Amber wasn't just surviving—she was experiencing freedom in my protection.

I knew that feeling. Recovery had protected me while I healed.

Amber's story wasn't just about survival—it was about deliverance.

And for the first time in my life, I wasn't just witnessing redemption—I was part of it.

Reflection

Divine orchestration is real. Six and a half years have passed since those early days with Amber, and my feelings have only deepened with time. Tonight we'll go to dinner at our favorite local spot—a small taco shop. Nothing fancy. Just something we both enjoy. The warmth of a thick homemade corn tortilla with steak and cheese, the comfort of familiar faces who know our order before we speak—simple pleasures that would have been unimaginable to the man I was before recovery, frantically chasing validation in Los Angeles, one drink away from oblivion.

Looking back at those pivotal moments in our story, I'm struck by something that wasn't obvious to me then: how precisely God had been orchestrating our lives, even when we thought we were lost. After she told me her heart-wrenching story, our bond strengthened in ways human words can't fully explain. We weren't drawn to each other—we were being divinely aligned.

Amber and I used to joke that Los Angeles is the biggest small town in America. As we shared our past, something remarkable emerged—our paths had crossed countless times over the years without meeting. During my early years in Beverly Hills, chasing empty dreams, Amber was there.

You have to understand the vastness of Los Angeles—eighteen million people spread across an urban sprawl where twenty miles can mean a ninety-minute commute. Amber lived twenty miles from me, but she was working to become a makeup artist. So there she was, her perfectly made-up face behind the makeup counter at the Century City Mall—a few blocks from my first apartment—while I walked past, the smell of espresso mixing with cologne. Both of us at the same coffee shop on Camden Drive, her by the window at noon, me walking past her at lunch. Even at Saddle Ranch on Sunset Boulevard—same nights, same bars, same broken dreams.

The connection—missed.

Or was it?

Twelve years later, geography itself became God's paintbrush again. I had moved from the heart of Los Angeles all the way down to Long Beach and then ended up in the city of Orange for rehab—many, many miles away from where I originally started in LA. There I was on my knees, detoxing in a sterile white room with strangers who barely knew my name. And Amber? She was a few blocks away, fighting her own battles behind different walls. I walked past her apartment daily, the same sidewalk beneath my feet that led to her door, neither of us aware how close we truly were.

Connection missed.

God's timing has teeth—sharp, purposeful, unyielding. It tears through our plans to reveal what was meant to be, patient until we finally listen.

When I left rehab, I moved nine miles away to Seal Beach. In a metropolis of millions, moving nine miles away from a location typically means you'll never cross paths with people in the previous area again. The odds of reconnection become astronomical. And yet—Amber took a job less than one mile from my apartment in Naples—a job she didn't even want and to this day and still cannot explain why she accepted. For an entire year, I rode my bike past that small, obscure business tucked away on the second floor in a row of storefronts. Not by choice or coincidence, but because it was literally the only route possible. Naples is an island—a half-mile strip connected by two bridges. One way in and one way out. To get from my apartment to downtown Long Beach, where I was working out, I had no other option but to ride through Naples. There was no alternative path, no other way. Every single day, divine orchestration forced me through the exact spot where she would eventually be.

Coincidence? In a city that vast, with millions of people?

No chance.

Looking back, I now see clearly what I couldn't then—divine timing rarely makes sense when you're living it.

The question that haunted me after surviving the crash was simple: Why? Why am I still here? Why on God's green earth am I still breathing?

Good people die every day. People who checked their mirrors and wore their seatbelts and didn't eat cocaine straight from a cupholder. People who deserved second chances far more than I did. But I'm still here.

Science calls it probability. Random chance—the perfect angle, speed, and give in the metal.

But that doesn't explain the light. That doesn't explain the choice I was given. That doesn't explain why, out of all the addicts, all the crashes, all the neck breaks and near misses, I got a second shot.

Here's what they don't tell you about surviving: it haunts you.

Not with guilt—

But with purpose.

Every breath feels borrowed, every heartbeat counting down.

The atheist in me back then wanted to call it luck. The addict in me wanted to call it happenstance. But something deeper—something I had buried under years of chemicals and pain—knew better.

When you've seen the light, when you've been offered the choice between staying and going, when you've felt that golden warmth wrap around your soul like a mother's embrace—you know. You know it wasn't by chance. You know it wasn't luck. You know you were kept alive for a reason.

I wasn't lucky. I was chosen.

Her ex thought he could separate us. He tried to use his thousand-dollar monthly payment like a leash, he sneered, *"No one will ever want you with two kids and you're over thirty. You need me."*

He removed his support from her and his kids when he found out we were dating. This event forced us to make a choice, and living in two separate apartments in California was far more costly than working together under one roof. I didn't see it as a burden. I saw it as an opportunity to be the man I was meant to be. He gave me the beauty to rescue. When he cut her off financially overnight, he thought it would cause her to come begging him for help. I didn't flinch. I simply stepped up. Amber didn't need a savior—she needed a partner. And for the first time in my life, I was capable of being that partner. I paid her rent for the first few months as we scoured Orange County for something suitable.

I won't sugarcoat it. We started living together before marriage. But even in our imperfection, even in our misunderstanding, God met us where we were—so He could take us where we needed to go.

As Amber and I prepared to move in together—a cat, four kids, two adults, one household—I began to understand that purpose more clearly. The divine orchestration wasn't about saving my life; it was about bringing two broken people together at the precise moment to heal each other and create something new that would glorify God.

Those early months weren't without challenges. We both carried defense mechanisms forged in the fires of previous relationships. But something was fundamentally different this time. Where before I would have slammed doors, now I found myself taking deep breaths. Where before I would have hurled accusations, now I caught the words before they left my lips. We never called each other names. We never screamed or threatened to leave—behaviors that had defined every relationship before this. Even when I got heated, I found myself stopping, breathing, finding a calm in a walk or stepping away.

It wasn't just love—it was healing happening in real time, the Lord restoring what had been broken in both of us. I struggle to explain the depth. Her experience mirrored mine, from the opposite side. We could see through each other's weaknesses, and yet instead of preying on that to gain control in the relationship, we naturally harnessed our awareness to heal each other. I could see every heartache she ever went through—her loveless marriage and desire to be truly adored as one flesh with a man who would lay down his life for her.

She was the living proof that my suffering had purpose, that my survival had meaning, that the broken pieces of my life weren't random but part of a greater design. Every missed connection, every wrong turn, every seeming failure had been precisely positioning us for this moment.

We weren't lost. We weren't drifting. We weren't missing each other by accident.

We were being shaped—one painful lesson at a time.

Every step. Every near miss. Every seeming coincidence.

God was writing our story long before we knew we were characters in it.

Amber didn't save me. She wasn't my Messiah. She was my mirror. Through her, God showed me what love looks like when it's not trying to control, impress, or manipulate—but simply heal. She wasn't my rescue. She was the proof it already came. She wasn't the answer to all my problems. But she became one of God's answers to prayers I didn't yet know I was praying.

"And I will restore to you the years that the locust hath eaten..." **(Joel 2:25).**

I had given years away—to addiction, pride, brokenness, and sin. Years stolen by the enemy, devoured like crops in a famine. But God doesn't waste pain. He doesn't just heal. He restores. Not to what was, but to what was always meant to be. His divine order—unfolding.

We didn't meet because we were flawless. Far from it. We met because we were finally done running. We'd run out of excuses. Run out of distractions. Run out of room to hide from the wounds inside of us. God waited until we were tired enough to stop sprinting and start listening. He waited until our hands were empty enough to receive something real. Not the counterfeit love we had known before. Not the conditional affection of broken people trying to fix each other. But the kind of love that comes down from above—

"...that bears all things, believes all things, hopes all things, endures all things." **(1 Corinthians 13:7).**

...that tells the truth even when it hurts, and holds space even when it's hard.

...that isn't afraid of scars, because it's familiar with the Cross.

Amber didn't redeem me—but she reflected the Redeemer. And in that reflection, I saw what real love could look like—love that chooses presence over perfection.

Love that doesn't need to fix you to stay with you. Real love sits comfortably in the ashes, still calling it holy ground.

This leads me to ask you directly—what about you?

Have you ever looked back at what felt like failure—only to realize it was positioning you for something greater?

Have you ever questioned why you're still here?

Maybe the answer isn't lost. Maybe it's just waiting to be seen.

God is mysterious. A marvel. Have you ever noticed that the people who cursed God can sometimes become the most relentless for Him? The ones who mocked Him, who swore they'd never believe, who lived without restraint—those same people end up being the ones who will die for His name.

I believe one of the best examples in Scripture is David. A warrior. A king. A leader. And a man who fell HARD. He didn't just commit adultery—he arranged a man's death to cover his sin. And yet, God still called him a man after His own heart. Why?

One of the clearest examples of this transformation in Scripture is David. God didn't use David because he was perfect. God used David because he was repentant. He owned his mistakes.

Look at Paul. Look at Moses. Look at Peter.

Look at me.

I was the farthest thing from a godly man. But when I finally saw the truth, when I finally understood that He had been calling me all along, I became more on fire for Him than I ever thought possible.

Because when you've lived in darkness long enough, you don't take the light for granted.

I don't take this second chance lightly. And neither should you.

You're not still here by accident.

Your past doesn't disqualify you—God specializes in using the broken.

The only question is: will you answer when He calls?

CHAPTER 11

The Indwelling

Creating A Home Together: The Next Battle

Answering God's call isn't just about believing—it's about stepping into a life you never imagined possible. It's about leaving old battlegrounds behind and choosing new ones worth fighting for.

The first night in our new Anaheim Hills house, we didn't wait for furniture.

A blow-up mattress on hardwood floors, the hollow echo of empty rooms surrounding us like the promise of possibilities not yet fulfilled. I'll never forget the look on Amber's face as she lay there, staring up at the ceiling—grateful simply to be somewhere her ex couldn't reach her. Something had left her eyes that night—a vigilance, a haunting watchfulness that shadowed every moment of her previous life.

That was peace.

No furniture? Didn't matter.
No bed frame? Who cares.
No more looking over her shoulder?
That's worth everything.

I lit logs in the fireplace in our room, flames dancing across bare walls as night flooded into our curtainless bedroom. The simplicity felt serene.

"What do you think our life will look like here?" she asked softly, breaking the silence.

I paused, absorbing the warmth of the fire, the soft darkness wrapping around us. "Different. Real. Honestly, I've never felt this way before—about anyone."

She shifted toward me, flames flickering gently in her eyes. "For so long, I didn't let myself imagine a future. Everything was about surviving. When I met you, I thought I'd lost my mind."

"Me too!" I replied, laughing. "I swore I'd never do this again, but then you steamrolled into my life. Actually, there's something I need to admit."

She took a sharp breath, suddenly tense. "Is this when the other shoe drops? Are you about to suddenly change now that we're living together?"

"No, no—nothing like that," I reassured her quickly. "Honestly, I've never been in love before now. Not truly."

Her eyes filled with tears. "Me neither. I didn't even know what real love was until I met you. I'd pretend I was happy, pretend it was love. But whenever my ex would leave on work trips, I'd feel relieved. That wasn't love." She exhaled deeply, releasing years of built-up tension.

"I just want a normal life," she whispered finally. "Nothing flashy—I just want to be with you, no matter what comes."

"We'll do better than normal," I promised, gently brushing the hair from her eyes. "We're going to build something extraordinary—even if it feels ordinary."

She smiled softly. "You promise?"

"I promise."

The absence of fear makes the simplest spaces feel like palaces. Freedom transforms empty rooms into cathedrals of possibility.

Those first few months weren't perfect. They were real.

Two people who had spent years drowning, learning how to breathe again. Each inhale—deliberate. Each exhale—a victory. We were novices at normal life, stumbling toward something neither of us had ever truly known: stability.

I transformed our garage into a gym, training clients at home. Nothing glamorous—just rubber mats, basic equipment, and determination—but it worked. We were building something real, something strong, something that felt lasting. Something neither of us had dared hope for.

But life doesn't let you build without testing the foundation first.
The enemy never sleeps. Soon we faced a new battlefield.

Fighting for Breath

Just as we found our footing, another war began—a brutal fight for Amber's life we never saw coming.

Barely a month after we moved in, a mystery illness descended—something savage. My ex had recently traveled to Greece, likely an early hotspot for COVID-19, and passed the virus to us through my children. This wasn't just another cold. Amber, already battling multiple autoimmune disorders, was hit like a wrecking ball slamming into a weakened structure.

> **RED FLAG MOMENT:** The enemy attacks through perfect timing. When everything is going your way—he sneaks in a devastating sucker punch. Be ready for it.

We all got sick. I barely suffered physically, experiencing mild symptoms that quickly passed. But emotionally, I suffered deeply, watching helplessly as this invisible enemy invaded our sanctuary.

My son was so ill he lost his spot on the high school basketball team. Instead of winning a trophy for his athleticism, he won it for *"most creative puker,"* destroying his mattress in the process. My daughter was equally unlucky, sick for weeks. But they recovered.

Amber **didn't.**

Our dreams shrank to a daily struggle to keep her breathing. She became **bedridden,** unable even to walk upstairs, coughing so violently she fractured ribs—turning each breath into agony.

Cough. Pain. **Repeat.**

I'd hold her through coughing fits, feeling spasms rack her body, tears streaming down her face. All I could do was remain present—a human pillar to hold onto.

One night—eyes hollow, face pale, body broken—she asked me weakened, *"Am I going to die?"*

Her voice, barely a whisper between labored breaths, confessed, *"I've been afraid since I found true love with you that it would be taken away. I survived all that hell—and now I'm going to die."*

I stayed strong in front of her, promising we'd get through this. But privately, hidden in the bathroom with the shower running to mask my pain, my frustration turned to anger—not at Amber, but at whatever force threatened to tear her away just as she'd found the fortitude to truly live. *Why now? Why her? Why us?*

Though I wasn't actively praying—too unaware, too scared—the Holy Spirit was there, quietly calming me, steadying my hands as I measured medications, helping me stand firm when everything inside me wanted to collapse.

Doctor after doctor. Specialists. ER visits. Urgent care centers at 2 a.m. No one had answers.

"Severe pneumonia." "Atypical respiratory infection." "Just wait it out."

How do you cope when someone you love can't breathe? When they're wasting away, breaking bones from coughing, and medical science shrugs helplessly?

Some battles aren't fought in rehabs or courtrooms but in quiet bedrooms—with thermometers, cold compresses, untouched soup, and whispered promises in the dark.

Amber's drinking—already minimal—stopped completely. No room for that demon in a body desperate to survive.

Eventually, frustration broke through. I started to voice my anger. She felt it. I saw it in her eyes. This wasn't helping. Shame washed over me. I heard a voice speaking to me: *This isn't about you. Are you suffering? No. So why are you frustrated when you should be loving?*

The old me would have run—retreated into a bottle or distraction. The enemy was trying to creep back in. His attack—structured to destroy God's gift.

The new me stood firm. The new me fought. The new me refused to let the enemy win.

I wasn't just fighting for her survival—I was fighting for us. For the purpose God had for our lives—a purpose I couldn't articulate but sensed in my soul. The spirit was beginning to connect to my soul.

In those dark nights, watching her struggle to breathe, something dawned on me: This wasn't just a relationship. This was a covenant. This was *"in sickness and in health,"* even before we spoke vows.

Three months later, the fever finally broke—not dramatically, but slowly, steadily, like the aftermath of a hard fought battle littered with faint cries and smoke lingering. Color returned to her face. When she could finally breathe without pain, tears filled her eyes.

"I was seriously worried you would leave me."

That thought never crossed my mind—not once. Something solidified during this trial, a certainty no previous relationship had ever inspired.

We had survived, and our foundation now felt unbreakable.

This wasn't some simple skirmish we fought. This was a war. One of many the enemy would continue to pound us with.

The enemy always attacks hardest when you are about to step deeper into faith.

The Real Spiritual Awakening Begins

I closed the garage door, sweat still cooling on my skin after the last client of the day left our gym. Amber had just finished assisting me with the couple—her first clients since recovering from the illness that nearly took her from me.

Orange County's golden hour spilled through our windows, painting the living room a warm, burnt-orange glow. I collapsed onto the couch, muscles satisfyingly sore. The scent of Amber's vanilla candle mingled with the light fragrance of her perfume—small comforts in a life still finding its shape.

"You were good with them today," I said, watching her move effortlessly around the kitchen without having to labour for breath. The illness had carved away something physical but the profound illness she fought had her thinking beyond our day-to-day lives. "They respond well to you," I said.

Amber handed me a glass of water, then sat beside me, tucking her legs beneath her. "They're determined to look buff like you. Did you see her checking herself out in the mirror when she thought no one was looking?"

I smiled, sipping water. "The Orange County special—an endless pursuit of Botoxed foreheads and fake perfection."

Amber leaned closer. "You know what she asked while we were doing lunges? If we were married. When I said no, she nodded and said, smart—everyone here is on their second or third."

"Charming," I responded.

Amber's fingers traced invisible patterns on the armrest, her gaze distant. "But she's not wrong. Do you know the divorce rate in Orange County? Seven out of ten marriages here fail. It's one in five nationally for first marriages, and worse for second."

I watched her carefully. This wasn't idle chatter; she'd been weighing this conversation. "Are you saying you want to marry me?"

She looked up sharply, eyes holding mine—no games, real raw honesty. "I'm serious, Matt. What we have... I don't want to lose it. And I don't think protein shakes and willpower alone can protect it."

She was right. All my life, I'd believed that determination alone could conquer anything. But some battles can't be won with sheer strength.

Amber continued softly—urgently, "Look at us. Look at everything we've survived. You know what separates us from every couple who swears they'll be different? Absolutely nothing—unless we build this on something stronger than ourselves."

The Bible lay on our coffee table, untouched except for the times Amber opened it. Even five years into recovery, it had mostly been a prop in my life—not a pillar.

"We should try church," Amber said gently, firmly. Not a mere suggestion—a lifeline.

My chest tightened. Pride flared like an old wound in cold weather, the monster I'd buried in rehab waking again. Shut up, I told myself. Think. **Don't react.**

A megachurch? In Orange County?

I revolted immediately, imagining rock bands pretending to worship, coffee-sipping Californians dressed for brunch, a sermon on prosperity, and bigger houses in Laguna. Everything in me rebelled against that superficial image.

"Church," I repeated slowly, the word foreign on my tongue, something I'd tried as a child and discarded without a fair chance because of my grandfather.

"Just once," Amber urged, holding my gaze. "Please, just try."

Outside, our neighbor's sprinklers clicked on rhythmically. Down the street, someone's Tesla pulled into their driveway. The scene felt painfully Orange County.

But Amber wasn't like them. She wasn't chasing appearances. She was offering something real, something deeper—something that had sustained her when my strength and determination hadn't been enough.

In that moment, I recognized the truth: This was a test of the leadership I claimed to have. Real leadership isn't about control; it's about knowing when to follow. Maybe I didn't have all the answers. Maybe I wasn't supposed to.

Amber's hand found mine, fingers intertwining. The last light of day illuminated the scar on my forehead. She touched it gently—a reminder of how close I'd come to losing this moment.

"Okay," I finally whispered. "We'll try church."

Her smile ignited a spark of hope I couldn't yet name. But I knew enough to recognize that whatever was unfolding between us was bigger than me. It was the start of a foundation that would complete my transformation.

I didn't know then that this simple "yes" would finally open my eyes to the spiritual battle I'd been fighting blindfolded for far too long.

The Megachurch Experience

*"The world tells you to find yourself. The Bible tells you to die to yourself. **Only one of those works.**"*

Mariners Church wasn't what I expected.

For starters, they had free breakfast burritos. Not greasy fast-food knockoffs—these were buttery bundles of heaven. And the coffee? Rich, smooth, probably sourced from some exclusive farm where each bean was hand-massaged by monks. It wasn't good coffee—it was Orange County coffee. The kind that quietly announces wealth.

Then the daycare—free and immaculate, a sanctuary for exhausted parents. Disneyland-level service designed so you could sit through service without kids throwing Goldfish at the pastor.

The entire place felt serene, warm, inviting—not fake, exactly, just very... put together. Sure, the aesthetics screamed wealth—but beneath the surface, something deeper stirred. Among the polished families, I sensed genuine seekers.

I didn't yet grasp the Gospel or grace. God's holy standard felt challenging, even threatening. Rules, authority—everything I'd rebelled against my entire life. That discomfort—the tension between who I was and who I was called to become?

That was the beginning of change.

The Power of Surrender

At the end of the sermon the pastor's voice echoed through the venue's speakers: *"Who's ready to believe? Ready to surrender?"*

Like surrender was some graceful choice—not something that happens when God breaks you down to your bones. Yet, Scripture says God honors a broken and contrite heart—not a perfect record.

I'd dodged this battle for decades, clinging stubbornly to the illusion of control. I glanced around—thousands seated calmly. I resisted, pride flaring. But then, something deep within me stumbled forward, breaking through my resistance:

"You are to stand and surrender."

I'd heard this voice before. My heart pounded as if my nervous system had been hijacked, rationality—overwhelmed.

"No one can come to me unless the Father who sent me draws him."

What was happening?

My hand **shot up.**

Amber stared at me, startled. She'd seen the Buddha statue in my old apartment—another leftover decoration from my old life. Initially, she'd wondered if she was dating a non-believer—a Hollywood guy with a Viking beard and little faith. She hadn't known I'd been quietly wrestling with God for years, burning inside without admitting it.

My surrender wasn't tidy or easy. Flashes of my past filled my mind:

My mugshot—handcuffed to a hospital bed.
Sliding off the blood-soaked mattress in a cheap motel.
My children's eyes when they saw me—totally broken.
The suspended prison sentence.

Surrender wasn't giving up. It was handing my failures to the only One equipped to carry them.

"I BELIEVE!"

It burst forth like an exorcism—something I'd been holding back my entire life. Relief washed over me.

I wasn't just saved or forgiven—**I was adopted**.

"You aren't just rescued. You're recommissioned."
"You're not just forgiven—you're assigned."

True leadership wasn't born in the spotlight but in the stillness following surrender—because, finally, I listened.

Always follow the light—
even when you don't understand,
even when you don't feel worthy,
even when the battle seems lost.

The Holy Spirit hadn't moved in to comfort me, but to equip, refine, and transform me—not for my sake alone, but for others. To cut through my pride. My numbness. My ego.
To divide **soul from spirit**—to show me what was real and what was reaction.

My surrender wasn't emotional—it was surgical.
My raised hand wasn't the end of my story. It was the beginning of my reconstruction.
Because the Spirit doesn't just settle in—He **renovates everything.**

He doesn't just soothe.
He shapes.
He **sanctifies**.
He sends.

And what He sends you into isn't a platform.
It's a **calling**.
Because we're never saved merely for ourselves—**we're saved to lead.**

Real leadership isn't built on control; it's built on submission to something far greater.

I'd walked into church for coffee and a burrito.
I walked out connected to the Holy Spirit.

Are you ready to learn what real leadership means?

BLUEPRINT STEP 5: PRACTICE TRUE LEADERSHIP

(Master Yourself To Lead Others)

"A man who cannot follow cannot lead, and a man who cannot surrender cannot serve."

WAR STRATEGY:

Most men have leadership backward. They think it's about position, power, control, and dominance. That's not leadership—that's the world's counterfeit. True leadership starts with surrender, service, sacrifice, and submission to something greater. The greatest leaders in history weren't just strong—they were submitted first. You cannot lead others effectively until you've mastered yourself. Your private victories precede your public ones. Your authority comes from your authenticity. Your influence flows from your integrity. Master these principles, and you'll lead even when you hold no title.

ACTION ORDERS:

1. Win The Battle With Self

Your biggest enemy isn't external—it's internal:

- **Pride** that refuses correction.
- **Fear** that prevents bold action.
- **Control** that drives others away.
- **Self-reliance** that rejects God's guidance.

Victory strategy: Die to yourself daily. Every morning, surrender your agenda, your ego, your need to be right. The man who cannot be led cannot lead.

2. Establish Your Leadership Foundation

Your leadership is only as strong as what it's built on:

- **Root yourself in Scripture**—leaders without God's Word build on sand.
- **Develop personal discipline**—private habits determine public success.
- **Create accountability**—find men who challenge you, not just cheer you.
- **Define non-negotiables**—know what lines you won't cross, even under pressure.

Leadership without character is a disaster waiting to happen. Build the foundation before the structure.

3. Master The Leadership Paradoxes

True leadership embraces opposing truths:

- **Strong yet humble**—confident in your calling without arrogance.
- **Decisive yet collaborative**—make clear choices while valuing input.
- **Visionary yet practical**—see the future while managing the present.
- **Demanding yet merciful**—set high standards while showing grace.

Learn the rhythm of leadership—when to advance and retreat, speak and listen, challenge and encourage, lead from front and empower others.

4. Lead By Example First

Before directing others:
- Get your own house in order
- Master your time, finances, health
- Conquer your worst habits
- Live what you'll eventually teach
- Serve before you direct
- Find ways to add value without recognition
- Solve problems without being asked

If you can't lead yourself, you can't lead anyone else. Jesus washed feet. Follow His example.

WAR CRY:

The world doesn't need more bosses. It needs more warriors who know how to kneel. More kings who understand service. More leaders forged in the fires of surrender. A true leader doesn't change circumstances—he transforms lives. He builds legacies. He fights for those he leads—against lies that hold them back, systems that oppress them, and enemies that want to destroy them.

Your leadership isn't measured by who follows you but by who you're willing to serve. It's not proved by who submits to you but by what you're submitted to. It's not displayed in your strength but in your sacrifice.

You want her trust? Walk in truth.

You want her respect? Walk in righteousness.

You want her to follow? Get on your knees first.

Leadership isn't what you claim—it's what you demonstrate. Now demonstrate.

BLUEPRINT RECAP:

BEFORE: *(The Failed Leader)*

"I thought leadership meant having all the answers. I thought respect came from control. I thought strength meant never showing weakness. In my relationships, I demanded to be followed without becoming worth following. I wanted submission without providing true leadership. I expected respect without walking in righteousness.

Most people make this same mistake. They want the benefits of leadership without the sacrifice it requires. They want their wives to submit while they refuse to lead. They want others to follow while they remain unchanged."

Pro Tip: Want to know if you're truly leading? Try this test: Ask those closest to you: **"How could I lead better?"** Listen without defending yourself. Implement their feedback, even if it hurts your pride. Return in 30 days and ask again. The degree to which you struggle with this exercise is the degree to which pride is sabotaging your leadership.

AFTER: *(The Surrendered Leader)*

"When I finally stopped fighting God and started fighting for Him, everything changed. In learning to listen—not just to God, but to Amber—I learned how to lead. And in learning to lead, Amber gained a new level of respect for me. She would eventually ask to center our marriage on Christ. Not because she had to, but because she saw the man I was becoming.

Leadership didn't start when I spoke—it started when I listened. It didn't show up in commands—it showed up in consistency. I had to walk in the manner worthy of the calling with which I had been called. And the gift that comes to a man who does this? It is greater than any amount of money. Greater than any amount of fame. Greater than any amount of power.

There is nothing more powerful than being trusted and respected by your wife because of your submission to Christ. That's where legacy begins. Her submission didn't make me a leader. My leadership—marked by humility, service, and spiritual strength—made room for her to trust again.

This isn't about control. It's about divine order. Leadership isn't demanded. It's demonstrated. I didn't become a leader because she submitted. She submitted because I finally became someone worth following."

VICTORY INDICATORS:

You Know You're Succeeding When:

- You make decisions based on principles, not preferences
- People follow your example, not just your orders
- You take responsibility instead of placing blame
- You elevate others instead of promoting yourself
- You seek wisdom before asserting authority
- You serve those you lead rather than expecting service
- You build systems that work even in your absence
- You're led by the Spirit, not only your strategy

RED FLAGS:

- You need constant control
- You get defensive with feedback
- You take credit for successes while blaming others for failures
- You lead through fear rather than inspiration
- You're threatened by others' success
- You talk about leadership more than you demonstrate it
- Your public image contradicts your private reality

REALITY CHECK:

True leadership is lonely. You will face resistance from people who are addicted to mediocrity. You'll be misunderstood. Criticized. Even abandoned. When you choose to lead, you paint a target on your back—for both human and spiritual attack.

Sometimes it shows up in little setbacks. Sometimes it's resistance to your work, or your momentum stalls. Sometimes it's even physical—like injuries during training or sickness when you're just starting to gain ground. That's not coincidence. That's war. Fight through it—with prayer, not pride.

You'll doubt yourself. You'll make mistakes that affect other people. You'll feel the temptation to compromise your values for faster wins. That doesn't make you a failure. It makes you a leader in the proving ground.

Every great leader has moments of crushing doubt. The difference? They don't stay down. They recalibrate. They own their mistakes. They return to their foundation—and then they lead again.

Leadership isn't about perfection. It's about accountability. Get up when you fall. Repent when you're wrong. Refocus when you're scattered. And never forget—the attacks confirm the calling.

WAR ORDER (FINAL COMMAND):

Serve someone this week **without recognition**. Find a need and fill it without being asked. Then, identify one person you can mentor, and take the first step—today. **Take responsibility** for something you've been avoiding. Leadership isn't a title—it's action when action is required.

"Real leaders aren't born—they're forged in the fires of surrender. The strongest men aren't those who never kneel—they're the ones who know how to kneel before something greater than themselves."

CHAPTER 12

All In

The Ring Weighs More Than Metal

*"Leadership isn't just guiding others. Sometimes, it's stepping forward into your own uncertainty—trusting the road ahead even when you **can't see the destination clearly.**"*

Picture this: March of 2019.

A few thousand bucks in my account.
An engagement ring burning hot in the back of our SUV—and even hotter in my thoughts.

Ahead, the 10 Freeway cuts through the desert, shimmering like broken glass under the relentless sun. Hot wind rushes through the cracked windows, carrying the sharp scent of creosote and dust. The desert has its own baptism—purifying through heat, stripping away every pretense. With each passing mile marker, I feel my old self burning away.

My brain runs the scenario on repeat:

Ask her before dinner, or after? After—definitely after. But where exactly? At the table? By the pool? I'll know when we get there.

Amber and I have crossed state lines in comfortable conversation before, never needing background music to fill the air.

But today?
I'm lost in thought.

I'm trying to play it casual, but Amber's watching me like a human polygraph.

"Are you okay?" she asks, her voice gentle but probing.

"Yeah, of course," I say, probably a little too quickly. "Great. Never been better."

Does she know? Does she sense the gravity of this moment? Would she say no?

We'd both sworn **never** to marry again.

When we arrive at her mom's boyfriend's second home—graciously offered for our getaway—the sun welcomes us warmly on the patio, infusing our skin with Vitamin D. For a moment, everything feels peaceful, as if life is finally settling down.

Amber's phone buzzes—sharp, insistent, like a rattlesnake's warning.

After months of silence, after blocking numbers, some random guy she dated briefly decides **this exact day** is the perfect moment to declare his lingering feelings:

I miss you so much.

The digital equivalent of an **emotional drive-by.**

I remember pausing before reacting. I recognize his tactics now—the strategic timing, the attempt to sow doubt at pivotal moments. The enemy always knows exactly when to strike. Not the day before. Not the day after. Precisely when your hand is reaching for something ordained by God. I remember feeling that strange calm settle over me. This text wasn't a coincidence—it was confirmation. I was on the right path.

This is how **the enemy works.**

Perfectly timed text messages.
Social media hearts.
Little doses of past poison when you're about to step into your future.

Years earlier, I'd have spiraled into anger or insecurity. But now, I exhale slowly, smiling.

You had your chance. You won't get another.

Amber reads it, frowns, and deletes the message without replying. She takes my hand, and just like that, the snake **loses its venom.**

Dinner & The Proposal

Azucar—an upscale Mexican restaurant tucked inside La Serena Villas, a Michelin-starred boutique hotel built in 1933 and rescued from demolition by locals—perfectly blends Old Desert charm with modern California elegance.

I chose Azucar carefully: They offer our favorite contemporary Mexican cuisine, and crucially, it's adults-only.

They seat us outside at the quiet table I requested.
The desert air cools, but my palms sweat.

Not from doubt.

From anticipation. From knowing this isn't a proposal—it's a transformation, with God as its witness.

Dinner passes in a blur, my mind already standing at the edge of the life I'm about to commit to. Afterward, we step out near the pool. Soft blue lights ripple gently across Amber's face.

Gorgeous.

For a split second, I flash back to that hospital bed years ago, wrists handcuffed, certain I'd destroyed every chance at a real life. The man in that memory feels like a stranger now—connected to me only by the thread of God's grace. The distance from that moment to this is immeasurable, except by **mercy.**

I breathe deeply, lower myself onto one knee, and look directly into Amber's eyes. This simple gesture declares war against everything I once was.

"Will you marry me?"

Her response is immediate, unhesitating, clear as the desert sky that night:

"Yes."

A pure, unfiltered yes. Two people who swore—*never again*—committing forever.

Amber's smile lights up the night. "I would've married you the first week we met."

Afterward, we drive to Dairy Queen and scarf down a large Heath Bar Blizzard, laughing like teenagers. This is what redemption feels like—not some grand, dramatic scene, but the quiet joy of ordinary moments made sacred—the ability to find wonder in a fast-food parking lot, licking ice cream off plastic spoons, laughing over nothing.

This is the miracle: not merely surviving but **truly living again.**

True love doesn't need a production budget,
 a viral moment,
 or anything beyond honesty.

My earthly father saved me from every disaster I engineered: jail, addiction—a highlight reel of my worst decisions.

But my heavenly Father?
He orchestrated dominoes I didn't even realize were falling,
pulled invisible strings I never knew existed.

Sometimes, God sends someone to guide you toward who you were always meant to be—not through pressure, but through pure, unfiltered truth.

Amber was that person.
I was truly, irreversibly in love with her.

The path to true love is rarely easy, but it's there—

Even if it leads through Palm Springs in March.
Even if it requires letting go of everything you thought you knew.
Even if it means becoming someone entirely new.

Real transformation doesn't ask for permission.
It arrives quietly, slipping a ring onto a finger beneath desert stars, rewriting
everything you once believed about love—
about God—
about yourself.

And sometimes, if you're very lucky,
it tastes like Dairy Queen in the desert,
with laughter on your lips
and a **second chance on your finger.**

Reflection

I'm looking at a piece of art hanging on my studio wall—a black and white painting of a couple suspended in clouds, caught in that electric moment before a kiss. I commissioned it from an artist I liked. Across the bottom, five words capture what we both knew from the beginning: *"We've got a lot of time on our hands."*

Those words weren't planned. They spilled from my lips one night in that Seal Beach apartment when Amber casually mentioned how marriage was supposed to last forever. *"I guess we've got a lot of time on our hands,"* I said, the truth escaping before I could catch it. We were still dancing around what we felt then, still pretending we could keep this thing casual, contained. When those words landed, we'd stopped pretending.

As I sit here today, looking at this painting, I see more than a relationship that defied the odds. I see the visible evidence of an invisible battle—one that had been raging inside me long before I even knew I was at war.

Before Christ, I wasn't merely influenced by darkness. I was possessed by it.

That's not hyperbole or dramatic storytelling. That's the raw, unvarnished truth. Addiction wasn't just bad behavior or poor choices—it was demonic. There's no doubt in my mind. After my car crash, after the bottle, after the cocaine—I couldn't even count how many demons had their grip on my soul. Each vice was a chain, each sin a shackle, binding me to enemy powers I couldn't see. As my addiction grew, the roots of his evil also grew, giving him near complete autonomy over my soul.

And yet, here I am. Looking at this painting of impossible love with clear eyes and a connected spirit.

We became gravitational forces, Amber and I, constantly pulling toward each other against all logic. I'd drive across town for thirty minutes in her presence, as if proximity was oxygen. What we found together wasn't just comfort—it was sanctuary. In the astronomical chaos that defined our separate lives, we'd somehow created an unsinkable vessel. Two broken people who'd found their missing pieces in each other, navigating a perfect storm with something neither of us had truly known before: unconditional love.

I thank God for this love multiple times a day, sometimes out loud, sometimes in silent gratitude when I wake beside her. He blessed us with something that defied every statistic, every pattern, every assumption about what happens when two people with our histories collide. The relationship wasn't unlikely—it was near impossible. And yet, here we are.

Looking back, I can see how the enemy wouldn't leave such an outpouring of love unchallenged. If our exes' venomous texts and midnight provocations were warning shots, what came next was nuclear—a global pandemic designed to crush newly forming bonds, to isolate and divide, to turn love's sanctuary into a pressure cooker.

He thought isolation would break us. Instead, it welded us together. What was meant as a weapon against us became the forge that strengthened us.

"What the enemy meant for evil, God meant for good." **(Genesis 50:20)**

I used to talk about generational curses because I lived under them. I used to talk about torment—because I was bound. I was a man drowning in the very air everyone else breathed easily. The whispers from the deep weren't mere thoughts—they were invasions, infiltrations of my consciousness by forces intent on my destruction.

But all of that changed the moment I truly received the Holy Spirit.

I remember the exact sensation—like cool water rushing through veins that had only known fire. Like light flooding rooms that had been dark for decades. Like chains dropping to the floor with a decisive clang that echoed through my entire being. That serenity. That calm. That love.

"Greater is He that is in you than he that is in the world." **(1 John 4:4)**

This truth echoes through every chapter of our story. The car crash that should have killed me led to sobriety. The broken relationships that nearly destroyed us prepared us to recognize true love. The pandemic that should have driven us apart only fused us more completely. The enemy's strategies repeatedly transformed into stepping stones toward redemption.

And what about you? What storms have come to break you? What battles have tried to pull you back into old patterns? What moments have forced you to decide—do I break, or do I build? Because love isn't tested in silence. It's tested in war. And real love? It doesn't crumble. It doesn't retreat. It doesn't surrender. It fights. United.

Satan may still whisper. He may still try to press in. He can tempt, deceive, oppress, and attack—but he **cannot possess me any longer**. He can win battles if I let him. But he cannot win the war—because that war is already won. I am sealed. I am filled. I am **not owned by darkness any longer**.

The chains broke the day Jesus came into my life.

This is the legacy of redemption. Not just surviving our wounds, but allowing them to be transformed into wisdom. Not just escaping our prisons, but using our experience to help free others. Not just finding love, but becoming living proof that broken people can be made whole again.

The story you're living right now—with all its pain, all its setbacks, all its seemingly random twists—is being woven into something beautiful. Something meaningful. Something eternal. You may not see the pattern yet, but God does. And one day, you'll look back and understand that not a single moment was wasted.

When I look at our life now, I see more than a marriage that beat the odds. I see a testimony. I see proof that God still works miracles. I see evidence that the enemy doesn't get the final word—**and he no longer has dominion over my life**.

Our legacy isn't built on perfection—it's built on grace. It's not about avoiding the battle but learning to face it with conviction. It's not about never falling but about rising every time we fall. And it's not just for us—it's for everyone, everyone wondering if their story can change too.

The answer is yes. A thousand times, yes.

You're not here by accident. Your story isn't over. Your scars aren't wasted. And the brush is still wet.

Your legacy of redemption is waiting to be painted. The only question is: will you start working with the only artist who can help you create a masterpiece?

The End Of The World

A month after we got engaged, we moved to Huntington Beach, hoping to be closer to the kids' schools. That's when it happened. The world didn't just stop—it spun in reverse.

If our new engagement would ever be tested by fire, this was it—like getting engaged at the start of the Great Depression. Except, instead of breadlines, we had fistfights over toilet paper. Instead of long days working fields, we had endless hours trapped together with no escape.

No breathing room.
No "see you later."
No easing into forever.

Now we had four kids trapped on computers eight hours a day. "Remote learning," they called it—more like **crisis homeschooling.** Four young souls, vibrant and restless, caged in digital classrooms while the world convulsed around them.

Some nights, I'd find Amber staring out the window, face bathed in moonlight, eyes fixed on something distant.

"Do you think this is it?" she'd whisper. "The beginning of the end?"

I had no answers. Only questions. Only a growing certainty that whatever was happening went deeper than a virus.

Looking back now, I see God's timing with breathtaking clarity. Had the pandemic hit just two years earlier, where would I have been? Alone, trying to stay sober? No gym? I would have been completely alone, probably self-medicating in isolation, with no anchor to hold me steady. But God had prepared a foundation—sobriety, a budding faith, and Amber—exactly when I would need it most.

California was tough.

Taxes kept **rising.**
Laws kept shifting.

Rules kept changing.

First we were inside.
Then outside.
Then singing was outlawed.
Then worship itself was criminalized.

First, they called us **selfish.**
Then **extremists.**
Then **dangerous.**

I watched the progression with chilling clarity.

This wasn't about health—

It was about control.

This wasn't about safety—

It was about compliance.

The enemy found a perfect vector for his oldest strategies: isolation, fear, **division.**

Was it time to pack our bags? To move—not just toward another state, but a new life? The question lingered unspoken, like a third presence in our home.

When you strip away people's daily purpose—their ability to provide, create, move—you don't weaken them.

You break them.

Amber had worked as a medical aesthetician for twenty-two years. Her career vanished overnight. I trained clients at the gym. That ended, too. People stopped working out and connecting. Their bodies atrophied as their fear grew.

One day in Whole Foods, I sneezed beneath my mask. My allergies were terrible—the mask made it worse. I shifted it slightly to breathe.

A man nearby jumped away from me—hissing at me. He took a long pause and, with wild eyes, shook his head side to side and said, "I hope you die a slow, painful death!" He shuffled away crying, his cart filled half with organic produce, half with irrational fear.

I stood frozen, the violence of his words hanging in the sanitized air between us. This wasn't panic—this was demonic—fear injected into hearts. **A soul attack** on humanity—a spiritual attack on God's creation. The same darkness I'd battled in addiction now walked freely through grocery store aisles—acceptable, even **celebrated.**

Outside, marriages **imploded.** Friends disappeared into their vices. The world fractured, splinter by splinter, each crack widening into sinkholes too vast for mere words or reason.

My phone buzzed. Barry's name lit up my screen after a year of silence. I knew something was up. Within thirty seconds of chatting, I knew I wasn't talking with the same Barry. There was a false confidence that I couldn't pinpoint. A false bravado. Then he told me he started drinking again, assuring me casually he had it "under control." "Just a couple beers now and then," he said, "nothing serious. It's not like before."

I knew better. Relapse calls to you long before addiction devours you.

"Don't," I urged. "That's the disease talking, Barry. You know exactly where this road ends—rehab or jail."

He brushed me off, but his denial haunted me. The beast he was fighting—I lived in its jaws. Barry's text was a God Shot, a reminder of my alternate path had I not been listening.

Outside our door, people unraveled.
But inside our home?
Still **sobriety.**

Still love.
Still laughter.

Amber and I never let the chaos outside infect us.

We often said how grateful we were we'd met before the world crisis. Being alone in this madness would have broken either of us. Instead, we built a sanctuary within the chaos. While others found reasons to fight, we found reasons to grow closer. Every dinner became sacred. Every movie night, a celebration. Every morning workout—an act of defiance... against the darkness pressing in from all sides.

During the stillness of lockdown nights, I realized—painfully—how the enemy uses isolation as a weapon. Separation from community. Disconnection from purpose. These aren't just inconveniences—they're battlegrounds where faith is tested and souls are shaped.

The pandemic revealed something crucial about spiritual warfare: it happens in the everyday moments. In how we respond to fear. In how we choose love when hate seems easier. In how we hold onto truth when lies are more comfortable.

Something deep within me was shifting. Even before fully grasping spiritual warfare, I felt the Gospel rooting inside me, guiding my thoughts, steadying my hands.

"Do you not know that your body is a temple of the Holy Spirit within you, whom you have from God? You are not your own." **(1 Corinthians 6:19).**

These words resonated now with unmistakable clarity. I wasn't fully immersed in the Gospel yet, but the seeds were planted. Deeply.

This was no longer just a global crisis.

This was spiritual warfare on a global scale—and my new faith gave me the discernment to see it.

One night, as the kids slept upstairs and the neighborhood lay silent beneath curfew, Amber and I sat on our back porch, watching stars appear one by one across the California sky. Those same stars had witnessed every plague, every war, every rise and fall of civilizations far greater than ours.

"Do you think it's time?" she asked quietly, not needing to say more.

I took her hand, feeling the engagement ring I'd placed there months earlier. "I think God is taking us somewhere else."

She nodded slowly. "Tennessee?"

"Tennessee."

I felt the weight of the moment settle into my bones. This wasn't running away. This was about strengthening our position to fight spiritual warfare on a battleground chosen not by us, but by God.

We weren't fleeing the chaos.
We were stepping forward—**deeper into our calling.**

The world around us might unravel, but we had something stronger. Something deeper. Something eternal.

We had a choice: cave to the chaos or rise in the Spirit.
And we chose to **fight.**

What about you?
When the enemy advances, when the noise gets louder,
when the ground beneath your life starts to crack—
Do you run, or do you rise?

Because when you surrender to God, you don't escape the war.
You walk straight into the battle.
Are you ready to wage holy war?

BLUEPRINT STEP 6: WAGE HOLY WAR
(Spiritual Warfare Is Real—Fight Back)

"The moment you choose God's path, you enter enemy territory. Be prepared—salvation isn't the end of the war, it's the beginning of a new battle."

WAR STRATEGY:

The moment you surrender to God, you declare war on the enemy. When you choose light, darkness notices. When you step into purpose, hell takes aim. I thought surrender meant peace. I thought choosing God meant the war was over. That was the first lie the enemy told me.

Here's the critical truth: **When you accept salvation, the enemy can no longer possess you.** He loses ownership. You now belong to Christ. This is a decisive victory—you're no longer fighting for freedom; you're fighting from freedom. But the battle shifts. The enemy becomes more desperate because he's lost his claim on your soul.

Spiritual warfare isn't religious superstition—it's the invisible reality behind every struggle you face. The enemy doesn't want your failure—he wants your soul. He doesn't only attack your body—he targets your mind, your faith, your purpose. To win, you must recognize the battle, understand your enemy, and wield the weapons God has provided. You're not crazy. You're finally seeing the battlefield.

ACTION ORDERS:

1. Know Your Enemy's Playbook

Satan's attacks follow predictable patterns:
- **He recycles past temptations**—he doesn't need new tricks, just old patterns that worked before. Lust—porn. Greed—more money. Alcohol—numbing agent.
- **He disguises distractions as opportunities**—sometimes wearing a suit, speaking through ambition
- **He causes spiritual interference**—nightmares, fear, insecurity, sudden attacks on faith
- **He works through deception**—his ultimate goal isn't your stumble but your hypocrisy—not just your hypocrisy—**your blasphemy**.

The enemy's most effective strategy isn't temptation—it's making you believe he doesn't exist. When you can identify his patterns, you weaken his position.

2. Learn Your Spiritual Weapons

What looks optional is essential for survival:
- **Prayer** isn't peaceful meditation—it's artillery.
- **Scripture** isn't self-help—it's battle plans.
- **Worship** isn't performance—it's warfare.
- **Community** isn't social hour—it's your platoon.

These aren't religious activities—they're weapons systems designed to defeat an enemy who wants you destroyed. Deploy them daily.

3. Put On The Full Armor (Ephesians 6:10-18)

This isn't metaphor—it's battle gear:

- **Belt of Truth**—no compromise, no deception, no self-delusion.
- **Breastplate of Righteousness**—guard your heart, protect your integrity.
- **Shoes of Peace**—move with purpose, walk boldly in your calling.
- **Shield of Faith**—deflect the enemy's lies before they penetrate.
- **Helmet of Salvation**—guard your thoughts; the battle starts in your mind.
- **Sword of the Spirit**—Use Scripture as a weapon; know it to deploy it.

You don't fight thoughts with thoughts. You fight them with God's Word. Arm yourself completely—partial armor means vulnerable areas. There were days when prayer was the only thing that kept me from picking up the bottle. There were nights where worship was the only light in the darkness.

4. Take Strategic Ground Daily

Spiritual warfare requires offensive action:

- **TAKE NEW GROUND**—face the void. Step into the fire.
- **HOLD THE LINE**—be honest. Shut down the enemy's self-talk tape.
- **NEVER RETREAT**—stay vigilant. Don't get soft.
- **ALWAYS ADVANCE**—know when to lead. Know when to be led.

The enemy never sleeps. Neither can your vigilance. The enemy doesn't quit. Neither can you.

WAR CRY:

The enemy whispers. We roar. The enemy prowls. We stand. The enemy fights dirty. We fight holy. Your pain isn't your weakness—it's your weapon. Your story isn't over—it's ammunition. Now get up. Put on your armor. Take your position.

The battle is **already won**. But you still have to **fight**.

This isn't about physical force. This is about standing when the enemy says fold. Fighting when your flesh says quit. Advancing when the world says retreat. Building what the enemy tried to destroy.

"The kingdom of heaven suffers violence, and the violent take it by force." **(Matthew 11:12)**

BLUEPRINT RECAP:

BEFORE: *(Fighting the Wrong Battles)*

"I thought my enemies were physical. The cop who arrested me. The casting director who passed on me. The agent who betrayed me. The ex who destroyed me. I wasted years fighting flesh and blood—throwing punches at shadows while the real enemy laughed.

When that black mass appeared in Los Feliz, when it pressed down on my chest until I couldn't breathe, when it spoke in my own voice that no one was coming—I still didn't understand what I was facing. I blamed bad luck. I blamed circumstance. I blamed everyone but the true enemy. I treated spiritual warfare like superstition. Like stories to scare children. Hollywood had me convinced evil was just a movie trope, not an active force working against me.

So I stayed defenseless—walking the battlefield naked, wondering why I kept getting hit."

Pro Tip: Want to know if you're engaged in real spiritual warfare? Test your reactions: When problems arise, do you immediately blame people or circumstances? When tempted, do you recognize the pattern of attack? When you pray, do you feel active resistance? When you speak truth, does unusual opposition appear? The enemy doesn't want to be identified—that's when his power weakens.

AFTER: *(Armed and Dangerous)*

"Now I see it clearly. The whispers weren't my thoughts. The 'coincidences' weren't random. The patterns weren't accidents. I was in a war I didn't recognize. I was walking through a warzone daily—and I couldn't even hear the bullets whizzing past my face.

But when I finally put on the armor of God—when I started fighting with Scripture instead of fists, with prayer instead of pride, with truth instead of tactics—everything changed.

The attacks didn't stop.
They intensified.
But now I knew who was attacking me.
And make no mistake: ***it was an attack.***

I've said it before in this book, and I'll say it again:
Satan's ultimate goal is death—and he wants to watch you suffer before he takes you out.

That voice suggesting I wasn't good enough?
Enemy fire.

That urge to go back to old patterns?
Enemy fire.

That fear that I'd never truly change?
Enemy fire.

The battles were real—but now I had weapons that worked. I stopped fighting people and started fighting the powers behind them.

And when I spoke the name of Jesus—not as a concept but as Commander—everything shifted. I discovered that **one word**—**'Jesus'**—held more power than all my strength, all my willpower, all my strategies combined. The enemy that once had me pinned down? **Now he retreats when I advance.** Not because I'm strong—but because I finally know **whose authority I stand in.**"

VICTORY INDICATORS:

You Know You're Succeeding When:

- You recognize spiritual attacks for what they are
- You respond to challenges with Scripture rather than emotion
- Your prayer life becomes a daily discipline rather than an emergency response
- You feel the resistance but push through it anyway
- You can identify when pressure is from God (conviction) versus the enemy (condemnation)
- You're more aware of the spiritual dimension of everyday situations
- You find community that strengthens your faith
- You relax in the face of torment
- You handle your emotions without overheating or retreating

RED FLAGS:

- You still view challenges as merely physical or emotional
- You ignore Scripture in your daily life
- You fight battles alone without spiritual support
- You blame people instead of recognizing spiritual forces
- You can't identify the patterns in your temptations
- You treat prayer as a last resort rather than first response
- You're embarrassed to acknowledge spiritual warfare is real
- You still wonder if God is really on your side
- You get down on everyone because you had a bad day

REALITY CHECK:

This war will seem invisible to most people around you. They'll think you're overreacting, being "too religious," or seeing demons behind every bush. Some battles will be sudden and violent—overwhelming temptation, crushing doubt, or paralyzing fear. Others will be subtle—gradual compromise, slow-fading conviction, or quiet distraction from purpose. You will have days when you feel completely overwhelmed, when prayers seem to hit the ceiling, when God feels distant. These aren't signs of defeat—they're normal conditions on the battlefield. Every warrior of faith experiences dark nights of the soul. The enemy will use these moments to whisper that you're fighting alone. Remember: feelings aren't facts. Your Commander hasn't abandoned you. Stand firm when you can't feel His presence. Fight hardest when faith is tested most.

WAR ORDER (FINAL COMMAND):

Identify your specific spiritual battlefield. Where is the enemy attacking you most? Write it down. Then find the Scripture that directly counters that attack. **Memorize it.** Speak it out loud when the enemy strikes. Fight back with truth, not feelings. Put on the full armor of God **before** you enter the day, not after you're already under attack.

"The enemy doesn't show up with a warning—he waits until you're tired, distracted, and vulnerable. Then he strikes. **Armor up before the ambush."**

Let's head back into the story.

The Decision to Move

The spiritual battle wasn't personal—it was geographical. As we waged war in the spiritual realm, God was preparing us for a physical move that would strengthen our position. You can fight from anywhere, but some battlefields give you better ground than others.

California is collapsing.
It always has been.

I have a contract looming. One client. One deal. $15,000 a month if I move closer. And if I take it? That number will only go up.

Amber and I aren't just talking about leaving anymore. We're running the math, checking Zillow, pulling up maps of Tennessee, calling my parents, who already live there.

Then we visit.
And we laugh.
Out loud.

Houses for a fraction of what we'd pay in LA. Gas for dollars less. Staying in California isn't brave. It's stupid. We make the decision.
We're leaving.

Amber has lived here all her life, but she wants out to give our marriage the best chance to thrive. I promised myself I would make it in LA, that I would never leave. Goals change when the Holy Spirit begins dwelling in your life.

I have one thing left to do, and it's a decision I made the day I met her.
Marry Her.

CHAPTER 13

The Calling

The Ticket Booth Wedding

*"Society sells you worldly success, but **love is the only treasure worth finding**."*

Sometimes spiritual battles lead you to surprising places. Sometimes victory doesn't look like conquest—it looks like covenant. The Honda Center in Anaheim, California, isn't built for weddings. It's built for blood on the ice and eighteen-dollar beers. But in **backward land,** it's the closest thing we have to holy ground.

We aren't the only ones here.

Masks hide anxious smiles. The powers that be—trying to cheapen the moment.

But here's what the adversary doesn't understand about true God-gifted love:

It doesn't need **perfect conditions.** It doesn't need **traditional venues.** It doesn't even need faces uncovered.

It needs two warriors ready to fight on the same side.

Two people choosing forever in the middle of temporary insanity.

Two souls saying *"I do"* while the world screams *"You can't."*

The air smells like hand sanitizer and **government overreach.** Amber doesn't care about the venue—we made the appointment together the day her divorce was finalized.

We stand in line as if we're waiting for concert tickets, not a covenant. But nothing about this moment feels cheap.

Because this isn't about aesthetics.
It isn't about a venue.
It isn't about guests or flower arrangements or a Pinterest board of rustic wedding inspo.

This is war.

Us versus the world.
Us versus every lie, every wound, **every doubt.**
Us versus every curse, every past mistake, every demon still scratching at the door.

They call our number.
We step forward.

Amber looks stunning. Not in the overproduced, airbrushed, Hollywood way. But in the real way—the way a woman looks when she is exactly where she is meant to be.

No cold feet. No doubts. No second-guessing.

I look at her, and for the first time in my life, I understand why God compares marriage to Christ and the Church.

Because when a man stands before God and says, *"I will fight for her. I will lead her. I will die for her."*

That's not a contract.
That's a calling.

A promise with tears in our eyes.

The second they handed us that paper, Satan lost.
The generational curses lost.

The past lost.
The statistics lost.

Love won.
God won.
We won.

The parking lot was our send-off aisle.

Not lined with rose petals or confetti, but with unseen angels—witnesses to a war won in silence.

I didn't carry her over a threshold.

We walked across one—together.

Into something holy.

Into something real.

And we walked away from that ticket booth, not only husband and wife.
But **WARRIORS.**

The Wedding Night War

Newport Beach. Mastro's. An hour after we get married.

Premium steaks topped with butter float past us steaming as the sun sets on the Pacific below the bluff. Amber and I are perched in front of the window. A breeze kisses us. My new wife—glowing like she's swallowed starlight.

My phone detonates.
One message. Then another.
I flip the phone over.
Buzz.
Buzz.
BUZZ.

My children have told my ex that we've gotten married.

A siren song of chaos follows.
The old life trying to claw its way into the new.

Then—the call.

My kids. Panic in their voices.
Static in the background.

"Dad, Mom is going crazy! She won't leave us alone."

My stomach turns.

Their grandmother has flown in a week earlier, claiming she wanted to visit.

In reality? She has an agenda.

To convince them they're better off staying with their mom than going with us to Tennessee.

But the kids have already decided.

And when she realizes she can't change their minds,
She does what bitter people do.
She rains acid on their lives.

And they have the video proof.

"Send me the video," I say.

The Video Goes Something Like This:
"Your mom would be better off without you."
"You are ungrateful bastards."

"Your dad is a loser. A drunk."

I close my eyes.
Take a deep breath.

Their grandmother doesn't present the strongest case.
The same antics I've dealt with for years.
This is an **attack on me.**

This makes sense. She would do this on this day.

"Dad, are you there?"

"Yeah, I saw it. Try to stay in your rooms and don't argue with her."

"But she won't leave us alone. She keeps screaming."

The children—**collateral damage.**
Torment them to get to me—shake my serenity and my new wonderful relationship.
A relationship I'm blessed with because I've changed.

For a brief moment, guilt twists in my stomach as I set the phone down to think— *am I failing my kids by not racing to them immediately?* I glance at Amber, the woman who promised me forever just an hour ago.

A memory surges forward at the perfect moment.
Tom's voice from recovery takes over:

Sometimes, protecting the people you love means becoming a shield. If I let her pull me away from my wedding night dinner with a fit aimed at destroying this important evening, I will set the tone for the rest of my relationship with her. I have to honor my wife.

The manufactured chaos can wait.

"If things don't get better by the morning, I will come get you."

"Ok."

That's it.

I set the phone face down.
Still concerned—Amber smiles.
This is our night.
We finish our dinner.

The Breaking Point

The phone **BUZZES** against the nightstand. Too early for anything good. Picking up where we left off last night.

I grab it, groggy, heart rate quickly rising. The cold floor against my bare feet grounds me in the physical world as adrenaline floods my system. My son's voice cutting through the static—**sharp, urgent, terrified.**

"Dad, we need to leave. Now!"

No hesitation. No buildup.

A shuffling sound. Then my daughter's voice, tight with fear, the words tumbling out between shallow breaths.

"She was attacking us again. We packed as much as we could and ran away. You have to come get us. We're at the park."

Attack. Park. What?

This wasn't an argument. This wasn't another chaotic night. **This was war.**

Then, more videos come through. Blurry. Shaky. The timestamp reads 7:17 a.m. A house in **full detonation mode**— Screaming. Terrorizing. Their mom— **unhinged.**

"Your dad is a loser! LOSER! I've been a good mother to you. You think you'll be better off. We'll see. You're abhorrent. You're minors. You can't make up your own minds. You're stupid."

A **hurricane of illness** unraveling in real-time. The raw hatred in her voice sends a chill down my spine—not for myself, but for what my children are enduring.

I don't watch the whole thing. I don't need to. The first ten seconds tell me everything. Amber and I are already **out the door.**

The drive?

Thoughts race as I race:

Gaslighting the kids. Nice. I know what you're doing. Beat them up until they can't think straight. Make them believe they are too young—too stupid—to make a decision. Without you, they'll die. Torment them into a state of catatonic agreement. I lived it. You can't fool anyone anymore and now the kids see it too. Your lies are old news.

I go too fast. The speedometer climbs as my thoughts spiral, the early morning streets mercifully empty.

Amber sits shotgun. **Agitated.**

I can feel her tension radiating beside me, her fingers drumming against her thigh—a physical manifestation of the maternal instinct now in full protective mode.

I grip the wheel tighter. Amber's breath quickens beside me.

"I can't imagine saying these things to my kids. Does she think this is going to make them want to stay here?"

Keeping my eyes on road, knuckles white against black leather:

"She's desperate. If she loses the kids, her story crumbles. The house her sister had to buy for her because of the kids, that I'm a deadbeat. She needs their support. The kids are her ticket to a life of luxury provided by her family."

Amber snaps back.

"Then she should try to come at them from a different perspective."

I grin, a humorless expression that feels foreign on my face.

"Of course. You're SANE. It was easy to manipulate them when they were younger. Now they see her mask slipping and she knows it. The act is over."

Stop **lights blur.** Red and green smear together as we race through intersections, the normal rules of the road seeming trivial against the urgency of reaching my children.

By the time I pulled up to the park around the corner from my ex's home, the kids are already there. **Pacing.** Their shadows long in the early morning light, moving restlessly like caged animals.

Backpacks slung over shoulders. Hastily packed. Zippers not fully closed.

They don't walk to my car.

They bolt.

Carrying all they could grab before they left. Their clothes wrinkled, hair wild, faces pale like they've seen a ghost. Eyes wide, darting in panic, searching for safety. They dive into the car as if something is chasing them—and in a way, something is.

Doors slam shut behind them—The sound reverberates with finality. They're breathing hard. From running. From fear. The car fills with the scent of their panic—that distinct smell of cold sweat and adrenaline.

I turn, quickly scanning them. No bruises. No blood. Terror locked in their expressions. *"Are you both okay?"*

My daughter speaks first. *"Yeah, but last night was crazy."* Her voice sounds distant, disconnected, as if she's reporting events that happened to someone else.

"I'm sure it was." I keep my voice steady, a counterbalance to the chaos they've escaped.

"No Dad," my son interrupts, urgency sharp in his voice, his hands still trembling, "like, crazy. She tried to get us to do some full moon ritual with her."

"What?" Amber's voice cuts in sharply, her head whipping around to face the backseat.

My daughter clarifies, eyes wide, voice unsteady: *"She said it would help us see we were wrong—that it would guide us to a better decision or something."* She hugs her backpack to her chest like a shield.

Amber shoots me a look—one of those wordless communications between adults that contains volumes. Her eyes say what her lips don't: this is beyond dysfunction; this is dangerous.

It's worse than we thought.

Their mom left scars. Not the kind you see—the kind that sits heavy in your chest. The kind that wakes you at night years later. The kind that alters how you see the world, how you trust, how you love.

The kind that lasts forever.

The kids go quiet, staring out the window, too sick to speak. The weight of what they've had to do—flee their mother's home—settles over them like a heavy blanket.

I watch them in the rearview mirror as we pull away, the park growing smaller behind us. They're safe now. Their bodies protected from immediate threat.

But safe **isn't healed.**

And the road to healing would be longer than the drive home.

The Court-Ordered Showdown

Because my ex won't stop calling the cops—claiming kidnapping—we're back at that park the very next day.

Court-ordered by our judge.

"Let the kids tell her themselves if they want to go to Tennessee," he barked, clearly fed up. Not that they haven't voiced it already, but she won't hear it unless the court orders it.

Forced back **into the nightmare.**
I beg my kids to do this. We sit outside the park, silent.

My son finally speaks. *"Do we have to get out?"*

"Yes," I say gently. *"If you want to leave California with me, you have to face her. I'm sorry."*

Reluctantly, they step out.
I watch from a distance as they approach their mother—her body coiled like a spring about to snap.

Five minutes.
That's all they can handle. They turn back.

She **erupts.**

Her control over me—**GONE.**
Her control over them—**GONE.**

Charging the car, screaming:
"THEY'RE MINORS!"

I crack my window slightly. Calm. Controlled. A surgeon's hand steadying the scalpel.

"They've made their choice—if you don't respect it, you're gonna lose them forever."

Silence. A sharp breath.

Then—**detonation.**

"RESPECT?! YOU'RE A DRUNK! A LOSER! I'M A GOOD MOTHER!"

But my mind remains calm: *Other people's chaos doesn't have to become your emergency.*

She can't stop. Or won't.
Same result either way.

I roll up the window and we drive away.

I can still see her yelling in the rearview mirror as we pull away, her figure growing smaller but her rage expanding to fill the space between us.

In the backseat, my daughter silently stares off wide-eyed. My son, the same. Their quiet solidarity speaks volumes about what they've endured and survived together.

That confrontation marked the last real interaction we would have with her for years to come.

No heartfelt apologies.
No birthday cards.
No **accountability.**

Carefully curated social-media illusions—a virtual reality replacing actual reality. While she posted throwback photos of *"perfect"* moments that never existed, my kids were building new lives, healing old wounds, finding their voices in our home. School administrators became collateral damage in her psychological warfare as she bombarded them with emails full of accusations they quickly recognized as hollow.

Letters sent to each child:

Fix your brain. I'm perfect. You're broken. Your father is evil.

Then—**radio silence.**

It's easier to pretend a monster stole your kids than admit you drove them away.

Some endings don't fade to black.
They sit there.
Paused. **Unanswered.**

Will she walk through that door?
Will this ever change?

One day you realize:
The sequel isn't coming.

I pray for change. But some people don't want saving.

They'd rather burn than admit the fire exists.

My kids didn't get closure.
They didn't get a mother who fought for them.

They still carry that wound, but they're learning that some questions won't be answered in this lifetime—and that healing doesn't require those answers.

But they got something else:
A home.
A **foundation.**
A family.

And Amber? She was changing.
Her motherly instincts kicked into high gear.
The woman who once ran from pain was facing it.
The woman who once hid from God began seeking Him.

I watched her transformation with awe, sensing something profound taking root in her—in all of us.

That's when it happened—the moment that would change not just how we lived, but who we were becoming **together.**

Planting the Seeds

When you want to help someone find salvation, God will always present you with an opportunity. A perfect time to **share your testimony.**

That evening, our house was quiet except for the gentle hum of the air conditioner. The emotional exhaustion from the confrontation at the park still hung in the air like a heavy fog.

Amber waits until we get inside. She sits them down at the kitchen table, the warm glow of the pendant light above creating a sanctuary of sorts. She looks them straight in the eyes, her hands steady but her voice soft with purpose, and says, *"I need to tell you something."*

She gives them **her testimony.**

No sugarcoating. No polite, easy words. No carefully edited version of reality.

"I was a mess," she told them, her voice occasionally catching on the jagged edges of memories still raw. "I tried to kill myself. I thought my life was worthless. I was drowning in my own pain, and I was sure that nothing could save me."

Their eyes locked on her. They had never heard this part of her story before. I watched from the doorway, both an observer and a participant in this sacred moment, feeling the weight of her vulnerability and the strength of her faith.

"But Jesus did," she said, her voice growing stronger with each word. "He pulled me out of this mess, and He saved me. He gave me a second chance at this life. And He can do the same for you. You're not worthless. You're not abandoned. **Christ loves you.**"

The kitchen clock ticked steadily in the background as her words settled over them. Outside, the neighborhood sounds faded away, as if even the world knew to be still for this moment.

The kids listen. Really listen. Teenagers... they don't resist. They don't argue. They don't roll their eyes or shut down. They... listen.

I've seen them dismiss adults countless times before, their teenage armor impenetrable. But something about Amber's raw honesty broke through where nothing else could.

As Amber finishes, silence settles over the table. My son's eyes glisten, his jaw working silently as he processes emotions too complex for words. My daughter quietly wipes away a tear she doesn't think we notice, her fingers trembling slightly. They don't speak—not because they don't have anything to say—but because, maybe for the first time, they're genuinely hearing that someone understands their pain. That their pain has purpose. That there's something beyond it.

I stand there, humbled by the Holy Spirit working through Amber—doing what my years of lectures and life lessons never could. This wasn't just conversation—this was divine intervention disguised as a kitchen table talk.

The **seed** is planted at the opportune time. It was fertile ground, prepared by years of hurt and questions that the world couldn't answer.

Enough to get them to church with us the following Sunday—not dragged reluctantly, but walking in willingly, curious about what had transformed this woman who had so honestly shared her brokenness.

That seed **GREW.** Not overnight, not without questions and doubts, but steadily, relentlessly—the kind of growth that can't be forced or faked. The kind that changes everything.

The Moment Of Truth

I step out on the back patio, sliding the door closed behind me. The perfect California evening weather kisses my face—that golden-hour light you can't find anywhere else, painting everything in honey and amber. The same light that once illuminated film sets and red carpets now bathes our modest backyard in glory.

I am going to miss you.

I breathe in the ocean air, salt and jasmine mixing with a distant hint of eucalyptus. No smog in the sky. I look around the backyard at the begonias that have remained gorgeous since we moved in—flourishing, their vibrant blooms a testament to what can grow when properly tended. I hear them laughing inside the house, the sound floating through the windows—my family, a word that once terrified me, now my anchor.

The laughter stops. I see Amber through the window, gathering dishes, her movements purposeful. She catches my eye and smiles—that smile that still cuts through my defenses like they never existed. Same as the first day we met.

Watching her, a clarity descends on me. That hand on my shoulder again: *Every battle we'd faced was leading us to this exact moment. We were growing closer to our calling—not despite our struggles, but **because of them.***

The realization flows with a wave of revelation. This isn't another basic thought—it's truth breaking through.

I've been climbing out of the muck and mess for so long I've forgotten to look back down the mountain of madness to see how far I've come. But it is not over. Is it? It's never over. Amber brought Christ to my doorstep and opened the door. There is only so far she can take it.

The man who once lived for himself, who chased Hollywood's empty promises, who drowned his pain in substances and status—that man is no more. Not recovering. Not improving. **Gone.**

There comes a time in a man's life when he must make that decision to lead or be led. A time to listen and a time to act.

The old me would have waited for someone else to validate this feeling. Would have questioned, second-guessed, maybe even run from it. Not anymore.

I'm no longer the man crawling out of that wreckage broken and beaten. I have been placed here by God to lead this family. To step up and share the Gospel to the world.

In this moment, standing on my California patio for perhaps one of the last times, I am overtaken by the current of truth that flows through me. What I have just witnessed is not only profound but sanctifying. To me, **a sinner** in the worst ways, my life riddled with bad decision after bad decision, the uniqueness of this moment is **not lost on me.**

For the first time in my life, the enemy's voice does not sneak through the void in an attempt to slither past an inkling of doubt. The whisper of inadequacy, of unworthiness, of *"who do you think you are?"*—silent. Christ has defeated this enemy long ago on the cross.

That victory wasn't distant. It echoed into this moment—on this patio, in this body, in this breath.

A double minded man is unstable in all his ways.

The words come to me with perfect clarity, not as a condemnation but as a promise now fulfilled. I am no longer double-minded. No longer torn between worlds. No longer fighting for control while simultaneously begging to be rescued.

Remain steadfast under trial and you will be rewarded. I have called you to lead.

The sun begins its final descent, crimson and gold bleeding across the horizon. As it sets on the west coast, a place I have lived for over twenty years, I bid my silent farewell. Every sunrise, every sunset, every moment of my life has been leading to this decision.

The line has been drawn. I must step into my calling.

I turn back toward the house, toward my family, toward the future God has prepared.

This is what it feels like when a man finally walks toward who he was created to be.

It's not about achievements.

Not through accolades.

But through surrender. Complete. Total. **Final.**

I smile to myself.

I saw **surrender** as weakness.

Turns out, surrendering to God is the most **powerful act** of courage a man can make.

Have you ever wondered why God saved you from destruction?

Walking in my calling didn't start with clarity. It started with chaos. It started with rehab. With blood on the windshield. With courtrooms and custody hearings. With me standing in front of a mirror I couldn't recognize, wondering if I even had a future. And then—God whispered: *You're not only being rescued. You're being repurposed.* Everything in this Blueprint came from fire. It's not theory—it's battlefield-tested. And Step 7? It's the one I waited too long to take. Don't make that same mistake.

Are you ready to walk in your calling? This is the step that changes everything—not just for you, but for everyone who will follow you.

BLUEPRINT STEP 7: WALK IN YOUR CALLING
(Stop Waiting—Become Who You Were Made To Be)

> *"The final step in any comeback? Walking through the door you've been too afraid to open."*

WAR STRATEGY:

You weren't just saved to be saved. You were saved to **lead**. You weren't just rescued—you were **recruited**. You weren't just given grace—you were **given a mission**. This final step isn't about winning your battle anymore—it's about leading others into victory. The world doesn't need more spectators—it needs warriors who will act. It needs men who recognize their scars aren't just wounds but qualifications for the battlefield. Your past has prepared you. Your pain has equipped you. Your testimony is now ammunition in someone else's war. The time for hesitation is over. Your calling is waiting.

ACTION ORDERS:

1. Confront The Lies That Keep You Sidelined

Three deceptions keep warriors from their purpose:

- **I'm Not Ready**—News flash: No one is. If you wait until you feel ready, you'll never move. God doesn't call the qualified; He qualifies the called.
- **I'm Still Too Broken**—Your scars don't disqualify you—they prepare you. The best leaders aren't those who never fell, but those who learned how to get back up.
- **Someone Else Is More Qualified**—The world doesn't need another hesitant leader. You're qualified not because you're perfect, but because you're willing.

The greatest tragedy isn't failure—it's potential untapped because of fear.

2. Discover Your Specific Mission

Your calling isn't random—it's revealed through patterns in your life:

- **What has God already equipped you for?** Your scars are training marks. What have you overcome?
- **What breaks your heart?** The pain you feel most deeply is tied to your purpose. What injustice hits you hardest?
- **What would you do even if no one paid you?** What battle would you fight for free? What hill would you die on?

Your unique combination of passions, pain, and preparation points to your purpose. Find the intersection.

3. Declare Your Mission

Make it real by making it concrete:

- **Write it down**—Vague callings never manifest.
- **Speak it out loud**—Claim it with your voice.
- **Own it**—Stop apologizing for your purpose.

What is the thing God saved you for? What is the fire inside you that won't die? What is the thing you know you were put on this earth to do? Define it. Declare it. Own it.

You don't need a stage.
You don't need a title.
You don't need a platform.

You just need to start where you are.

For me, it looked like recording a video with trembling hands, telling the truth about my crash—for the first time.
It looked like posting about faith when I knew I'd lose followers.
It looked like showing up to church not to receive—but to serve.
And now? It looks like helping other men walk out of their wreckage and into their purpose.

4. Step Into It Immediately

Action is the only proof of intention:

- **No more waiting**—tomorrow never comes.
- **No more planning**—perfect plans paralyze.
- **No more excuses**—they only serve the enemy.

Start today. Not tomorrow. Not next year. **Now**. Take one immediate action that moves you toward your calling. Small steps create momentum. Momentum creates breakthroughs.

WAR CRY:

Stop **waiting**. Stop **doubting**. Stop **hesitating**. Reading these words **isn't enough**. Feeling called **isn't enough**. Getting fired up **isn't enough**. Truth without action is **just information**. Calling without movement is **just intention**. Leadership without followers is **just potential**.

The world doesn't need **more people who know what to do**. It needs **people who do it**.

Right now, **someone is waiting** for the breakthrough that only **your** story can bring. Right now, **someone is praying** for the help that only **your** calling can provide. Right now, **someone is losing hope** because **you haven't stepped up yet**.

That ends **today**.

BLUEPRINT RECAP:

BEFORE: *(The Unregenerate Heart)*

"I was a man obsessed with all the wrong measurements of success. Fame, fortune, fitness, followers—these were my gods. I chased them relentlessly, convinced they held the keys to happiness.

'If I make enough money, then I'll be happy.' 'If I become famous, I'll be happy.' 'If everyone sees me as successful, I'll be happy.' 'If I have the perfect body, I'll be happy.'

I bought into every corporate slogan about 'living my best life.' I believed salvation could be found in a bank account, in Instagram likes, in a perfectly sculpted physique. The world's algorithm for success became my religion: work hard while you're young, accumulate wealth, retire comfortably, then... what? Shop and eat until you die?

I was a man who knew his purpose on paper but hesitated to live it. I recognized my calling but kept waiting for the 'right time,' the 'perfect circumstances,' the 'complete healing' before I would step into it. Meanwhile, the world suffered from my silence, and my gifts gathered dust while I made excuses."

Pro Tip: Watch how the world sells you everything but what truly matters:

- They'll tell you to save for retirement, but not for eternity
- They'll tell you to build your platform, but not your character
- They'll tell you to chase happiness, but not holiness
- They'll tell you to be relevant, but not righteous

All these worldly pathways lead to the same destination: emptiness at the end of achievement.

AFTER: *(The Regenerate Heart)*

"The Gospel didn't change my mind—it rewired my soul. Everything I once valued became worthless compared to the mission. I realized that all the things I'd been chasing—fame, money, success, validation—were elaborate distractions from my true calling. To the children of God the Gospel is: Light. Warmth. Encouragement.

The regenerate heart gave me the ability to truly love. It removed the burdens of proving myself to the world. I no longer feel pressured to be someone important, to validate my existence through achievements or possessions.

I now understand that this world and its systems are temporary. The culture of fear, empty success metrics, and digital distractions—these aren't salvation. They're designed to keep us distracted, guilty, and confused.

When I stopped believing all these lies, I found serenity. More importantly, I found purpose—not only for myself, but for others. I stopped waiting for permission to make an impact. I stopped believing I needed to be perfect before I could be powerful. The truth set me free: my calling isn't about me. It's about what God wants to do through me.

Now I wake up with clear purpose. Not to chase wealth, not to build my brand, not to improve my image—but to serve others, to fight for truth, to bring hope to those still trapped in the matrix of worldly success.

My scars, my story, my struggles—they're not personal baggage anymore. They're credentials for the battlefield. They're proof that transformation is possible."

VICTORY INDICATORS:

You Know You're Succeeding When:

- You've defined your mission in clear, specific terms
- You're taking action without waiting for perfect conditions
- You're helping others apply what you've learned
- Your purpose extends beyond personal success
- You face resistance but move forward anyway
- Your life has visible impact on others
- You're living in alignment with your values daily

RED FLAGS:

- You're "still waiting" for the "right time"
- You constantly change direction
- You keep your transformation to yourself
- You talk about purpose more than you pursue it
- Your calling remains vague and undefined
- You're paralyzed by perfectionism
- You fear criticism more than you desire impact

REALITY CHECK:

Walking in your calling will cost you. People will question your motives, doubt your abilities, and criticize your methods. You'll face opposition from unexpected sources—sometimes those closest to you. You'll have days where you wonder if you misheard God's voice. You'll make mistakes in public. You'll help people who don't appreciate it. You'll invest in some who never change. These struggles don't mean you're on the wrong path—they confirm you're a threat to the enemy. Every leader throughout Scripture faced resistance when walking in their calling. Moses stuttered. David was overlooked. Paul was imprisoned. The greatest callings attract the fiercest opposition. Don't mistake difficulty for disqualification. The resistance you face isn't proof you should stop—it's evidence you're finally doing what matters.

WAR ORDER (FINAL COMMAND):

Write your mission statement in **ONE** bold sentence. What were you rescued from, and who were you rescued for? Then, take **ONE action** today that moves you toward that purpose. Not tomorrow. Not someday. **TODAY.** Finally, find someone still struggling in an area where you've found freedom. Reach out. Share your story. Share it with me on social media. I want to hear from you. Offer help. Your comeback isn't complete until you're helping someone else make theirs.

"You weren't saved to sit on the sidelines. You were pulled from the fire for a reason. Your scars, your story, your struggle—they're all weapons in the war for souls. It's time to stop waiting and **start leading**.*"*

EPILOGUE

Right Now

4:58 a.m.

My feet touch the floor in the home I own. *"Praise be to God."*

The house is quiet—filled not with silence, but peace. My life is no longer tossed by the winds of worry—it is cradled in the hands of grace. My brain no longer rings with panic when I wake like it once did when I was in the clutches of the enemy.

Amber sleeps beside me. No fear. No chaos. Simply breathing, steady as grace.

I walk to the living room and drop to my knees. Not because I must, but because I can.

"Lord, thank you for this day. For the grace you have given a sinner like me. I am not worthy. Give me the strength to speak your son's truth today. Help me share your message to those in need. Those the enemy has imprisoned. Those suffering. Awaken them to the enemy and strengthen them to join this battle."

A simple prayer. I walk to the kitchen, fire up the espresso machine, and pause to savor the warmth of routine—something I once dismissed as mundane, now sacred.

Now I understand clearly what was always true. For years, I fought faith, resisted surrender, believing control was victory. I was wrong.

Surrender didn't defeat me—it saved me.

Looking back, I see now what I couldn't see then: **God was sovereign all along.**

Every failure, every betrayal, every reckless choice—I thought they were mine alone. My free will unchecked, running wild through destruction. But **God never lost sight of me**. He wasn't scrambling to repair my story. He was **masterfully redeeming** it from the beginning.

Like Joseph in **Genesis 50:20,** I can say with full clarity: *"You meant evil against me; but God meant it for good."*

The enemy didn't win when he nearly killed me—he participated in my calling without even knowing it. God used my free will to **expose the lies** I had built my life on. He allowed me to be torn down—not to punish me, but to **prepare me**.

They say the sound of your neck breaking is like a tree branch snapping in winter. **POP. CRACK. SILENT SCREAM.**

Let me tell you about salvation. Let me tell you about eating cocaine straight from a cup holder at eighty miles an hour while God decides your fate.

The **KING BABY** I used to know seems like a stranger to me now, viewed across the vast canyon of grace. From where I stand today—my feet on solid ground, my heart at peace, my soul anchored in Christ—I barely recognize him.

Yet—I must never forget him. His scars are my testimony. His rock bottom became my foundation.

This is why I share my story with such brutal honesty. Because the distance between that broken body on the asphalt and the man who kneels in prayer each morning isn't measured in years or miles. It's measured in mercy. Divine, undeserved, transformative mercy.

But even with all the healing… one question still echoed in the silence:

Why me, Lord?

Why did I survive the crash? Why did You spare me when better men—more faithful, more prepared—never made it home? Why them? Why not me?

I don't have the answer. And maybe that's the point.

The truth is, **He is God, and I am not.**

Some of us are taken home early. Others are left behind to carry a message forged in fire. But we're all part of the same plan, woven by the same hands.

"Oh, the depth of the riches and wisdom and knowledge of God! How unsearchable are his judgments and how inscrutable his ways!" **(Romans 11:33)**

This is what some call unjust. Some call cruel. But what it really is… is **love with a long view.**

I open the doors to the deck as the sunlight crests the top of the hill illuminating the forest. These moments are God's connective tissue for me. Moments that passed me by when the enemy seduced me.

Resistance to God was profound for me. Even after moving to Tennessee, I was quoting verses, attending church—but was I truly walking the walk? After every miracle, every near-death escape, every second chance, I still fought. Christ had claimed me, but I had yet to fully claim Him.

Would I rise to become the man worthy of my calling? Or would I let my stubbornness crumble our future? The Bible rested on the table in front of me for a year, radiating the truth. Do you find it a coincidence that in the hotel room in my darkest hours a Bible slid out of a drawer for me to see?

I finally opened it. I studied it. And it spoke to me.

The part of me that had resisted surrender vanished, replaced by something I hadn't known before—clarity. The pages came alive. The Holy Spirit spoke directly to my heart.

I believe that's what finally broke me. It wasn't strength that brought me to my knees—it was the **collapse of every illusion** that I could fix myself. I was still trying to be my own savior. But it wasn't until the **Holy Spirit rushed in and wrecked me with truth** that everything came full circle.

That moment wasn't defeat. It was **rebirth.**

"Not my will, but Thine be done." **(Luke 22:42)**

The last of the scales fell from my eyes—like Paul on the road to Damascus, when *"something like scales fell from his eyes, and he regained his sight"* **(Acts 9:18).**

Romans 8 became the anthem of my freedom: *"For I am sure that neither death nor life, nor angels nor rulers, nor things present nor things to come, nor powers, nor height nor depth, nor anything else in all creation, will be able to separate us from the love of God in Christ Jesus our Lord."*

These weren't mere words—they became my guide. The last of my chains fell away the moment I stopped fighting God's mercy.

Nothing can separate us. Not addiction. Not shame. Not even myself. Because freedom isn't perfection—it's surrender. And surrendering to Christ changed everything.

I had accepted Christ—but Christ didn't merely pay my debt, He erased it. Legally. Spiritually. Completely.

My chains weren't loosened—they were **obliterated.**

Redemption isn't partial. **It's total.**

He could've stopped Satan at any time. Like with Job. But **He allowed the refining fire**, because He knew I would emerge not only saved—but *sent*. Not only healed—but *commissioned*.

"Behold, I have refined thee, but not with silver; I have chosen thee in the furnace of affliction." **(Isaiah 48:10, KJV)**

He allowed me to be shattered, because the vessel I once was **couldn't carry the message He was preparing me to deliver.**

I thought my destruction was the end. It was the **turning point**. Not the grave—but the garden.

Every morning, I train. After I pray. Before I work. Not for vanity. Not ego. But readiness. Because warriors don't soften in peacetime. Because the enemy never stops watching. Because my mission isn't finished.

Amber and I look back on seven years, and it feels like yesterday. A man who'd sworn off women. A woman who'd sworn off men. But God had other plans. Two broken people. One unstoppable story.

Time moves differently when you're living your purpose. When you finally become who you were created to be. This isn't just redemption—it's stepping into your calling. Not perfection. Not ease. But peace. Salvation.

My children accepted Christ—not because we preached, but because they saw the difference. They saw faith in action. The generational curse—**BROKEN.** The chains once destined for them—**ERASED.** My kids will not inherit their father's chains. They inherit freedom.

I did not want to write this book. Who wants to relive those moments of despair and hopelessness? So, why did I write this? Because the truth of my story carries the power to transform others' lives. If people suffer in the enemy's grasp, and they do, how would I be righteous in keeping the story of profound salvation to myself?

God doesn't owe me an explanation. What He gave me instead was **grace**, and **a calling**. Not to make sense of it all—but to make use of it. *And that's enough.*

I shared this story with you, as painfully cathartic as it was, in hopes that it might inspire you to the belief that there is more than what your eyes perceive of this world. You may ignore the demon knocking at your door but does ignoring him make him go away?

This war isn't only mine—it's yours. You've seen the battlefield. You've been handed the weapons. You know what's at stake.

Now, you **must choose.**

You can close this book, ignore the war, numb yourself again—or you can stand up and fight.

Your soul is the prize, and eternity hangs in the balance. This isn't about improving your life—it's about reclaiming your life. Every decision you make after closing this book isn't about today—it's about your legacy. Your children. Your children's children.

Heaven and hell don't wait for you to be ready. Salvation doesn't pause while you debate your next step. Every moment you delay, darkness takes more ground.

The same God who rescued me waits to rescue you. The same power that broke my chains is available to break yours. But you must choose it.

Your moment is here. Your comeback awaits. Your redemption begins right now.

I pray that this book sparks a light inside of you no matter where you are in the journey, and that you find comfort in knowing that in brokenness hope remains and in darkness there is always light.

The grace God has given me is accessible to all. What you have done—the sins you may linger on as unforgivable—are what make you uniquely you. Christ's darkest moment, the only time in the Gospel He cries out *"My God, my God, why have you forsaken me?"* is the very moment he was taking on all the sins of the world so that you may be saved. God turned His back on His only Son so that we may be saved if we choose to believe.

His self-sacrifice was for you. Do not let the world **cause** you to ignore **or** mock the Son of God who willingly gave you this opportunity. Christ is the gate. His crucifixion is the death of the old you. His resurrection is your comeback.

My shattered life became the mosaic through which God's glory now shines.

Close this book. Take up your sword. Fight for the life you were meant to live. All glory to Christ. **King of Kings.**

Your **COMEBACK** is waiting for you.

What are you waiting for?

– Matt

> *"What the enemy meant for destruction, God uses for restoration if we **humble ourselves before Him**"*

READY TO CONTINUE YOUR COMEBACK?

Your journey doesn't end here.

This book is the blueprint—**NOW it's time to execute**.

TAKE YOUR NEXT STEP

JOIN THE WARRIOR COMMUNITY

Get exclusive Blueprint strategies, video training, and personal insights directly from me by **scanning the QR code below**:

BRING THIS MESSAGE TO YOUR COMMUNITY

Transform your **team, church, or event** with a life-changing presentation.

Book Matt at www.mattfarnsworth.net

SHARE YOUR TRANSFORMATION STORY

Your honest **Amazon review** helps others take their first step toward redemption.

Go to Amazon and leave your review now.

"The battlefield awaits. Will you fight alone, or will you stand with warriors?"

www.ingramcontent.com/pod-product-compliance
Lightning Source LLC
LaVergne TN
LVHW041331080426
835512LV00006B/395